Ten Things You Need to Know as In-House Counsel

Practical Advice and Successful Strategies

Sterling L. Miller

Cover design by Cathy Zaccarine/ABA Design

The materials contained herein represent the opinions of the authors and/or the editors, and should not be construed to be the views or opinions of the law firms or companies with whom such persons are in partnership with, associated with, or employed by, nor of the American Bar Association or the Business Law Section unless adopted pursuant to the bylaws of the Association.

Nothing contained in this book is to be considered as the rendering of legal advice for specific cases, and readers are responsible for obtaining such advice from their own legal counsel. This book is intended for educational and informational purposes only.

© 2017 American Bar Association. All rights reserved.

No part of this publication may be reproduced, stored in a retrieval system, or transmitted in any form or by any means, electronic, mechanical, photocopying, recording, or otherwise, without the prior written permission of the publisher. For permission contact the ABA Copyrights & Contracts Department, copyright@americanbar.org, or complete the online form at http://www.americanbar.org/utility/reprint.html.

Printed in the United States of America.

21 20 19 18 17   5 4 3 2 1

ISBN: 978-1-63425-792-3
e-ISBN: 978-1-63425-793-0

Discounts are available for books ordered in bulk. Special consideration is given to state bars, CLE programs, and other bar-related organizations. Inquire at Book Publishing, ABA Publishing, American Bar Association, 321 N. Clark Street, Chicago, Illinois 60654-7598.
www.shopABA.org

Contents

Introduction	v
Acknowledgments	xi

General Skills Ten Things You Need to Know About:	1
How to Be a Successful In-House Counsel	3
Becoming General Counsel	5
Ten Habits of Highly Effective In-House Lawyers	13
How to Be More Productive Every Day	21
Writing Skills for In-House Counsel (It's Different In-House)	27
What In-House Lawyers Want from Outside Counsel	35

Litigation Ten Things You Need to Know About:	43
Drafting Documents and Emails	45
Your Company Has Just Been Sued—Now What?	49
Explaining Litigation to the Board and the CEO	53
Settlement Agreements—Making Sure It's Really Over	61
Litigation Financing—A Primer for In-House Counsel	69

Contracts and Deals Ten Things You Need to Know About:	77
Help Your Clients Get Their Contract Through Legal Quickly	79
How to Negotiate—Practical Tips for In-House Counsel	85
Insurance Contract Basics for In-House Counsel	93

Legal Department Operations Ten Things You Need to Know About:	101
Setting Goals for the Legal Department	103
Simple Ways to Reward and Retain Your People	109
Effectively Managing Outside Counsel Fees	115

Running an Effective Staff Meeting	121
Increasing the Efficiency of the Legal Department Through Use of Technology	129
Creating a Client Satisfaction Survey	135

Regulatory   Ten Things You Need to Know About: — 143
- All I Want for Christmas Is an FCPA/Anti-Bribery Health Check — 145
- Trade Associations and Antitrust Risk — 149
- Data Privacy—The Essentials — 155
- Record Retention—Programs, Policies, and More… — 163
- Europe's New Data Privacy Law—What You Really Need to Know — 171

Intellectual Property/Employment   Ten Things You Need to Know About: — 181
- Trade Secrets and Protecting Your Company — 183
- Protecting Your Company's Reputation and Brand — 191
- Website User Agreements — 201
- Partnering with HR (1 + 1 = 3) — 209

Governance   Ten Things You Need to Know About: — 217
- Basic Corporate Governance for In-House Counsel — 219
- Dealing with the Board of Directors — 229

Crisis Readiness and Risk Management   Ten Things You Need to Know About: — 237
- Spotting, Analyzing, and Managing "Risk" — 239
- Crisis Preparation 101 — 247
- Preparing for When "Bad Things" Happen — 253

Representing the Organization   Ten Things You Need to Know About: — 261
- The Attorney-Client Privilege—What You Need to Know — 263
- How to Run a Government Affairs Campaign — 271
- Common Ethics Issues for In-House Counsel — 279

Additional Resources   Ten Things You Need to Know About: — 289
- Best Legal Blogs for In-House Counsel (2015) — 291
- A To Do List for In-House Counsel — 295
- "Cool Tech" for In-House Lawyers (2016) — 301

Index — 309
About the Author — 321

Introduction
(How Did We Get Here?)

In the Beginning...

I know this will sound clichéd but I knew I wanted to be a lawyer since the 1970s, when I was a young boy growing up on the "hard scrabble" streets of York, Nebraska, with a population of around 6,000 hardy, Midwestern souls and at least several times that many cows. I don't remember exactly what drove my decision: it could have been watching repeats of *Perry Mason* with my mom, or possibly all of the writing I did on my first typewriter, or maybe it had something to do with my grade school teachers telling me I talked so much that I should be a lawyer. But now that I think about it, it was probably rooted in playing the board game Life. In the game Life two of the things you do are get paid and buy stock. I realized that lawyers got paid a good bit more than a lot of the other jobs handed out in the board game and I was completely fascinated by the small certificates of stock you could buy, giving you a partial ownership stake in some generic company. And I knew that lawyers had something to do with stocks.

This came in handy when I was about 11 years old and decided, along with my brother Paul and few friends from the neighborhood, to start a lemonade stand one summer to see if we could earn some extra money. I had the bright idea to create certificates of stock in the stand, using paper from my trusty "Big Chief" tablet and the soberest colors from the 64 Crayola Crayon box. Each share cost $1.00 and gave you part interest in the Miller Lemonade Stand Company. Long story short, it didn't really work out and everyone got a quick—though relatively painless—lesson in bankruptcy.

Career Advice

Jumping ahead a bit, in high school you start to get "career advice" from all of the grown-ups. I still wanted to become a lawyer—even though I had no idea how to make that happen. All of this changed toward the end of my junior year when our "government" teacher asked me about my plans for the future. I answered something about wanting to be a corporate lawyer (leaving out any acknowledgment of the Great Lemonade Stand Failure of 1973). He told me this would be a huge mistake. Lawyers are "a dime a dozen," he explained, and what I really needed to do was to go into engineering—electrical engineering to be exact—because that was "where the jobs were going to be." Since I was 16 and highly impressionable (i.e., clueless), I thought this sounded like good career advice. So, forget about lawyer, it was now electrical engineer or bust.

No One Told Me There Would Be Math

I hated everything about engineering in college. In particular, I really hated the math: calculus, statistics, and my true enemy—differential equations. It was at the first week of that class when the teacher wrote on the chalk board (yes, I'm old) "96–12" and said that this was the range of scores on the first test of the year. I turned around to my buddy sitting behind me and said, "If you got a 12, you might as well pack it up now and go pick a different major." When I got my test paper handed back to me, I eagerly unfolded it and saw a nice, big red "12" in the upper right-hand corner. Without saying another word, I packed up my stuff, walked out of the class room, and headed to the administration building to change my major to political science. Screw engineering, I was going to law school! I even used my newfound "legal powers" to help a group of friends of mine beat the rap for holding an "illegal" keg party in our dorm. Turns out the Honor Court didn't know how to follow procedure (hello "mistrial") and, like something out of *Animal House*, they were definitely not prepared for my cross-examination of the head resident assistant, which, literally, brought tears to his eyes. You see, law is about the details and I had an "iron butt" and could happily sit for hours rooting them out.

Due to some actual good advice from a professor, I ended up at law school in St. Louis, Washington University to be exact. I took every class I could on corporations, corporate finance, securities law, and so on, figuring I would need all of it when I became a big-time corporate lawyer. Of course, once I graduated and joined a law firm I ended up in the litigation section—as I quickly realized that was where all the fun people were! I spent six years at the firm and near the end of that time got married to an awesome woman from Dallas, Texas.

Moving on Up

We moved to Dallas and for a change of pace I ended up working in the litigation and regulatory section of the in-house legal department at American Airlines. I had often thought about working as an in-house attorney, mostly because I thought it would be really interesting to be able to focus on one client, be part of the internal decision-making process, and (the real reason) be done with tracking how I spent my day in six-minute increments. I enjoyed everything about being an in-house lawyer right from the start. American Airlines had a small technology division called Sabre, and I was assigned to work on a lot of projects for Sabre over my first few years in the legal department.

American Airlines decided to spin off Sabre and I was asked if I wanted to help form its legal department. I knew that if I wanted to get ahead, that is, become the general counsel, my path would be a lot easier getting in on the ground floor of the Sabre legal department versus sticking around at American Airlines. So, I accepted and was put in charge of litigation and regulatory matters for Sabre. While in-house, I adopted a motto that I picked up from Tom Wolfe's classic book about the early days of the U.S. space program, *The Right Stuff*. In the book, the astronauts talk about "never refusing a combat assignment," meaning whenever something hard or challenging is offered to you, you take it. It was simply the easiest way to advance your career in the military. Over time my team and I took the motto to heart and picked up things that no one else wanted to do, like immigration, bankruptcy, sweepstakes and contests, certain contracts, compliance, export/import, data privacy, and host of other legal areas. Taking this path not only kept us busy, it gave everyone on my team a broad set of skills and valuable experience in many areas and facets of the law. We were the proud garbage men of the department: if you didn't want it, put it on the curb and we'd come by and pick it up!

Getting to Sit on the "Big Chair"

Eventually, I was moved over to be general counsel for Sabre's wholly owned subsidiary, Travelocity.com, where I quickly established my value to the company by being the first to say that the (then) new Travelocity Roaming Gnome advertising campaign was "dumb" and had "no chance" of ever being successful. I managed to get over that stellar moment and enjoyed running a fairly autonomous legal department with a team of attorneys sitting all over the globe. After about four years at Travelocity, the Sabre Corporation general counsel decided to retire and I was asked to move back over and head up the entire legal department, including integrating the Travelocity team more fully into the larger Sabre legal department. Being general counsel for Sabre was a much bigger job than being general counsel for Travelocity, especially after the Great Recession at the end of 2008 and a number of hard decisions having to be made. I loved it but it was a demanding job—as anyone who sits in the general counsel chair can tell you. Still, I was able to implement a number of programs and ideas I had for how a large, international legal department should function. One of the things I was most satisfied to see was that no matter how hard we worked (including some really spectacularly successful legal projects and litigation wins), my legal department always had the highest employee satisfaction ratings of any staff group or business group in the company. I was fortunate to work with a large group of extremely talented people who were great coworkers and were always willing to go the extra mile to help out a colleague or do whatever was need to help the business achieve its goals.

Time for a Change

The last few years I was general counsel at Sabre were difficult. We had some bet the company litigation and regulatory investigations, we restructured several parts of the business (and other lines of business), we bought and sold a number of companies, and we ramped up for and completed a successful IPO (after being held by private equity for almost seven years). To cut to the chase, I needed a change. And so, after twenty-plus years as an in-house attorney, ten of which were spent as general counsel, I decided that it was time to turn the page and retire from Sabre. And that's what I did near the end of 2014. It was a difficult decision because I did (and still do) love the company and the people I worked with, especially the incredible members of my legal team. However, as I sit here almost two years later, I know it was the right choice. Since I was still fairly young at this point, I had to ask myself, "So, what's next?"

I Need to Write This Stuff Down

Shortly after I retired from Sabre, I was asked to serve as a speaker on a panel at a conference in Dallas sponsored by a large international law firm. My panel discussed cross-border mergers and even though I was not an M&A lawyer by training I was surprised at how much I knew about the topic based on my many years of in-house work and my involvement in numerous deals (not including the lemonade stand). Afterwards at the cocktail reception, several young in-house lawyers came up to me and introduced themselves. They started asking me about any advice I had for them about things they needed to know or do if they wanted to become general counsel. I starting talking about several things and, to my surprise, they were actually writing down what I said. The light bulb went off: I should be writing this stuff down! And that was the beginning of the Ten Things You Need to Know as In-House Counsel blog, where basically twice a month I try to write down lessons learned (hard ones and easy ones) over my twenty-plus years as an in-house lawyer. I know from experience that in-house lawyers do not want a ten-page memo. They need quick points written in a practical manner that they can digest and work into their everyday practice. Consequently, I titled my blog Ten Things since I try to pick interesting topics to cover and then discuss the key things in-house lawyers need to know in ten simple points.

So, Here We Are

When I started the blog in November 2014, I wasn't sure if anyone would read it, let alone care if I wrote a second one. It's definitely gotten much bigger than I ever imagined (and it has allowed me to prove to my Mom that I had not become a "shiftless hobo" in semi-retirement). As I look back on some of the early posts, a few things stick out—I jam a lot more words into each new post (though I do try to stop at around 3,000 words), I have slowly developed a consistent style in terms of laying out issues, I have gotten much better at the technical end of blogging—and I knew *nothing* about blogging when I started, and, man, I did a lot of different stuff over twenty years!

So, that is the story of how we got to this book. I have taken a big selection of my blog posts from November 2014 to August 2016, put them under categories, and updated them where necessary and adapted them to "book form," and I hope the result is a useful guide to a wide range of issues for any in-house lawyer, from those just starting out to those that have been living the life for a number of years. I continue to write the blog and I have a long list of topics for future posts—in fact there are probably a dozen or so new posts on the site since I submitted the book for publication. I guess those will be for the second volume!

October 2016

Acknowledgments

There are numerous people I wish to acknowledge and thank in the creation of this book:

Joe Berry (RIP)—English teacher, York High School: thank you for encouraging me to write, and write some more.

Professor Robert Oberst—Nebraska Wesleyan University: among many things, thanks for the advice to go to Washington University School of Law in St. Louis.

Professor David Becker—Washington University in St. Louis, School of Law: thanks for taking an interest in me as a first year, for telling me to be sure to have a hobby, and for helping me fix Becker Bingo much to the surprise of my classmates.

Charles "Chip" Seigel—Partner, Gallop, Johnson & Neuman, St. Louis: thanks for teaching me how to be a lawyer and a professional. A lot of your advice is set out in these blog posts.

Andy Steinberg (RIP)—General Counsel, Sabre Corporation: thanks for teaching me how to think through issues, be a humane leader, and how to show decency and compassion as a lawyer. You are missed!

David Schwarte—Deputy General Counsel, American Airlines, and General Counsel, Sabre Corporation: thanks for teaching me how to be an in-house lawyer and for always trusting me with more responsibility.

Sam Gilliland—CEO, Sabre Corporation, and **Michelle Peluso**—CEO, Travelocity: thanks for taking a chance on a kid from Nebraska and hiring me to be your general counsel and for making me part of your leadership team, where I could learn the key part of being an in-house lawyer that has nothing to do with the law and everything to do with doing what's right by customers, shareholders, and employees.

Readers of the Blog—The blog is nothing without you! Thanks for your notes that always make my day.

Greg Adams—Government teacher, York High School: thanks for telling me lawyers are a "dime a dozen" and that engineering is the career of the future!

*****

I want to thank my parents, Tom and Carole Miller, for encouraging me to read everything I could get my hands on, for giving me my first typewriter, and for always helping me take the path that was right for me no matter where it led.

Thank you to my daughters Maren and Zoey for putting up with an absent Dad so many times and still always making me feel special and part of your lives.

My biggest thanks for my amazing wife, Inger, who made me realize that there is more to life than work and that sometimes you need to step away and focus on what's really important in this world. Thanks for tolerating my need to write books and blogs!

This book is dedicated to in-house lawyers everywhere. You are in an exclusive club and only you know how challenging and rewarding it can be. And to the many in-house lawyers I worked with at American Airlines, Sabre Corporation, and Travelocity, especially those who worked for me and always made me look good even when I didn't necessarily deserve it. I think about all of you often and am grateful for the time we had together, the friendships we made, and for everything you taught me about being a good lawyer and a good person.

General Skills

Ten Things: How to Be a Successful In-House Counsel

Whether you are new to an in-house department or a long-term veteran, the general counsel or just a basic contract lawyer, there are a number of things that can help make you more successful in your career. I have distilled a lot of hard-learned lessons into ten key tips. These tips are not exhaustive and there are always more, but these are the ten things I have consistently taught to my teams over the years.

1. **Learn the business.** Make time to talk with your client and really understand what it is your company does. If you know how the company makes money, you can draft, defend, and advise much better.
2. **Say it and write it as simply as possible.** Get to the bottom line quickly. Business people are not interested in the arcane or minutiae. They just want the answer.
3. **Keep a sense of humor.** This will serve you well on good days and bad, and your clients will appreciate it.
4. **Don't let your boss be surprised.** Whoever you report to should be fully informed of anything of importance you are working on. It's not a great day when the general counsel hears about a legal issue for the first time from one of the business folks. Similarly, if the board of directors learns of a problem from the press, that's not a good day either.
5. **Listen (listen more than you talk).** Make sure you understand what your client is asking/telling you and don't be afraid to ask questions (but pick your spots in meetings).
6. **Deliver bad news and good news fairly and honestly.** Keep an even keel. Don't hide or exaggerate. This will build trust between you and the business.
7. **Communicate frequently.** Don't let the client have to ask you about status. Keep them up to date, even if you are only telling them that their project is simply still on the pile. They will appreciate your taking the time to keep them

posted. And be sure to promptly reply to emails or calls from your clients, even if you're just letting them know you are busy but will get back in touch soon.
8. **Know your numbers.** Know your budget, even if you are in charge of only one matter. Know what you are spending and why. And be able to explain why you picked the law firm you did for this project. Also, learn how to read a balance sheet, income statement, and cash flow statement. Learn the language of business.
9. **Step up when the opportunity presents itself.** Big litigation, a big contract, a big M&A deal: all of these are opportunities for you to show your stuff. Your boss, the CEO, the board will all appreciate hearing you say "I'll take care of it" and then deliver. Take the time to think through what needs to be done and get moving.
10. **There's never enough money, time, or people.** Get used to it. No one is doubling your budget or looking to add more lawyers. You are part of a cost center. Costs are for cutting. This is never going to change. So figure out how to work with what you have and focus on how you (or your team) can get more done, get the important stuff done, and get things done more efficiently.

November 28, 2014

Ten Things: Becoming General Counsel

One of my earliest articles was titled "How to Be a Successful In-House Lawyer."[1] Since then I have heard from many of you on a slightly different question: how do you become general counsel? In particular, what skills should someone develop if they have their eyes on the big chair? I thought this would be an excellent topic to write about. If you already are general counsel, congratulations! Hopefully, the points below ring true to you. If you aspire to become general counsel (or are looking for an upgrade), now is the perfect time to start thinking about your game plan for the future both in terms of developing needed skills and ensuring you are on the radar of the right people. If you are outside counsel, you can use these points to help your inside clients attain their goals.

I was fortunate enough to have been the general counsel of two companies. While each company required different skills for both the legal department generally and for the general counsel seat specifically, there was also a lot of overlap. I suspect the overlapping parts I experienced are the same for most companies. I also believe that the core skills needed for the position—including operational and strategic excellence—are the same here in the United States and across the globe. Here are some of the things you will need to think about, know, or master on your path to becoming general counsel:

1. **Be careful what you ask for.** First, you need to decide whether or not you are truly interested in the job. Being "the boss" definitely sounds good, but there are a number of things you need to consider. Being general counsel is a tough job and involves a lot of long hours and a lot of pressure. You will have to make very important decisions with little time and sparse facts. Your schedule will be tied to that of the CEO, CFO, and the board of directors, meaning you may need to spend many evenings, weekends, holidays, and vacations working. You

---

1 See page 3.

will need to keep your phone on and close by 24/7/365. It will be very hard to balance work and family. It's important that you go in with your eyes open. As general counsel, there is no place to hide (i.e., no one ahead of you to make the final decision or take the heat when things go badly—which they will at some point). Still interested? Good! There are definitely a lot of good things as well, including getting to be part of the executive team making the decisions for the entire company, compensation, prestige, rewarding work, managing your own budget, implementing your vision for how a legal department should operate, and putting together and leading your own team.

2. **Get on "the list."** If you are interested in being general counsel, you need to let the right folks know, as it is highly unlikely that someone just "recognizes" that you would be awesome in the role. Assume no radioactive spider will bite you and change your life overnight. You will have to progress through your career the old-fashioned way—hard work and with a little self-promotion. I am not saying you need to step on anyone to make your way to the top, but you need to show you're interested in the job. This will be either internally, that is, at your current employer, or outside, for example, working with a recruiting firm to look for opportunities elsewhere. If you really enjoy where you work now and think you would like to eventually sit in the general counsel chair, let your manager (or the general counsel) know about your interest. Seek out honest feedback about your performance and what things you need to do to make the succession plan for general counsel at some point (and any company worth its salt has a succession plan for the general counsel position—looking at those ready "now" and those who might be ready several years down the road). Take your annual review seriously and use the opportunity to go into those meetings with a plan to discuss your interest in the job and to highlight your skills and accomplishments. Self-selecting does not automatically get you on the list, but it will get you noticed and considered. Likewise, if you're not sure about staying with your current employer or perhaps you are told that your odds of making the succession plan are low, you should consider contacting several legal recruiting firms.[2] Be sure to use your personal email and personal contact details with the recruiting firms and put together a professional-looking, mistake-free, résumé.[3] You should also create a professional LinkedIn[4] page, as it is another good way for companies and search firms to find you. You can also stay on top of opportunities through several

---

2 http://www.lawcrossing.com/recruiter-ranking/.
3 http://www.inhouseblog.com/in-house-counsel-resume/.
4 https://www.linkedin.com/.

job posting sites, including the ACC.com and GoInHouse.com websites (or the international equivalents for such sites outside the United States). One last thing here—be sure your social media postings and profile are appropriate for someone seeking the top legal job.

3. **Become "Dr. Yes."** One of the oldest "lawyer" jokes in the world is that the legal department should be called the Department of No. Yea, it's funny the first 34,478 times you hear it but then it gets a bit old. Old or not, the fact that anyone thinks of the legal department as an obstacle to getting things done is bad. First, it reflects poorly on the department and all the great things it does. Second, it means people will likely look to bypass the legal department or keep it out of the decision process, which is bad because getting noticed requires a seat at the table. One way to set yourself apart in the eyes of the business is to become (and apologies to James Bond fans) "Dr. Yes": as in "yes, we can figure out a way to get that done." In its simplest form, it means don't be a lawyer who just says "no, you cannot do that" and ends the discussion. The better path requires that you dig deep to find out and consider what the business objectives are and whether what is proposed works or not. If not, bring a solution (e.g., "There are some problems with what's been proposed, but I think we have a work around that gets you to the same place"). Businesses remember the lawyers who solve problems versus those that just point them out.

4. **Learn the business.** This seems pretty basic, but it always amazed me when lawyers did not read their company's public filings, pay attention to strategic initiatives, or even know the name of their company's top customers. It is difficult to be effective and strategic unless you start to understand your company's business and the competitive dynamics it faces in the market place. Here are a few of the basics:
   - Know your company's products and services
   - Know who the customers are
   - Know who the competitors are (including strengths and weaknesses)
   - Know the current business objectives of your company
   - Understand the company's strategic plans (short-term and long-term)
   - Stay on top of trends that can impact your business
   - Subscribe to several industry publications and relevant blogs
   - Track how your company is perceived in social media

   If you're not sure how to do any of this, start by asking your manager or even better strike up relationships in the business with people who can help you understand these issues. They will be appreciative that a lawyer is taking time to understand how the business works.

5. **Think strategically.** One key thing your business partners are looking for is a lawyer who can think strategically. This means that you can see more

than just the immediate legal issue. It means you can "peer around corners" and see what's coming down the pike and how it may impact your business, not only legally but from an operational standpoint as well. For example, the new EU data privacy law[5] has been pending for around four years. A strategic lawyer followed the law through the legislative process and already understands its basic parameters and how it might impact the business and/or drive changes in operations. The strategic lawyer has already briefed their boss and/or management about the law several times and kept them up to date with what's coming. Additionally, he or she has gathered a cross-functional team that is ready to act now that the law has passed. The nonstrategic lawyer knows that a law has been pending but figures he or she will start to deal with it once it passes or actually goes into effect. To think strategically, you must constantly scan the horizon for risk. And remember that the horizon is global and not just your home country. One idea is to build a *risk map* (a bit like the famous board game) where you know (a) all the countries where your company operates, (b) the top three or four issues for each country (current and likely arising over the next three years), and (c) how you plan to monitor those risks and take action in the event the risk comes to pass. This doesn't have to be any more complicated than just simply keeping up with the news and relevant industry publications. For example, the currency exchange problems in Venezuela may seem remote to you, but they have caused numerous problems for foreign companies doing business there. A strategic lawyer is looking at the problem from multiple vantage points and is already thinking about what the currency problem could mean for his or her company (and not just legal issues), which outside parties might be helpful or hurtful if this is a problem, who in the business needs to know, and so on. The reason all of this is so important is because what the business ultimately wants is as much lead time as possible to consider and adapt to changes (legal or otherwise) that can impact the business.

6. **Build an executive presence.** You want to catch the eye of both the general counsel and other company executives. The first thing to remember is that every interaction/meeting/conversation with a vice president or higher is an audition for the general counsel job. They will remember if you came across as a clown or as someone they would trust running the legal process in the event of bet-the-company litigation or a major M&A transaction. I don't mean that you cannot have a sense of humor or be pleasant to be around, but just understand that everything about you—from how you talk to how you

---

5   http://www.nytimes.com/2015/12/16/technology/eu-data-privacy.html?_r=1.

dress—is being filed away for down the road. Be sure to take the time to come across as "executive material"[6] in your dealings with the business. A big part of this effort will involve how you "present" legal issues and advice to your audience—from a brown bag lunch with summer interns to a meeting of the board of directors. Everyone wants to see gravitas in their lawyers. Can you take complex legal issues and put them into a context that nonlawyers can understand? Can you be a "teacher"? Are you needlessly wordy or overly talkative (*hint*: embrace brevity)? At meetings, weigh in with good questions (show you're paying attention) and make solid points or observations when appropriate. You should be confident but not arrogant. Don't try to fake it either. If you do not know the answer, just say that and promise to get the answer quickly. Remember the basics—sit up straight, don't slouch, make good eye contact. Be able to think on your feet (but go into every meeting already thinking about the types of questions you may get and what the answers will be). If you want to be general counsel in the future, start acting, talking, and dressing like one now.

7. **Enhance your legal skills and credentials.** You may think being chair of the local bar association's employment law section is kind of mundane, but to nonlawyers (e.g., head of HR), it can be very impressive. Getting certified in data privacy law may just be putting a stamp on things you already know, but it is a great credential to have in the current environment of cyber risk. The point here is to always look for ways to enhance your legal skills and credentials because they will mean something when you go for the general counsel position (with your current employer or with another company). Look for areas that you are truly interested in enhancing or developing a skill, or which are important to the company (e.g., compliance programs). Join and get active in key legal organizations,[7] such as an ABA committee or your local ACC chapter. Write articles for your state bar association magazine. Pick an area of expertise and focus on that area. For example, there are a number of areas of the law that are usually part of a general counsel's background, such as corporate governance, risk management, regulatory, and investigations. Start a blog and become an authority on these types of issues, for example, "Smith on Governance." You don't have to write a treatise on the topic, but having credentials like this on your résumé can show CEOs, boards, and others that you can go deep in an important area of the law.

---

6 http://root.bryancavemedia.com/docs/acca.pdf.

7 http://www.washlaw.edu/legalassociations/.

8. **Enhance your nonlegal skills and credentials.** Just being a good lawyer is not enough anymore. The C-suite and the board want a general counsel who brings more to the table than good legal skills. In fact, they assume you have those skills if you're being considered for the top job. The way to be the more attractive candidate is being able to demonstrate important nonlegal skills. Some of these skills are discussed above, but here is a good list of areas you can focus on:
   - Judgment, including ethics and integrity (the general counsel job will involve making decisions with imperfect information in gray areas of right and wrong)
   - Legal budgeting and forecasting
   - Business and financial acumen (e.g., understanding balance sheets, profit and loss statements, and cash flow). Consider getting a "mini-MBA."[8]
   - Use of legal strategically to advance business interests (e.g., intellectual property issues)[9]
   - Thinking about the big picture
   - Partnering easily/influencing decisions/being self-aware
   - Hustling/ability to "get stuff done"
   - Ability to spot risks and take action before they become problems
   - Ability to effectively "triage" problems/weighing multiple data points and outcomes
   - Discipline and drive—first one in, last one out
   - Crisis management skills/calm in the eye of the storm
   - Thinking globally/cultural understanding[10]
   - Comfortable with technology/willing to try new things

   It's a long list[11] for sure and there are many other things I could add. The important lesson here is to look for projects and situations that allow you to develop and demonstrate these skills. No one is going to teach you ethics and integrity; you will need to demonstrate it every day. Similarly, consistently using

---

8   http://www.acc.com/education/businessedu/programs/minimba.cfm.

9   http://www.law.com/sites/articles/2015/12/17/board-up-the-brand-utilizing-legal-it-for-ip-protection-from-cybersquatters/?kw=Board%20Up%20the%20Brand:%20Utilizing%20Legal%2C%20IT%20for%20IP%20Protection%20from%20Cybersquatters&cn=20151221&pt=In%20Practice&src=EMC-Email&et=editorial&bu=Law.com&utm_source=Sailthru&utm_medium=email&utm_campaign=LAW%20ALL-PA&utm_term=PARALLALERT&slreturn=20160616145301.

10 https://hbr.org/2004/10/cultural-intelligence.

11 http://www.kornferry.com/institute/general-counsel-senior-leader-more-just-lawyer.

legal "strategically"[12] is something you will want to look for the opportunity to do, based on a good knowledge of the law, the business, and the competitive landscape.

9. **Seek out complicated projects that have exposure to senior management.** One concern I heard from some of the lawyers who worked for me involved how could they develop "management skills" when our department was lean and chances for promotion or for managing people were limited. It's a hard problem to solve, especially in smaller legal departments. One way around it is to seek out those "messy" cross-functional problems that every company has (and sets up a team to solve). Ask for the opportunity to be the person "from legal" on these projects or, even better, ask to head up the project team. These types of projects are usually high profile and can give you real hands-on experience with managing and motivating people, working and partnering across multiple business and staff groups, dealing with deadlines and pressure, preparing reports and presentations for business leaders, and—most important—having exposure to senior management. Lawyers who volunteer and work outside their comfort zone get noticed.

10. **Recognize the power dynamics in the legal department and in the company.** Sorry if I am the first one telling you this, but every legal department and every business comes with "politics"[13] and power dynamics. Some are not so bad; some are really bad. If you want to get to the top job, you need to be able to "read the room." Learn to understand what motivates some people, what drives them, what their objectives are. Start with being a good colleague within the legal department. Next, make friends and develop positive relationships outside of the legal department, especially with people who are likely to move up the chain around the same time as you would, that is, one day the 28-year-old analysts will be the 48-year-old executives running the company. Most important, work to be neutral and transparent in what you do as legal counsel. Remember that your client is the company, not any particular individual. The business will want a trusted advisor, a "consigliere" if you will. Earn trust by your actions and your discretion. But most of all, earn trust by giving good, thoughtful advice.

*****

---

12 http://sloanreview.mit.edu/article/finding-the-right-corporate-legal-strategy/.
13 https://www.mindtools.com/pages/article/newCDV_85.htm.

If you want to be general counsel, you may need to be realistic about your chances at your current company. You are probably not the only person in the department thinking about the job (and competition is always good). Sadly, companies will often overlook the talent in their own organization and go for a splashy hire or someone they—mistakenly—think has skills not present in the proposed internal successors. Be sure to promote the full range of your skills to your manager (and the general counsel) but know that in the end you are responsible for your career and for seeking out opportunities. One rarely gets "discovered." Moreover, you may have to leave to move up. There is nothing wrong with that. Get on the radar of legal recruiters in your area. All they need is a good résumé and to know that you're interested in hearing from them if any opportunities arise. It doesn't mean you'll leave your current position, but it keeps your options open. You may also decide that being the general counsel is not really what you're looking for in terms of a career. That's fine too. It's not a position suited for everyone and sometimes just being a damn fine lawyer is enough. But if you have the drive and desire, now is the time to start creating your plan to get to the top.

December 21, 2015

Ten Things: Ten Habits of Highly Effective In-House Lawyers

I have written a lot about the key to being a successful in-house lawyer[14] and the steps to take if you are interested in becoming the general counsel,[15] the latter being one of the most popular pieces I have written to date. I recently came across an old, dog-eared copy of Stephen Covey's 1989 business self-help masterpiece, *The 7 Habits of Highly Effective People*.[16] If you haven't read it, it's worth picking up a copy. As I flipped through the pages of the book I realized that most, if not all, of it is still relevant almost 30 years later. And it got me thinking about some of the things I learned as I advanced in my career as an in-house lawyer. Through luck, hard work, trial and error, excellent mentors, and other things, I stumbled upon a number of "habits" that I think make for highly effective and successful in-house lawyers. Here is what I think those habits are:

1. **Carry a notebook and write things down—by hand.** Wherever I went as an in-house lawyer I carried an 8½ × 11 black notebook. In fact, it was a very specific brand and model of notebook—the Mead Cambridge Limited Action Planner 06064. I still use the same model notebook today. I like this notebook because it is lined (and numbered) and lends itself to keeping lists and bullet points, with extra spaces for other notes, names, date, and so on. I use a notebook for two reasons. First, it's important to capture notes of meetings, phone calls, presentations, and so on. You will be amazed how often you refer back to your notebook and your notes. I also would print out and staple relevant emails, memos, and other documents to my handwritten notes to have an even fuller capture of what transpired. Second, writing things down by hand is a much more effective way to keep notes than using a laptop or tablet. When you

---

14 See page 3.
15 See page 5.
16 https://www.stephencovey.com/7habits/7habits.php.

write notes by hand, it forces you to tighten up the points (i.e., verbatim notes are too much to write) and allows you to focus on the speaker(s) versus having your head down typing. This, in turn, allows you to better absorb what's being said and to be a participant in the meeting versus a scrivener. Several recent studies reveal that taking notes by hand allows you to retain far more[17] and with deeper comprehension than typing notes. Simply put—typing your notes in real time during a meeting gives you a lot of text but more is not better.[18]

2. **Have a routine to start your day.** The most effective in-house lawyers have a routine to start their day that rarely varies.[19] The routine is designed to get them into their job as quickly as possible so they are "up and running" as the day begins. They get up at the same time every day. They are out the door and on the road (or at their computer) at the same time. Once they get to the office, they have a ritual. For many it's a cup of coffee and scanning a newspaper or trade papers, for example, *The Wall Street Journal*, *News 360*, *Financial Times*, and Law.com. For some, it's quickly checking through their calendar and email, or daily company reports. Others like to check out the sports scores or read a few joke news stories at *The Onion*. Some just carve out 15–20 minutes to think. The important thing is that they block out time first thing in the morning to do some task or tasks that get them ready to face the day. One part of my morning routine (which included bits of all of the above) was to write out the *top three* things I wanted to accomplish that day. This became my to do list. It was manageable, relevant, and flexible: everything you want in a to do list. I highly recommend it. The downside to having a routine to start your day is that if it gets disrupted, you can feel pretty out of sorts—as my wife can attest to. But the benefits of the routine far outweigh the downsides of the few times things go askew.

3. **Seek the help/opinions of others.** When it comes to the habits of effective in-house lawyers, there is a lot to be said about the ability to delegate work. While this certainly is an important skill, don't ignore the flip side to delegation, that is, the willingness to ask other people for help with whatever you are working on. By this I do not mean asking other people to do your work, but rather the ability to recognize when you may not have all of the knowledge or skills needed to complete the assignment or, more important, realizing that a second pair of eyes critiquing your work and ideas can be beneficial. As to

---

17 http://www.wsj.com/articles/can-handwriting-make-you-smarter-1459784659.
18 http://www.scientificamerican.com/article/a-learning-secret-don-t-take-notes-with-a-laptop/.
19 http://www.businessinsider.com/how-successful-people-spend-their-first-hour-at-work-2014-12.

the former, it's a matter of recognizing your limitations. We all have them, and there is no shame in reaching out for help. As to the latter, asking someone to review your work and ideas is one of the best ways to find out if you missed something and if your answer "holds together." Having the opportunity to correct or deal with any weaknesses in your work product before it goes to the ultimate "decider" is very beneficial. As to both, the bottom line is to not be too proud to ask for help or seek other's opinions. They'll appreciate being asked.

4. **Pick battles carefully.** One of my wisest in-house colleagues used to say that the hardest negotiation we would have regarding the deal was the one that would happen internally at the company. He was right. One thing you realize quickly as an in-house lawyer is that everyone has an opinion and an agenda, many think that they can do legal's job better than legal, and there are numerous internal politics you need to navigate every day. The higher up the chain you go, the more pronounced all of this becomes. A good habit to develop and perfect is to pick your battles carefully. If you decide that it's going to be your way or no way on every word, point, issue, and matter, then you are in for a painful career as an in-house lawyer. It just doesn't work that way. You need to pick your battles carefully and fight for things that are truly important and let the rest go. While you do not want to get a reputation as a pushover who gives in on everything, you do want a reputation as a balanced thinker who tries to find ways to get what the business wants done but will push back when you spot an issue of real importance, legal, strategic, ethical, administrative, or otherwise. Your best friend here is common sense. Most in-house lawyers have a ton of it, so use it liberally.

5. **Take risks.** Few people are effective or successful without taking chances, that is, risks. If you read my article on risk,[20] you will know I believe that people take risk because of the positives that can occur when the risk pays off. In other words, taking the most conservative position is not always the best position. Taking risks can be anything from accepting new responsibilities in the legal department, trying to utilize new technology, or throwing away the "old way" of doing something because you realize that the old way may no longer be the best way. It can mean taking a chance on a certain litigation strategy, such as a motion to disqualify a biased judge (which can have a real downside if the motion fails), to pushing hard for certain positions or language in a heated contract negotiation. The common thread occurring in all of these risk-taking scenarios is that the in-house lawyers taking the risk have thought

---

20 See page 239.

through the steps and consequences of what they are doing *before* they take the risk; they know how to game theory the risk.[21] They also have the ability to stay calm under fire or when things are not working out exactly as planned (even if their stomach is churning like mad inside). Most important, they don't try to fool themselves (or others) by overstating or underselling the risk and the benefits. Basically, they lawyer the crap out of the risk before they take it.

6. **Develop good people skills.** Effective in-house lawyers typically have good people skills. Strike that. They have amazing people skills. They look people in the eye when they speak with them. They learn and remember names. They say "hello" and "good evening" to everyone, from the CEO to the janitorial staff. And they always say "please" and "thank you" for even the smallest consideration from anyone. They are willing to laugh at jokes made at their expense, are self-aware,[22] and are generous with deflecting credit to others on their team or in the company. For some people, this is all perfectly natural. For most of us, it takes a lot of practice.[23] For example, whenever I sat down at the table for a meeting, I would draw the table in my notebook (yes, the same black notebook mentioned above) and I would write everyone's name next to where they were sitting. If I didn't know someone's name, I would just lean over and ask. Likewise, if I happened to be in the elevator with someone I didn't know, I would just introduce myself. It's amazing how well people respond to something so simple as just saying "Hi, I'm ...." Similarly, if I thought someone outside of legal was really helpful or did a good job on a project or at a meeting, I would send a short note to his or her boss just recognizing that fact. It costs nothing but a few minutes of time but the payoff in goodwill down the road is huge. People skills are in large part thinking about how you would like to be treated in any situation and then simply treating the people around you in that same manner.

7. **Get things done.** The ultimate measure of a successful in-house lawyer is "did she get stuff done"? No matter your people skills, risk taking, daily routine, or whatever, if it doesn't add up to concrete results it's not going to matter much at the end of the day. The math is simple. Since in-house legal services are a limited commodity, the more you can get done the more valuable

---

21 http://gametheory101.com/courses/game-theory-101/.
22 http://99u.com/articles/30437/its-all-our-fault-self-awareness-as-a-secret-weapon-for-habit-change.
23 https://www.mindtools.com/pages/article/newTMM_36.htm.

you become. In my experience, the in-house lawyers who got stuff done share three characteristics:

- They don't procrastinate—they just put their head down and get started. To recast an old Chinese proverb,[24] every email starts with the first keystroke. In other words, you need to take the first step to get to where you want to go. So, just get going.
- They don't worry about hours; they worry about minutes, that is, they are looking to use every minute they can to get things done. Those 5 minutes you're waiting for the meeting to start can be spent playing *Candy Crush*, or you can use those minutes to read a short article or return an email. Getting things done in large part requires finding the time to do the work. Don't waste the minutes.
- They have a fire in the belly that is unmistakable. They enjoy being a lawyer and have a passion for solving problems. They enjoy working for the company and the legal department. They have an enthusiasm that is contagious and even if the project turns into a "slog," they have the ability to keep things moving forward often through the sheer force of personality and goodwill.

8. **Don't over-rely on outside counsel.** Having the assistance of outside counsel can be extremely helpful, especially when you are faced with tough litigation or a challenging corporate transaction. Their experience and depth of bench can be a godsend. It's also easy in such situations to be overly deferential to, and overly dependent on, your outside lawyers, especially those silver-haired lions who are recognized as experts in their field. This is a mistake. First, it's your job to be sure to challenge your outside counsel on important matters, including briefing, strategy decisions, and drafting. You need to be sure you fully understand and agree with what they are proposing. The worst thing you can do is just simply assume they know everything about everything and just accept whatever they decide or give you. As an in-house lawyer, you have a unique understanding of the business, the industry, the personalities, and the politics. Your outside counsel does not. You need to bring that to bear throughout any representation as your outside lawyers will miss things simply because they don't know what they don't know. Second, while it is okay to defer to your outside lawyers during meetings with the business, it is not okay to abdicate. You need to participate in the discussion and you need to take a lead role in how things are laid out for the business leaders. If all you are doing is sitting like a potted plant, then the logical question for the business to ask is "why do

---

24 http://www.successconsciousness.com/blog/goal-setting/journey-begins-with-one-step/.

I need that person?" You need to have a point of view. Yes, it takes extra work to be prepared like this but not only is it worth it from a career standpoint, getting heavily involved is also rewarding from a personal satisfaction angle, that is, the ability to exercise your legal skills as part of a high-caliber team. The easiest way to ensure this happens is to discuss in advance with your outside lawyers your role during any meeting or teleconference.

9. **Read—a lot.** Another thing I have noticed about the most effective in-house lawyers I came across is that they all read—a lot. And they read a wide variety of things: newspapers, magazines, industry blogs, books, legal publications (including areas of the law they do not necessarily specialize in), or whatever else comes over the transom. Their reading included points of view that might not always agree with theirs, for example, the editorial pages of *The Wall Street Journal*, *The New York Times*, *The Guardian*, or *The Times*. Reading a wide spectrum of points of view helps you have better and more impactful conversations with many different people. You may not always agree with them, but you can better understand where they are coming from in their thinking and, potentially, empathize with them. Empathy is a powerful skill in business.[25] Being well read also allows you to be a better "story teller." If you can tell a good story, you have the ability to effectively communicate with just about anyone. This is not about telling 20- or 30-minute tall tales to amuse your audience. It's about short 3-to-5-minute narratives that help make your point in a way that is engaging and memorable. For example, if you can tell the other party a good "story" around why a certain clause is needed in the contract, it can go a long way to getting their acceptance to include just such a provision. The ability to tell stories is gaining acceptance as a critical business skill.[26] To be an effective in-house lawyer, it's a skill you need to develop as well.[27]

10. **Be yourself (*most of the time*).** There is an old adage out there that says if you want to truly be successful, you must *be yourself*. I agree with this to a point. I suggest that you be yourself—*most of the time*. No one other than the most insensitive clod is "themselves" 100 percent of the time. For example, I grew up in a household where swearing was pretty common and accepted. That said, I am sensitive to the fact that not everyone shares my enthusiasm for a good "#$%^&!" every once in a while. In fact, they might find it downright

---

25 http://www.huffingtonpost.com/douglas-labier/why-humble-empathic-busin_b_6042196.html.
26 http://blog.hubspot.com/opinion/why-storytelling-will-be-the-biggest-business-skill-of-the-next-5-years.
27 http://www.forbes.com/sites/danschawbel/2012/08/13/how-to-use-storytelling-as-a-leadership-tool/#56c14dc07ac9.

awful. Accordingly, I am not "myself" in all situations—I watch my manners or as some call it, I self-monitor my behavior. There is a great op-ed by Adam Grant in the June 5, 2016, *The New York Times* titled "Unless You're Oprah, 'Be Yourself' Is Terrible Advice."[28] In the article, he discusses another author's attempt to be "totally authentic" 100 percent of the time. For example, that person told his in-laws he found their conversations very boring. You can imagine how that went over. That author ultimately concluded that "deceit makes our world go round. Without lies, marriages would crumble, workers would be fired, egos would be shattered, governments would collapse." I don't know if it's as dire as all that, but I can vouch for the fact that the most successful in-house lawyers are "situationally aware"[29] and are constantly monitoring the room and themselves, understanding how best to pitch an idea or give criticism, when to make a joke and when to keep quiet, when someone needs a pat on the back or a kick in rear. I am not asking you to be a fake. It is definitely important to be yourself generally. If you're a laid-back person generally, you cannot go through your career pretending to be a "Type A" personality. But you always need to consider your audience and make a decision as to whether being 100 percent truly authentic is the best way to go at that moment, or maybe 85 percent authentic is good enough.

*****

I know there are a number of other "habits" one could include in the list above. Actually, some of the things on my list may actually be "traits" rather than "habits" but that's putting too fine a point on the message here. The point is, what do you need to do to be effective and successful? If you want to be more than Fred Flintstone clocking in 9 to 5 at the quarry, then these are the habits you can adopt, develop, or enhance that will make your in-house job more than just "a job." They can make it a career—a very successful career at that.

July 15, 2016

---

28 http://www.nytimes.com/2016/06/05/opinion/sunday/unless-youre-oprah-be-yourself-is-terrible-advice.html?_r=0.

29 https://www.linkedin.com/pulse/20140326204034-13387671-staying-situationally-aware-in-business.

Ten Things: How to Be More Productive Every Day

As in-house counsel, one of the questions you frequently ask yourself is "how am I ever going to get all of this stuff done?" Don't worry, you are not the only one asking that question. In the in-house world, there is never enough time, money, resource, or people to get to everything that needs to be done. If you're someone who cannot live with this type of situation, then you will not be happy as an in-house attorney. On the other hand, if you do not faint at the sight of an endless to do list and a decreasing legal budget, you've overcome the biggest hurdle and you're probably interested in trying to figure out ways to get more done within the hours you currently work and still leave some time for your family and yourself. I have written about using technology[30] to increase productivity but there are other things you can do.

First, let me say that I struggled with this problem almost every day I was in-house—especially when it came to balancing out time spent on work versus time spent with my family. I put a lot of thought and effort into trying different things to help me be more productive at the office so I could get myself out the door at a reasonable time every night. I didn't always get it right, but over the years I found a number of things that did help. This article will share some of my ideas on how to be more productive every day.

1. **Get up an hour earlier.** This is not a very popular option but it does really work. If you can manage to rise an hour earlier every day, you will get a dramatic increase in your ability to get things done. I found that the time period before 9:00 am on any workday was always more productive than the hours between 9:00 am and 5:00 pm (i.e., the time most of your clients are in the office or otherwise working). How productive? I estimate that I could get twice the amount of work done before 9:00 am than I could in any 2-hour window

---

30 See page 129.

during the day. It's quiet, there are few if any phone calls or meetings, and the email "pile" has not reached Mt. Everest proportions—yet. There is also the math to consider: If you can add an hour to your workday, that's 5 extra hours a week, 20 extra hours a month, and (cutting out days for vacations, etc.) around an extra 200 hours a year (or a month of extra time). You do not have to spend all of this extra time on work; it's just extra time you have to spend however you think best, for example, on yourself, with your family, or on work.

2. **Start the day with a "top three."** You can start each day with the most awesome, beautiful looking, detailed, comprehensive to do list in the world but we all know it gets blown to hell once the emails, meetings, and phone calls start (and more about to do lists below). One of the best pieces of advice I ever got was to write down the "three things" you really need to get done today and let that be your guide for the day. A to do list of 30+ items can make you feel like you're never going to get anything finished. Having a focused list of three things lets you adapt more easily to the ebb and flow of the day but still keep your eye on the most important tasks. If something doesn't make your top three list, then it can probably wait until tomorrow. And if you cross off all three things on your list, you can call it a good day at the office!

3. **Stop multitasking.** I hate to be the one to break this to you, but you actually *cannot* join a conference call, check email, and sign bills or do other paperwork all at the same time. If you're on a call, those people deserve your full attention. If you're at a meeting, put down the iPhone and pay attention. If you're at your desk and on a call, turn off the screen or close your laptop—an easy way to stop getting distracted by incoming email. Turn off social media and save it for lunchtime or a break. While you may think multitasking is letting you get more done, you're actually just doing a crappy job on multiple things. You'll actually get more done and be more effective by staying on task and in the moment. Put another way, slow down and focus. You'll be much more productive and a better in-house lawyer for it.

4. **Learn to truly delegate work.** You may have heard of the "Four Ds"—do it, delegate it, defer it, or delete it.[31] This is a pretty good way of looking at things as they come across your desk. I happen to think that "delegate it" is the most important one. Why? Because if you do it correctly and you truly let someone run with the project (i.e., telling them what you need and let them figure out the best way to do it), not only do you take work off your plate, you give challenging opportunities to your team so they can learn new things and new skills and feel like they are adding value to the department. I used to

---

31 http://lifehacker.com/avoid-feeling-overwhelmed-at-work-with-the-four-ds-me-1705678087.

look at something in my inbox and first think—"Is this something only I can do?" If not, who on my team can or deserves the chance? Next, "Is this only something a lawyer can do?" If not, who on the support staff can do it? Finally, "Is this something legal should be doing at all?" Meaning, don't fall victim to the business sending things to legal that they can actually do for themselves. There are a lot of things that come into legal that do not require a law degree to handle. Push those tasks back to the business. Be willing to help them; just don't be willing to do their work for them. That's a disservice to them and to the company.

5. **Dedicate set times to key projects.** If you have a "big rock" to break up, it can become the project you never start because you're always waiting for the "right time" to get to it. In the meanwhile you're filling up your day with smaller, less important tasks, or maybe just any task that you can use as an excuse to not tackle the big problems. Block out times on your calendar to work on these "big rocks" (yea, it took me a while to figure out that I could use my calendar for more than just setting meetings with others). Set aside an hour or two and only work on one project—no emails, no phone calls, and no interruptions. Once the time is up, stop and go on to other things. You'll be amazed at how much progress you make and how much better you feel that you finally got started busting up that rock.

6. **"Barf it up."** Apologies for the analogy but when I was just out of law school and in my first law firm job, I was having trouble getting started on writing an important memo. I felt a bit overwhelmed due to a strong desire to impress everyone with my writing skills. The young partner (who was waiting for me to get him the memo) came to my office and said "Just barf it up on paper dude and get started." What he meant was "don't sit there and try to write the perfect first draft or even the perfect introductory paragraph—just start writing." He was exactly right. You can waste a ton of time stalling and cursing the assignment or you can actually save time by just "barfing it up" and get going. Don't worry that you've just typed the longest run-on sentence in history or that you dangled that participle. You're going to need to edit what you write anyway, so just get going. It will come to you and it will get easier and go faster once you get started.

7. **Use the "small chunks" of time.** I never left my desk without bringing something along that I could work on or read or sign during the inevitable delay of the meeting getting started or any of the other many ways you can find yourself with 5, 10, or 15 minutes to kill during the workday. You can check your phone of course, but to me that's just spinning your wheels as you're going to look at all of those emails again when you get back to your desk. If you have an article you want to read, some invoices to sign, a brief or memo to edit, a

budget sheet to look at, whatever, use the little chunks of time to get things out of the way. And while we are on the topic of meetings, get out of the habit of scheduling every meeting for an hour. That seems to be the default setting for some reason. If you set a 1-hour meeting, the laws of human nature dictate that the group will stretch the proceedings to use up the full 1 hour, even if it could have been a 30-minute meeting. Start setting 30-minute meetings and just be more organized and ready to go.

8. **Lose the to do list.** If you're someone who spends time creating a detailed and comprehensive to do list and religiously updating it, you're probably spending way too much time on a thankless task. Take it from someone who's tried to make it work—lose the to do list. First, your email inbox is already a to do list (and Outlook has a lot of neat features to help you be more productive, including tracking the Four Ds mentioned above).[32] Second, I found that focusing on my top three and using post-it notes to write down other tasks and slap them on my desk worked far better than spending time trying to maintain a detailed to do list. As I completed a task, I tossed the post-it note in the trash. Another useful trick is to keep a folded piece of paper in your pocket and jot down things throughout the day, usually little notes to yourself to help you remember things. At the end of the day, take out the paper and decide what you need to do with each of the items you jotted down.

9. **Use forms and checklists.** As you go about your work over the next couple of weeks, start to jot down the times when a form or a checklist would have been (or was) helpful. If you're like most in-house lawyers, there will be at least a few times a week when this is true. If you have tasks or work that lend themselves to a form, a checklist, or any type of repeatable process, you can save a lot of time by putting those things into place—not only for yourself but also across the legal department if possible. Contract forms are the best example here. Having a checklist or form works in other areas too. For example, there are several things you're going to need to do when a new piece of litigation comes in. Have a checklist ready that reminds you exactly what to do, whom to contact (e.g., insurance, corporate communications, investor relations), and what information to pass along. Since you know there are several pieces of information about the suit that people will want to know, create a standard form/template where you can capture those things, for example, the parties, the court, a summary of the dispute, and a summary of the claimed damages. Putting the information into a standard form, with a standard look, and into a

---

32 http://unkcms.unk.edu/bf/_files/p_and_p_linked_files/4_Ds_records_management.pdf.

repeatable process will save time. You may even be able to delegate completion of the form to a paralegal or other staff member.

10. **Plan for next week/declutter your office.** I know that a lot of people like to get out the door as early as possible on Friday afternoon. I like to take 30 minutes at the end of the day on Fridays to plan for next week and declutter my office. First, since most people are bolting for the door, it will be fairly quiet, with few phone calls or meetings or urgent emails. Meaning you have some time to reflect back on the past week and think about what's going to be important next week and start to plan ahead (and more planning is a good thing). Go ahead and get your top three for Monday ready to go. Hopefully, whatever happens over the weekend will not change the list. Second, coming back to a clean desk on Monday will put you in a much better state of mind than coming back to a mess. Spend a little time getting things in their files or drawers and get your post-it notes updated/cleaned up. And begin to practice the "six-month rule," that is, if there are any magazines, articles, bar journals, and other clutter that you have not read or touched in six months—toss them into the recycle bin and move on. If it has sat on your desk or in your office untouched for six months, it just cannot be anything you need to keep around. Plus it feels really, really good to toss things out.

*****

There are many other ideas to increase productivity. One really good website to check out is Lifehacker.com.[33] To be clear, I am not advocating that anyone spend more time at work. Work is a jealous and fickle mistress, and it's challenging enough to balance the demands on your time without dedicating more of your time to the office. As in-house counsel, you need to accept that you will never get everything done. Learn to leave things for tomorrow. That said, there are ways to be more productive with your day without spending more time in the office.

October 30, 2015

---

33 www.lifehacker.com.

Ten Things: Writing Skills for In-House Counsel (It's Different In-House)

As general counsel I saw a lot of writing: emails, memos, policies, correspondence, and so on. Most of what I saw produced by my team was well written. Some of it was not. Wait, hold on. I take that back. It was well written for a lawyer but it was not well written for what the business needed. Here's an example: one day I received a very long email from a lawyer on my team discussing some litigation risks in a dispute brewing on the horizon. It was an email we planned to share with our executive team once it was finished. It began with a very detailed discussion of the facts and the law, including case citations and citations to secondary legal treatises. There were plenty of Latin phrases (I had to look some of them up in *Black's Law Dictionary*), and lots of "Wheretofores" and other legal jargon. There were even a few typos. And, at the very end was a long summary of everything I had just read along with a squishy conclusion saying essentially, on the one hand this but on the other hand that, with no clear recommendation on what to do next, no conclusion about the most likely outcome given the different risks at play, and no mention of next steps. There was so much information to wade through; it was like trying to find the score of the game in a Grantland Rice column. I knew that if we sent this out to the senior management, heads would explode long before they got to the end of the email.

I thought I knew what the problem was immediately. The lawyer who had written it had recently moved in-house from a big law firm. Sure enough, when I walked down to have a chat with him, I saw a treatise on legal writing on his desk, right next to a copy of *The Bluebook*.[34] Ah yes, problem confirmed. I asked him to pop down to my conference room to talk about the email. We sat down and I said, "The first thing you need to do is forget everything they taught you about writing in law school and at the firm." Second, "And here are some things

---

34 https://www.law.georgetown.edu/library/research/bluebook/index.cfm.

you need to know to write successfully as an in-house lawyer." Here are those key points:

1. **Listen.** The most important thing to know about writing as an in-house lawyer is to listen to what the client is saying. What is the problem and what does the client need from you? Sometimes we are so intent on getting started and jumping into the fray that we do not take the time to ensure that we really understand the question/assignment. Resist the urge to get cracking immediately. Instead, take a deep breath and start your "writing" by asking lots of questions right up-front and as needed going forward. Be sure you know the "who, what, where, when, and how" of the problem. Do you have all the facts? Are there key documents you need to better understand the issues? Is there someone else you should speak with to get more background? In short, be a lawyer. Some of your business colleagues will find all the questions annoying, but it is far better to be a bit annoying than to spend time preparing a document that misses the issue or doesn't help solve the problem. If the issues are complicated, send a short summary back to the client setting out your understanding of what the "go do" is and ask them to confirm that you got it right or to let you know if you are off-base.

2. **Always summarize the answer up-front.** When it comes to the actual writing, this is the key point for in-house lawyers to understand. Your business partners do not want to read through pages and pages of text to get to the answer. They need it "now." Figure out the main point of your email or memo and put it right up-front at the very beginning, in summary form. Get to the point as soon as possible. If the answer is simple and clear, that's great (and rare). If the answer is not clear, note that and set out the "most likely" answer/outcome. After setting out the "short answer," you can set out a detailed discussion of the facts and the analysis if needed.

3. **Keep it clear and simple.** Clarity is the goal of all written communication. Unfortunately, as lawyers, we frequently get bogged down in details, alternative theories, and "on the other hand" arguments. Yet, the most successful in-house lawyers are those who can take complex issues or voluminous information and turn it into something simple and straightforward using clear and concise language, all with the goal of enabling the business to make better informed decisions. Remember the basics. Who are your audience and what are you trying to tell them? What are my main points? Keep your sentences short and direct. Lose the $20 words and the footnotes. For example, don't say "The company, pursuant unto the common law of the State of Texas, unilaterally terminated Mr. Smith's situation" when you can say "The company fired Mr. Smith." Are there words you can cut? As someone said, all innovations are new, all friends are personal, and, as Colonel Jessup noted in *A Few Good Men*, all danger is

grave. Brevity is your friend. Edit your writing; then edit it again if you have time. A mentor once told me to write as if every word cost me $5. If you think like that, your writing will get tighter and clearer. Use examples, descriptions, or analogies if those can help the reader understand your point, such as illustrating how a clause in the contract is supposed to work. A footnote or two may be fine, but if you have extra information you think might be important, don't try to weave all of it into your document. Attach it to the email or memo or just note to the reader that additional information about "X" is available if they need it or want to see it. Finally, be sure to make your writing understandable to outsiders, that is, could someone outside the company understand what you are trying to convey? This is really important if your company gets into litigation where ambiguous or poorly written documents can sink you.

4. **Make it easy on the eyes.** No one likes staring at 3,000 words of text in block form. It just hurts your eyes and it's hard to read without getting lost. Break up blocks of text to make it easier to read and more interesting to look at. Use headings to transition to different sections or points; use bullets to quickly set out information; use **boldface**, *italics*, or underline to distinguish or emphasize things; try different margins for different sections; use a block quote now and then if appropriate; and so on. Your readers should be able to skim through the document and quickly get the gist of what you're trying to tell them. If you make the presentation of the writing easy on the eyes, you are more likely to engage the reader and have them grasp the key points.

5. **Grammar matters.** Grammar matters a lot for in-house lawyers. You are being judged and measured every time you interact with the business, especially when interacting with the executive team. One thing they look for is how well do their lawyers communicate. Your email may only be going to your friend in finance, but keep in mind that she may need to send it along to the CFO, who may in turn send it to the CEO or the board. While these folks may or may not know if you have a good legal mind, they will know immediately if you can write well. Bad writers generally do not advance in the company. Rule number one is to make sure you *always* check your spelling (and don't rely exclusively on "spell check"). Additionally, here are some common grammar errors[35] to lookout for when you write:
    - *It's vs. its*
    - *There vs. Their vs. They're*
    - *Are vs. Our*
    - *To vs. Too vs. Two*

---

35 http://blog.hubspot.com/marketing/common-grammar-mistakes-list.

- *Effect vs. Affect*
- *Which vs. That*

Be careful with overuse of exclamation points (!) and don't dive into the world of semicolons (;) unless you really know what you're doing. Note that in American English the commas and periods are always inside of the quotation marks, the opposite of our friends across the Atlantic (though I prefer the British style on this point). Finally, be sure to use active voice (subject-verb-object). I often lapse into passive voice when I write. It's not intentional; just comes from being lazy. Using the active voice makes your writing more direct and powerful. Many executives and board members look for this when they read memos or reports. I have seen it firsthand. My easy way of remember how to use active voice is to simply put the person or institution "doing" the action at the beginning of the sentence. It doesn't work all of the time but it works enough of the time. Following are a couple of examples:

- **Passive voice**: "It has been noted that summary judgment is rare in Alabama state court."
- **Active voice**: "Judge Smith notes that summary judgment is rare in Alabama state court."
- **Passive voice**: "The plaintiff was awarded $200,000 in damages."
- **Active voice**: "The jury awarded the plaintiff $200,000 in damages."

The rules of grammar can be tricky. One year I gave the members on my team a copy of Strunk and White's *Elements of Style*, still the best book on basic American English grammar I have found. Pick yourself up a copy, keep it nearby, and refer to it often.

6. **Eliminate jargon.** Another common mistake in-house lawyers make with their writing is using a lot of legal jargon—just like they are taught in law school and at the firm. As much as in-house lawyers laugh at business jargon like "drill down," "core competency," or "paradigm shift," just know that businesses groan at many things their in-house lawyers write. This includes common legal Latin phrases that always pop up when lawyers write, such as *prima facie*, *ultra vires*, *dictum*, *a fortiori*, and *res ipsa loquitur*. Likewise, dump the "Ye Olde Middle English" phrasing when you write to the business, including words and phrases such as the following:
   - *Herein above*
   - *Salient*
   - *Prerogative*
   - *Henceforth*
   - *Theretofore*
   - *Party of the second part…*
   - *Whereas*

- *These presents known*
- *Privity*

Put simply, when you use Latin or "Middle English," no one really knows what the hell you are talking about. Go with "plain English" instead.

7. **Lose the "Bluebook."** Yes, you did pay a fortune for your legal education and for someone to teach you about "Bluebook" form, "Shepardizing" cases, string citations, how to properly capitalize a treatise, etc. Alas, none of this is useful when writing to the business. Businesspeople do not want nor need to see this after a key point.

> *See Miller v. Sterling*, 678 A.2d 690, 701 (Del. Ct. App. 1998); accord *Coyote v. ACME Company*, 32 N.W. 456, 500 (Minn. 2001). But see *Nowitzki v. James*, 284 So.3d 879 (Fla. S. Ct. 2011).

Likewise, they do not care about the title of the treatise or law review article you used to get the answer. You are not writing for a partner at a law firm or for the court; you are writing for business professionals. There is little, if any, need to include case or other citations in your communications to the business. The exception to this rule is when you are writing to another in-house lawyer or to the general counsel and you know they are looking for legal research on the issue.

8. **Give an answer/options/recommendation.** No one likes to be wrong, especially lawyers. But, as we all know, the law is rarely black or white, so a lot of lawyers like to "fudge" on giving an answer. You see this when they write "On one hand, the court might do X. On the other hand, the court might do Y." This drives businesspeople crazy. They don't want to hear about how goofy the court is or how many different factors can affect the answer. They just want your best answer. Give them one. I would write it like this:

> There are a number of factors that can impact how the court will decide the issue. Based on what we know today, and in particular [Y], we think the mostly likely thing the court will do is [X].

Similarly, the business wants to know what its options are in any particular circumstance and, ultimately, what it should do. This often requires you, as the attorney, to set out and weigh risk. You need to describe the type of risk(s) at issue, the range of potential consequences (e.g., worst case, middle case, best case), and the probability of each, and then give a recommendation or conclusion based on your analysis. Could you be wrong? Absolutely, but businesspeople deal with risk, unknowns, and probability all the time.

9. **Call to action/next steps.** Always be clear with your reader about the next steps, that is, what happens or is needed next. For starters, if your email is urgent with action required, put that in the subject line or in the first sentence or two. If you need immediate action, you need to tell that to the reader. At the end (or in your summary at the beginning), tell the reader what steps are needed next, even if you are telling him or her nothing more is needed at this point. For example, if action is needed you might write:

> The next draft of the contract is due on Thursday. We need to give direction to the negotiating team by Wednesday noon. Our legal recommendation is we go with Option A. Please let us know if you agree or have a different preference, or if you need additional information.

10. **Watch for privilege issues/Stay professional.** As a lawyer you get spoiled by the fact that much of what you write is "privileged" and will probably never see the light of day outside of you and the client. Don't get too comfortable with this position, especially once you are an in-house lawyer (as those practicing outside the United States already know). Courts are becoming more hostile to applying the privilege to in-house counsel communications, usually tied to the issue of whether the in-house lawyer is giving legal advice or business advice. Two things you need to do: (a) take all the necessary steps to establish and protect the attorney client privilege,[36] including stating right up-front that you are "providing legal advice," and (b) be sure you are giving legal advice. If not, write with that understanding in mind. If the document is "mixed," try to separate the legal discussion from the business discussion, so the legal part can be redacted if necessary. Finally, always be professional with your in-house writing, even casual emails. Everything you write on the job as in-house counsel is a business document; treat it like one. Since you never know who might be reading something you write, be sure you "write smart"[37] and keep it classy at all times.

*****

Regardless of whether you work in the United States or elsewhere, the ability to write clearly is your most important tool as an in-house lawyer. Writing for businesspeople is challenging as legal writing and business writing are very different

---

36 See page 263.
37 See page 45.

creatures. You often need to put aside years of training of how to "write like a lawyer" and, instead, learn to "write like a businessperson"—who just happens to know a lot about the law. If you are an in-house veteran, you know you will get better over time if you keep the differences top of mind. Don't get too hung up on trying to be perfect. You won't be. I know, as I have made, and continue to make, a lot of the mistakes noted above. But I do try to apply the lessons I have learned every time I write something.

February 16, 2016

Ten Things: What In-House Lawyers Want from Outside Counsel

My friends who are outside lawyers are always interested in what it was like to be in-house counsel. Besides being envious of the fact that I did not have to keep track of my time, they would (and still do) ask me, "what do in-house lawyers want from outside counsel?" I also keep in touch with a lot of the in-house lawyers I worked with or met over the course of 20+ years on the "inside." They often share with me the things they like and don't like about outside counsel. I recently had conversations with both "sides" and it got me thinking about how in-house lawyers are not good at telling their outside counsel what they want, while outside counsel are not good at asking in-house lawyers what they need. So, I decided to try and crack this nut. This article focuses on what in-house lawyers really want from outside counsel. It is written based on my in-house experience and from the point of view of a general counsel (but I am pretty confident these points resonate with all in-house lawyers regardless of position, here in the United States and globally):

1. **Be practical.** The most important thing I need from my outside counsel is for you to be practical. You need to understand that law review answers may be interesting, but they are not very useful to me. I need practical advice, that is, things that work in the real business world based on real-world experience — and which show me that you understand the context of your answer within the realities of my business. For example, think twice about telling me I need to register my trademark in 108 countries when I only do business in 5. Be strategic in your thinking and options presented. Most of all, I need you to give me your counsel on what you would do under the circumstances. If all you do is tell me "You have Options A, B, or C" but don't tell me which option you'd recommend (and why), then you're missing the point as to why I hired you in the first place. I may disagree and go with a different option, but that's not necessarily a bad thing.

Data privacy expert Chris Zoladz wrote a really good article about anticipating several core questions business executives will ask regarding legal advice about compliance with certain data privacy laws:[38]
- *What is the cost of noncompliance versus cost to comply?*
- *How actively is the rule enforced?*
- *What are consequences of noncompliance?*
- *Which are the companies that have experienced compliance issues and what were the results?*

These same core questions apply broadly to just about any type of legal advice you give. If no one is enforcing the rule and/or the consequences for a violation are small, but you're telling me undergoing expensive compliance is "essential" because rule is the rule, then you're not being practical or "keeping it real." In fact, you are probably losing credibility quickly, and so will I if I adopt the same posture with my executive team.

2. **Keep me informed.** I am surprised how often I need to remind my outside lawyers to keep me up-to-date and in the loop—seems pretty basic, but not everyone gets it. Here is a list of things outside counsel working for me should consider each day:
   - *Have you returned my last email or phone call?* If not, do it immediately, even if you're telling me that you cannot get to my question right this moment. At least I know you got my message.
   - *Keep me updated even if I don't ask about an update.* Don't make me chase you for information about my matter. Keep me regularly updated even if you're telling me nothing new has happened. That way when the CEO/business calls me, I already have the answer. If your update or message is important, make sure I received it. Use a "read receipt" or follow up by telephone.
   - *If you are out of the office, have you turned on your out-of-office message for email and voice mail?* If not, are you checking it every day and getting back to clients? If you are not checking it and you do not have an out-of-office message turned on, you are basically telling me you "don't care."
   - *Don't let me be surprised.* I should know every important development, material deadline, hearing date, deposition date, and so on in advance and you need to remind me of the deadlines as they get closer in. I do not have access to the sophisticated calendaring systems law firms use. I may put it in

---

38 https://www.linkedin.com/pulse/anticipating-privacy-legal-compliance-questions-from-chris-zoladz.

Outlook or I might write it on a post-it note. If I get surprised—or worse the CEO or the board gets surprised—that is a bad day for me ... and for you.
- *The bottom line*. Bad service like this is rarely something I will call you out on directly; I will just stop using you and your firm. You are accountable for everyone on your team as well. If they are not responsive, you are painted by that same brush. You have a lot of competition out there, all of whom are ready to return my emails and phone calls and keep me posted.

3. **Communicate succinctly and in a useful manner.** Twenty-page memos are not helpful. Ten-page memos are not much better. Find a way to communicate with me in a succinct and to-the-point manner. I have written before about legal writing skills.[39] While aimed at in-house lawyers, the points in that article apply equally to outside counsel. You need to keep things simple. If you need to go deeper, call me. We'll get to the answer much faster that way. If there is a brief I need to review, don't wait until the night before to send it to me. The odds of me having sufficient time to review it at that point are low. Let me know something is coming and then build in enough time for me to review, respond, and comment on important papers or decisions. Don't assume that what works well for one client works for all the rest. Ask me how I want you to communicate with me, for example, via email, weekly phone calls, text messages, and written status reports. And for outside—and in-house—counsel under 30, I recommend you learn the proper use of the word "like," as in "I like to hear good speakers give a speech" versus "Like, I was standing, like, near the podium, like, and, like, it was such a good, like, speech."[40] Finally, don't send me a letter with an attachment you could have emailed to me (and then bill me for "memo to client"). I need George Jetson, not Fred Flintstone.

4. **Cost versus rate.** There's a difference between "rate" and "cost." While I am shocked by $1,000+ per hour rates, I am willing to consider paying high rates *if* there is unique expertise that comes with the price tag. But what I really pay attention to is the overall cost of the matter. That's because I need to see value for the money I am paying. If I do not feel there is value, it doesn't really matter what your hourly rate is. If I have to pay for three additional lawyers to get the partner with the $1,000 rate, I am not sure that is going to get me the value I am looking for either. I do want to see you get creative with billing options. Fixed fees or "capped" fees, for example, are great because I get certainty as to my final cost. Give me different rates for differing types of work, for example, charge me lower rates for the discovery phase and a higher

---

39 See page 27.
40 https://www.attorneyatwork.com/like-yikes-articulate-advocate/.

rate for trial or a different rate for due diligence versus drafting the merger agreement. And yes, it's true, I don't want to pay to train your first-year lawyers. I don't mind if they tag along with you, but don't bill me for it, or, at a minimum, give me a highly discounted rate for their work. Lastly, there's more you can do for me than just legal work. Make your associate training programs available to me and my team. Share work product (memos, briefs, etc.) with me—properly redacted. Give me guides, checklists, sample clauses and agreements, Continuing Legal Education (CLE) programs, and other practical and useful tools, like desk books and handbooks. Give me access to your facilities and conference rooms if I need them. Find ways to give me "more" than just the billable hour I am paying for.

5. **Don't tell me it's too hard to budget or predict costs.** In-house counsel are expected to budget for every matter or, at a minimum, for the month overall. That is why I need a budget for every matter. You should volunteer this instead of waiting to be asked. No in-house counsel wants to hear that it is hard to set a budget or predict costs. I know it's hard but since that line doesn't work for me with my CFO, it's not going to work for you either. You can tee up the assumptions and note that if something material changes, the budget changes too. I understand. That said, you really need to spend time developing the budget and the assumptions that went in to it. If you just ballpark the number it will be obvious. Show your work. How many depositions? Summary judgment motion? Document reviews for each MB of data? You should be able to accurately estimate the costs of the key milestone events. Don't forget nonlawyer costs when you budget, for example, travel, printing, data storage, court reporter, and experts. The budget is incomplete if you don't include these numbers. Next, you and your team need to live within the limits of the budget every day. There are no "black holes" for billing hours. If there are problems with meeting budget (i.e., a material deviation), do not delay in letting me know as soon as you see it. The sooner we can discuss it, the easier it is for me to deal with the problem and work with you to make smart choices to get spend back on track—or get the finance team on board if that's not possible. Follow the engagement letter and my outside guidelines (and ensure everyone on your team does too). Don't make me be the one who is reviewing the invoice and finding the wrong rates, misapplied discounts, or expenses that we agreed would not be charged to me on the bill. If you cannot get the bill right, I'm having questions about whether you will get the legal analysis right. It needs to be important to you—important enough that you have already gone through the bill and made sure everything lines up under our agreement.

6. **Ask me how you can improve.** I appreciate getting the opportunity to tell you how you are doing and things you can do to improve your services. Just ask.

I will complete your survey, especially if it asks relevant questions and seeks honest feedback in a manner that I do not feel will damage my relationships with the lawyers at your firm, that is, I want to be honest but if you're not preparing your team for honest feedback, then I become the "bad guy" client and that's not what I want. I also want to do an in-person, well-organized postmortem after big projects or litigation to figure out what we did right and where we (including me, my team, and my company) can improve in the future. That said, I don't want to pay you and your team to work with me on a postmortem. It's a chance to team up to create a better relationship, not a way to bill a few more hours.

7. **Learn my business.** I mentioned above that you need to give me practical advice tied to the realities of my business. In other words, if you want to be my lawyer over the long term, learn how my business works, how it fits in the marketplace, what countries we do business in, who my competitors are, and what are the challenges the company faces (business and legal). Read our public filings and our "press room" posts. Follow the company on Twitter. Ask me to grab some coffee and teach you the basics and give you insights into my company (I'd be happy to—and impressed that you asked me). Get the names of key industry publications and blogs and subscribe to them. Keep an eye out for things that you think might be helpful to me or that identify potential threats or bumps in the road. Send them to me, along with a short description of why you think the article is interesting. Become an advisor, not just a lawyer.

8. **Your marketing materials/plans need a little work.** You can send me all the marketing materials and brochures you want, but if it's more than a few pages long I am probably not going to read it. That might affect how you think about the ROI on your marketing dollars. Say what you need to say in two pages or less. I am interested in your credentials, but I don't want to read a list of every speaking engagement you've ever had, or about articles you wrote in 1989. I find your client alerts and blogs helpful, but only when they are relevant to my particular area of focus (litigation, corporate, etc.), the business generally, or a specific legal issue I am working on. Don't make me have to find them on my own. Ask me if I am interested in getting alerts/blogs and, if so, which ones. Make it easy for me. Your competition does.

When you invite me to dinner or the game, don't forget to invite my spouse/significant other if you can. They may not be able to come but they will appreciate you inviting them. And don't forget my team. It means a lot to me if you think of them when opportunities for tickets and the like arise. When we're together, don't hard sell me about your firm. I know why we're at lunch or dinner. Let me get to know you and vice versa. Not every "social" outing has to be a big production. Breakfast (or just coffee) can be better than a 3-hour dinner at the fancy steakhouse—and you get to be home that evening instead of entertaining me. Consider offering me 5 hours of free legal advice instead of dinner or tickets. That's something I can really use!

If you're going to cold-call me (literally or via email), you need to give me a really good reason to listen or read. If it's about a new lawsuit, send me a copy of the complaint. Give me your initial thoughts and strategy (or explain why you're an expert in this area). Show me how you can save me a significant amount of legal expenses, that is, I am probably not moving law firms because you're 5 percent cheaper than my current law firm.

9. **Value my input.** I am the best resource you have about the company. Not only can I help you get the information you need for our matter, but also I understand the marketplace, the board of directors, the C-suite, and just generally "how things work" at my company. If you ignore me and my input, you are putting yourself and my company behind the eight-ball right from the start. Make me a real part of the team. Note that the odds are good that I am not an expert in antitrust or tax or M&A finance or whatever else I hired your firm to work on. I will have questions and some will be very basic. Don't assume I know anything about the litigation process or the intricacies of tax-efficient corporate structures, but I may be embarrassed to admit that. Ask me at the start of—and throughout—the engagement if there are any points of law I would like to understand better or learn more about. I will be grateful for the opportunity to learn. Be patient and answer my questions, but don't talk down to me. Treat everyone on my team like you would treat the "general counsel" and don't try to circumvent them and come directly to me (they will tell me). Basically, make me look good and I'll make you look good. Be "ahead of schedule and under budget." Do this and I'll be a reference, I'll do the "Chambers"[41] thing for you, I speak well of you to the partner, and I'll let your firm use the company name in your marketing materials. But you have to earn it.

10. **Be honest and truthful.** I know when you're talking "bull" or not giving me the full story. No need to sugarcoat things. If something "bad" happened, I need to know what happened, why it happened, and what our plan is to fix it. Trust me, I am going to get asked those same questions from my boss or the board. If you dropped the ball, just tell me that. If I (or the company) dropped the ball, tell me that too. Be balanced with good news and bad; for example, if we have major problems with our case, don't wait until two weeks before trial to suddenly tell me that we need to seriously consider settlement because

---

41 http://www.chambersandpartners.com/guide/global/2.

our position is really weak. You cannot imagine how poorly (by factors of 10) that will go over with the business—and with me. And don't tell me every one of your associates is a superstar and every partner is top of his or her field. I know they are not. And that's okay. In fact, you get bonus points if you say "we're probably not the best suited for that type of matter but we can get you some recommendations." That will keep me coming back to you versus a bad experience with your nonsuperstar associate or less-than-stellar partner.

*****

The good outside counsel I worked with over 20 years (and there were a lot of them) did all or most of the above regularly. The other ones did not. Every in-house lawyer will have a slightly different "top ten." I encourage in-house lawyers to be proactive and look for opportunities to tell outside counsel what you want and need, what you value and what you don't, and what makes you happy or unhappy. Outside counsel, if you want to know what in-house counsel want—ask them. They'll tell you.

March 14, 2016

Litigation

Ten Things: Drafting Documents and Emails

As in-house counsel, you already know that poorly drafted documents, especially emails, can hurt your company; for example, M&A deals can get derailed or litigation extended. You can find examples every day of "bad" emails[42] being read in court. Labels like "confidential," "company private," "restricted," and "proprietary" will not protect documents from being obtained through proper legal process.

Document requests in litigation or government investigations are broad, typically calling for correspondence, handwritten notes, agreements, drafts, email (email backup tapes), sent files, deleted emails, calendars, spreadsheets, documents on tablets and smartphones, graphs, expense reports, voice mail, meeting agenda, calendar entries, copies of media articles, and so on. Consequently, it's important that your business colleagues understand the importance of properly prepared documents and emails (and the potential harm from not doing so).

Below are ten things you can use in your daily dealings and conversations with the business to help limit problems that can arise from poorly prepared documents. I have included some links to other resources as well. A lot is focused on emails, but the rules apply to pretty much any written communication (including instant messages and recorded voice mails). Feel free to cut and paste these into your own checklist or email (or however you best can get the word out at your company).

1. **Understand that emails are business communications.** Treat them as such, just as you would if you were writing a "formal" business letter. Your company should have an email/document policy[43] spelling out what is expected from

---

42 https://www.yahoo.com/news/apple-heads-trial-over-digital-music-claims-080615089--finance.html?ref=gs.

43 http://www.policypatrol.com/white-papers/why-and-how-to-create-a-corporate-email-policy/.

employees when preparing any work-related communication. If you have a policy, enforce it, and get the tone set from the top.

2. **Prepare emails and documents with knowledge that they may be seen by third parties and/or published on page 1 of the *New York Times*.** I used to tell folks to pretend that every email they write starts with "Dear Government Regulator" or "Dear Company Suing Us" and then think about how that affects what they write.

3. **Don't write emails when you are angry.** Take time to cool off. Writing an email when angry or upset may feel good at first, but you will inevitably regret firing off an email in the heat of the moment.

4. **Mark draft documents as "Draft—subject to revision."** Mark the document as a draft when it is not finalized (on every page) and delete drafts as soon as the next version is ready or, if necessary, when the final version is prepared. It's difficult to say something was just a draft when it's not marked as a "draft."

5. **Avoid absolute or dogmatic statements.** Things are rarely "black and white." Use words like "usually," "sometimes," "mostly," "apparently," and so on to show nuance and that circumstances matter. PowerPoint lends itself to short, declarative sentences. But, when your document is flashed up on a big screen in front of a jury, it's hard to later say "I meant 'sometimes' that is the case." That may have been what you meant, but it's not what you wrote.

6. **Don't speculate about legal issues.** Leave that for legal, for example, don't write "we breached the contract." You simply may not be aware of all of the contractual obligations and how to truly interpret the agreement or the facts. If you need legal advice, ask the legal department directly and be sure it is clear in the body of the email that you are seeking legal advice so as to best maintain any applicable privilege.[44]

7. **No profanity/off-color humor.** No matter how funny you may be in real life, regulators, judges, and juries will not appreciate it. These are business documents. Treat them so. Same thing goes for "funny" pictures in presentations. These can and will be taken out of context by the other side in a dispute.

8. **Avoid "gung ho" statements.** For example, "dominate the market," "destroy a competitor," "leverage our dominate position," or "impede a competitor/ competition"—these types of statement may get the testosterone pumped up but they can come back to bite you in court. Be boring and stick to the facts. It's a business document. Treat it so.

---

44 http://www.out-law.com/topics/dispute-resolution-and-litigation/privilege/legal-professional-privilege-some-practical-considerations/.

9. **Project names matter.** A name like "Project Death Star" may be funny to you, but will not be funny to the jury. Keep project names boring.
10. **Don't send an email telling someone to destroy or delete emails/documents.** For example, "delete this email after reading"—this type of email is probably worse than whatever was in the email you were trying to get deleted. Trying to explain what you really meant will likely be hard. And, once you send an email, you can pretty much bet it will be around for years and years regardless of any instruction to delete it. I used to tell my folks, "The only things left after full-out global nuclear war will be cockroaches and regrettable emails."

*****

No one is perfect. Despite your efforts, people will write "dumb" documents and emails.[45] It doesn't mean they are bad people. More likely, they just weren't thinking hard enough about what they were writing and how it may be perceived down the road. That said, you need to stay vigilant and keep working with the business to make sure they understand how harmful bad documents can be to your company. Communicate regularly with the business about this issue (e.g., email blasts or host a lunch and learn); do live training at staff meetings or large gatherings of employees (webcasts are a great tool too). Use real examples from the headlines (or company documents) to bring the points home. To be safe, ask your outside counsel to help you prepare any presentations or at least give yours the once-over. When you come across poorly drafted emails or documents, take some time to point out to the author what the problems are and how he or she can improve the drafting (especially with the senior management who will set the tone for the entire company). Use the occasion as a teaching moment and be kind when you do so. No one likes the "holier than thou" lawyer routine. The business will appreciate the help and advice and you'll sleep better knowing the quality and tone of your company's business documents will improve.

December 10, 2014

---

45 http://www.cbsnews.com/news/unsend-the-10-worst-emails-ever-sent-in-the-pharma-business/.

Ten Things: Your Company Has Just Been Sued—Now What?

It's hard to recall a more disconcerting feeling than getting a copy of a lawsuit filed against your company. If you have no experience with litigation, this can be a panic-inducing moment. And no matter how experienced you are in handling litigation, your stomach will start to flutter as you read through the allegations.

I was a litigator in private practice and I definitely saw my share of litigation, big and small, as in-house counsel. Over the course of that time I developed a standard list of "things to do" when a lawsuit came across my desk. I did this because it's easy to forget some basic things you need to do up-front to put yourself in the best position to defend the claim. Below are ten things to do when your company gets sued (I have added links to additional resources in key spots).

1. **Read the complaint.** Take a deep breath, find a quiet place, and read through the complaint. First pass is a quick skim to get the gist of what's alleged (and just because it's alleged doesn't make it true). Then, a second more careful reading. The first thing you will be asked by the business is "what is the lawsuit about?" Reading twice will help you answer that question. As you read, check to be sure the suit has named the right parties and that service is proper. Is there an arbitration provision or a dispute escalation process required by your contract? Did they follow it? Mistakes like these are common and they can buy you additional time to respond.
2. **Prepare a short summary of the lawsuit.** This will help you focus and distill the issues. Include basic information like the parties to the suit, where you are being sued and the judge, the claims made against your company, and the types of damages alleged (monetary, injunctive, etc.). You'll also start a list of potential defenses to the claims.
3. **Identify key documents and witnesses.** As you prepare your summary, make a list of documents (contracts, emails, presentations, etc.) mentioned in the suit. You should gather those up quickly and review them as soon as possible. Are any company employees named? If so, start a list of witnesses to interview.

If no one is named, think about the part of your business involved in the suit and who within that organization can help you identify potential witnesses and documents.

4. **Implement a litigation hold.** *Do this immediately.* Litigation today is as much a game about "gotcha" over discovery issues as it is about the merits of the claim. A proper litigation hold[46] is of paramount importance. Use the materials you prepared in the previous step to identify whom you need to contact to ensure they preserve documents (and remember, "documents" is broadly defined, that is, hard copies, soft copies, drafts, calendar entries, and instant messages). You should have a standard litigation hold notice on hand. Don't worry about gathering up "every" document at this point. Outside counsel will drive the collection process down the road. As the case develops, refine and update your list of people subject to the hold and what records need to be kept. Regularly remind all of the people affected by the litigation hold that it is still in place (e.g., via a monthly or quarterly email) and get them to affirmatively acknowledge that they received each notice/reminder (including the initial notice) and understand their obligations.

5. **Who needs to know?** If it's a small claims matter, probably only a few people. If it's major litigation, then certainly the CEO and CFO and other C-suite executives (and likely the board of directors). Keep in mind that it is rare that a senior executive fully understands the litigation process. You'll probably need to some Litigation 101[47] as you look to soothe nerves within the company. Since almost all lawsuits show up in some type of electronic docket (e.g., the PACER system), the media will likely receive a copy. For example, employee claims can be particularly appealing to the media. Bring your corporate communications team up to speed early on all but the most minor litigation. Having a response ready to go in the event the media reaches out to your company will save you a ton of late night work. If you work for a publicly traded company, contact your investor relations team and disclosure committee (and you may need to file an 8K or add to your next 10Q).

6. **Does insurance cover the claim(s)?** For any material litigation, check with your insurance broker or internal team responsible for insurance to see if any of the allegations are covered by any of the company's policies (directors and officers liability, errors and omissions, commercial general liability, etc.). Check them all. And remember, it is not the headings of the claims that

---

46 http://www.ned.uscourts.gov/internetDocs/cle/2010-07/LitigationHoldTopTen.pdf.

47 http://www.martindale.com/medical-malpractice-law/article_Foster-Swift-Collins-Smith-PC_1604692.htm.

control whether insurance is triggered, but the factual allegations contained in the complaint. Don't make the mistake of just looking at the title of Count I or Count II and concluding there is no insurance coverage. If there is any basis for coverage under the facts alleged, notify your carrier. The duty to defend is broader than the duty to indemnify. Your broker/internal team will help with this. Be watchful of how the insurance company responds[48] to any notice.

7. **Select outside counsel.** Unless your company handles litigation internally, you will need to hire outside counsel. You probably have a go to list already in place but don't hire a firm on knee-jerk reaction. There are many things to consider before picking a counsel, including where the claim was filed, does it involve claims based on unique statutes, who represents the plaintiffs, and how much/what is at stake. It may be that there is a temporary restraining order[49] involved and you simply need to make an immediate choice and go. But, if you have time, think hard about who would be the best choice. Time and other circumstances permitting, running a request for proposal process can be helpful. Not only will you be able to compare expertise and rates, firms typically provide some type of detailed preview of how they would attack the case—which you can use even if you don't select that firm.

8. **Can this be settled/resolved quickly?** Just because a lawsuit was filed, it doesn't mean the dispute cannot be resolved quickly. I was involved in several cases where all it took was a phone call or two to get litigation resolved (usually involved correcting a faulty factual premise). Would early mediation[50] be something the other side would find appealing? Does your company just owe some money and needs to pay it? It's worth spending some time before you crank up the litigation machine to try to quickly resolve the dispute if possible.

9. **Who is the client?** You typically think of the company as a whole as your "client." That's true enough. But, who will you work with on settlement authority, budget, mediation, discovery, and the like? You need someone in the business to be your "client." Work with senior management to identify that person and develop a strong working relationship going forward.

10. **Are any confidentiality issues triggered?** Litigation is a very public process. Start thinking about any sensitive trade secrets (e.g., price information or contracts terms) or reputational issues that could arise throughout the case.

---

48 http://www.americanbar.org/publications/gpsolo_ereport/2012/march_2012/bad_faith_under_commercial_general_liability_policy.html.

49 http://www.insidecounsel.com/2013/08/08/litigation-elements-of-a-preliminary-injunction-an?&slreturn=1467226819.

50 http://www.knightdisputeresolution.com/mediation/early_mediation_saves_money/.

If you think the plaintiff has already violated a confidentiality clause in the agreements at issue in the lawsuit (i.e., disclosed confidential information in the complaint), get a protective order[51] on file as soon as possible and try to get the documents sealed. Keep confidentiality issues top of mind as you go forward. Outside counsel will be invaluable here.

*****

The list above is a good start to get you on top of litigation filed against your company. There are, of course, many other things to start thinking about (e.g., budget/costs, counter claims, staffing the case from the legal department) but this list will put you in great shape, especially if the CEO calls down and wants to know what you're doing with respect to that new lawsuit filed against the company. Now you have ten things you're doing right off the bat. Above all, don't panic. Litigation in the commercial context is almost inevitable for companies, especially in the United States. It's going to happen at some point. When it does, it's your chance to step up and be the calm in the eye of the storm.

December 18, 2014

---

51 http://www.smithmoorelaw.com/Confidentiality-and-Protective-Orders-08-05-2013

Ten Things: Explaining Litigation to the Board and the CEO

One of the first things I wrote was called Your Company Has Just Been Sued: Now What?[52] which deals with the ten things you should do when a new lawsuit comes in the door. Equally important is what you should be doing a year or more into the lawsuit. In particular, how have you explained (and reported on) the litigation to your CEO and the board of directors? In many cases, neither senior management nor the directors have much, if any, experience with litigation. You can avoid a lot of frustration and second-guessing by taking the time up-front to explain the litigation process to them and providing regular updates thereafter. As you will likely need sign-off from the CEO or board regarding many decisions including settlement authority, alternative dispute resolution (e.g., mediation), budget, and so on, the better informed they are about the litigation—and the litigation process generally—the easier time you will have getting what you need and avoiding second-guessing on key decisions.

Below are ten things you need to do in explaining and regularly updating your CEO (including senior management) and the board of directors about important litigation. For purposes of the below, I will assume that the litigation is material to your company such that it warrants the attention of the CEO and the board:

1. **Describe the process/timing.** One of the biggest mysteries about litigation to senior management is simply "what is the process" and "what are the timelines"? As in-house lawyers we tend to just assume everyone knows the basics of the litigation process. That is a mistake, and a big source of frustration and confusion for the CEO and the board is simply not knowing how litigation "works." Accordingly, one of the first things you should do is set up some time with the CEO/affected business leaders (and ultimately the board) and walk them through the litigation process and the expected timelines. You should

---

52 See page 49.

create a presentation that includes, at a minimum, a description of the litigation (i.e., what it's about) and the timelines for following: (a) the complaint, (b) the answer, (c) discovery deadlines (written discovery/depositions), (d) expert witnesses, (e) motions to dismiss, (f) counterclaims, (g) summary judgment, (h) trial, (i) motions in limine, (j) jury selection, (k) estimated length of trial, and (l) the appeal process. Granted you will not know all of these deadlines with certainty at the start and you can either estimate based on experience or, worst case, put TBD. As you step through the timeline, be sure to spend a few minutes explaining what each of (a)–(l) are, so everyone can better understand what's coming. For a good summary of the different phases of litigation, see the article "How Does a Lawsuit Work?"[53] The goal is to create a reusable document that you can update during the course of the litigation as dates change and as new items appear or get resolved.

2. **Selecting outside counsel.** You might think picking counsel to prosecute or defend litigation is left completely to the legal department, but that is not always true. Be prepared to explain to the CEO/board the reasons you selected the firm and always anticipate pushback (though there may not be any). It may be that the board wants a "name brand" firm or that the CEO has a friend who's a partner at Firm "X," or any number of reasons why your selection may draw questions. Do not be defensive about it if this occurs. It's important that you can articulate why the firm you selected is the "right" firm for the job (and, quite frankly, you should already have those reasons down in your head from the start). It may be that the case is insured and you need to use counsel preferred by the insurance company. It could be that you know the case is going to go to trial and you want a firm with a lot of trial experience in this particular court. Or your lawsuit involves a certain statute or type of claim where you need a firm with expertise in that specific area. You should be able to set out the process you went through to select counsel (request for proposal, references, etc.) and be ready to explain your selection. It's also a good idea to have your outside counsel meet the CEO (or the board if the case is significant enough) very early on so they can get comfortable with the legal team. Consider putting together a packet with pictures, bios, awards, and honors about your outside counsel to give to the CEO/board (yes, finally a practical use for all of those outside counsel marketing materials).

3. **Define success.** Whether you are plaintiff or defendant, it's critical to know what the company's goals are with respect to the litigation. Defining these goals involves working closely with the CEO and the board. Is the goal about

---

53   http://www.stoel.com/how-does-a-lawsuit-work-basic-steps-in.

money (gaining/losing) or a specific action (such as advancing or defending a strategic objective)?[54] Is it about preventing damage to your stock price or business reputation? Is the goal about boosting employee morale, maintaining relationships, or preventing more lawsuits of a similar nature? Regardless of the goal, you (and outside counsel) must take the time to truly understand and agree with the business/board around defining success in the litigation. One suggestion is to commit the goals to a writing called a "Definition of Success Memorandum,"[55] which, like all litigation plans, can—and will likely—change over time. This memorandum acts as a measuring stick for legal and the business to determine "how things are going" with the litigation.

4. **Budget/Cost.** A common area for surprises and unhappiness is the cost of litigation. This is especially true when you wildly surpass the budgeted amounts and/or the business has no advance warning about a budget miss (which, for example, can make a huge difference for publicly traded companies and meeting earnings expectations). Consequently, it's important to spend time up-front—and every month—working on a realistic cost estimate and keeping senior management up to speed on how things are progressing on the cost side (good or bad) and "why." Resist the urge to underestimate the cost (so things look a little better) and try to honestly set forth the cost of proceeding with or defending the case. If your company is the plaintiff, the cost can be a factor in determining whether to go forward or not. If you are the defendant, the cost may require adjustments in spending for other parts of the business, so there is money to pay for the litigation. The key is to be open and honest about the cost and be able to show that you are using best practices to proactively manage costs. I have written about ways to manage outside counsel spend.[56] All of the lessons set out there apply here.

5. **Decision trees.** At some point the CEO or the board will ask you "what are our chances here?" or "what is our realistic exposure?" Telling them that litigation is too hard to predict so you cannot answer the question is not a good idea (except for early in the case where you would add that you will get back to them as soon as you have more information about the merits of the case and the amount of damages the plaintiff is seeking). The business operates in an environment of uncertainty every day. They will not be sympathetic to legal telling them "uncertainty" prevents coming up with an answer. I think the best way to

---

54 http://media.mofo.com/files/Uploads/Images/1306-ACC-Docket-Win-First-Win-Smart.pdf.

55 http://www.americanbar.org/content/dam/aba/publications/blt/2005/01/its-not-just-the-money-200501.authcheckdam.pdf.

56 See page 115.

respond to this type of question is with a decision tree. I like decision trees because the business is used to them (businesspeople use them all the time), and they allow you to change variables/assumptions/numbers as the case changes. They can be simple or they can be complex. Your finance colleagues may even be able to help you create a decision tree spreadsheet. Seeing the analysis on paper gives the CEO and board added comfort that you are on top of the case. Here are a few good resources for help with creating decision trees in the litigation context: (a) Decision Tree Analysis in Litigation: The Basics,[57] (b) Advanced Decision Tree Analysis,[58] and (c) Interpreting a Litigation Decision Tree.[59]

6. **Time diversion of management.** Everybody is gung ho when litigation starts, especially when they are the plaintiff. It has always reminded me of the opening chapters of *All Quiet on the Western Front* when everyone was giddy about heading off to the start of World War I. But, similar to the book, everyone starts to realize that big-time commercial litigation is a slog through "no man's land" and begins to question why the company is involved in litigation in the first place. It is very important therefore to educate everyone on the time diversion they can expect as the litigation moves forward. To successfully prosecute or defend litigation, there will need to be large commitments of time by the business (usually including the CEO and CFO and potentially the board) around things like educating outside counsel about the business and the issues; running down requests for information from counsel; depositions (including preparation time); assisting with responding to document requests; interrogatories; requests for admissions; assisting expert witnesses; attending hearings and attending trial (e.g., the company representative); and so on. Litigation is not something that will or can be handled solely within legal but rather it will reach deep into the business and the company needs to prepare for and accept that a number of different and valuable people will be taken away from big parts of their day jobs to assist with the effort.

7. **Confidentiality.** Be sure to tell the CEO/board up-front that they need to brace for seeing some (or potentially a lot of) company emails and documents made public during the litigation, even ones that seem to have little

---

57 http://settlementperspectives.com/2009/01/decision-tree-analysis-in-litigation-the-basics/.
58 http://settlementperspectives.com/2009/07/advanced-decision-tree-analysis-in-litigation-an-interview-with-marc-victor-part-i/.
59 http://www.litigationrisk.com/Reading%20a%20Tree.pdf.

relevance to the legal issues and are otherwise embarrassing[60] or cringe-worthy. Courts in the United States lean heavily in favor of making almost all case materials public. The business needs to understand and be prepared for this. Using documents to drag the other side through the mud is a typical tactic in litigation often done to increase settlement pressure or simply to inflict pain on the other side once the gloves are off. Very early on you will want to set straight anyone who believes that litigation is confidential. It isn't. The wrong time for this issue to come up is when CEO or board first hears about a "bad" document through the media. Prepare your board and executives for this problem up-front and, as you come across troublesome documents during the course of the litigation, report that back to them regularly. You can tell them that you will seek to file documents under seal, ask for protective orders,[61] and file motions in limine before trial, but everyone needs to be realistic about the risk of poorly written or poorly thought-through documents leaking out. Additionally, loop in the corporate communications team as they will need to prepare a media/employee communications strategy in the event any problematic documents or emails do become public. Note that any litigation media strategy (and the documents/emails regarding the same) may not be privileged, including when you use outside media consultants.[62] Meaning "writing smart"[63] is very important for the corporate communications team (and any outside consultants) as well. Finally, if your company is publicly traded, you need to prepare the CEO and board for the requirements around describing material litigation in public filings (e.g., quarterly and annual reports, 8K).

8. **"Why is this taking so long?"** On television most litigation wraps up in 60 minutes. Sadly, the real world doesn't work so quickly, and many executives and directors are surprised by how long the litigation process can play out. Get ahead of this issue early in the case. While most litigation settles, that usually does not occur until 12 months or more into the case (as the evidence gathered in discovery and depositions is important to framing up settlement positions). Most cases do not get to trial until 18 to 24 months have passed and sometimes up to three years. Appeals can add another 12 months or more

---

60 http://blogs.wsj.com/digits/2015/02/26/alleged-ellen-pao-harasser-contributed-to-key-performance-review-court-hears/.
61 http://www.smithmoorelaw.com/Confidentiality-and-Protective-Orders-08-05-2013.
62 https://www.mcguirewoods.com/Client-Resources/Privilege-Ethics/Privilege-Points/2016/6/Public-Relations-Consultants-Inside-Outside-Privilege-Protection.aspx.
63 See page 53.

to the process. Be frank about the fact that the pace of the litigation is not in your complete control. While you can control what your side does (i.e., your outside counsel's behavior, your motions, your pleadings, your schedules), you have no control over what the other side does or how the judge wishes to manage her calendar. There are many factors that impact timelines in litigation, most tied to the length of the discovery process (which is dependent on schedules of lawyers, witnesses, experts, and others) and the court's calendar and availability to hear motions and disputes or, ultimately, set the case for trial. When you set out case deadlines or dates for the CEO/board, be sure to add the dates are not in stone and are subject to being postponed due to scheduling conflicts, other cases on the court's docket, illness, vacations, and so on.

9. **"The judge did what?!"** I got this question a number of times, and it just goes to underscore that litigation is messy and frustrating, and, sadly, it's not always fair. They call them "hellholes"[64] for a reason. While most judges are smart, hardworking, and evenhanded (i.e., calling balls and strikes down the middle), every once in a while you get one that is not. Prepare your CEO and board for this potential problem. You and your outside counsel should do some diligence on the judge and determine how he or she has ruled in the past, his or her reputation in the legal community, his or her record on summary judgment, including being reversed on appeal or taken up to a higher court on a writ of mandamus. Find out if the judge has standing procedural orders and do those orders appear to favor one side or the other. Share what you find out with the business so they have a sense for what to expect from the judge. As you gain experience with the judge over the course of the case, the report can be updated (good or bad). For example, in litigation you should expect to win the motions that you should clearly win and lose the motions you should clearly lose. There will be a large middle ground of motions where it's truly 50/50 and some you will win and some the judge just saw it differently than you did. However, if you are losing *every* motion and feel like the Washington Generals, you may need to contemplate more drastic measures such as seeking recusal of the judge—which is a decision you cannot take lightly nor make without the input of the CEO/board, because if you fail, you will certainly have given the judge even less reason to like the company.

10. **Regular meetings/Reports.** Items 1 to 9 above all build up to preparing and presenting regular reports to the CEO and, as warranted, to the board. You will

---

64 http://www.judicialhellholes.org/wp-content/uploads/2015/12/JudicialHellholes-2015.pdf.

develop your own form of report over time but it should include updates on, among other things, the following:

- **Timelines:** Where is the case in the timeline, what's coming up, any changes in timing.
- **Key motions:** Pending, contemplated, risk/reward, and results.
- **Depositions:** Summaries of key "gives and gets" and overall rating of the deposition (I used a 1–10 scale).
- **Budget:** How you are tracking to budget, any changes in assumptions or any unexpected changes in spend (good or bad). You will want to update the CFO/finance team more frequently on this item.
- **Decision tree updates:** Use the most current information to add or take out claims, update percentages, damages amounts, and expectations.
- **"Hot docs":** Identify new documents that could significantly help or hurt the case and the plan to deal with them, and documents that could be problematic if made public (even if not really material to the litigation) and the plan to deal with them.
- **Damages update:** Provide an update on the damages sought by either side, for example, direct, consequential, punitive, injunctive, interest, and statutory.
- **Settlement/alternative dispute resolution:** Updates on prospects for settlement (including proposals made or received) or alternative dispute resolution (e.g., mediation), seek settlement authority.
- **Judge/jury research:** Updates on the judge and, if ready, updates on any jury research.
- **Strategy issues:** Any key strategic decisions that need to be made or for which you seek CEO/board input (key motions, jury waiver, subpoenas of third parties the company has a relationship with, etc.).
- **"Definition of Success":** Update your "Definition of Success" memorandum and use the meeting as a touch-point to note how things are going and to consider any changes.

It is also a good idea to have your outside counsel present (on phone or in person) during these updates as it gives the CEO and board a chance to get more comfortable with them and to ask questions that you may not otherwise have the answers to. If you do this, just be sure to take an active role in the presentation and discussion as you do not want the CEO or board to see you as a potted plant.

*****

If your company is sued (or is contemplating suing another company), make sure the CEO and the board understand from the beginning what to expect during the litigation process. The fewer surprises and the more input they have into the case (e.g., defining success, budget approval, and strategic decisions), the more likely they will feel comfortable and leave the day-to-day details to you and the legal department. Moreover, agreement on defining success will mean that when you "win," everyone will agree it was a great day.

July 7, 2015

Ten Things: Settlement Agreements— Making Sure It's Really Over

There are few things as wasteful and painful as litigation. And that's from someone whose career started as a litigator and, after a long tenure in-house, now works for a litigation boutique! While sometimes it is simply unavoidable and necessary, any in-house lawyer can tell you that litigation is expensive, time-consuming, distracting, frustrating, risky, and very difficult to predict outcomes. As a result, ending litigation is usually a great feeling (sometimes celebrated with bottles of expensive champagne). Still, litigation rarely ends with a jury verdict or bench decision. It usually ends with a settlement, that is, an agreement by the parties to the litigation to end the matter based on some agreed-upon terms. Sounds simple, right? It's not.

A settlement agreement is an extremely important document and should receive the same level of attention to detail as any other complex contract your company might enter into. There are many ways a settlement can go "wrong" and that is why the agreement is not something to leave solely to the outside lawyers once the "deal has been made." In-house counsel need to be intimately involved with the documentation and execution of the deal. Simply put, careers can end because of "bad" settlement agreements. You do not want to be on the receiving end of a settlement agreement that turns out NOT to be the deal you (and the CEO or board) thought you had to end the litigation. Since many in-house lawyers rarely deal with litigation, let alone settlement agreements, I want to discuss ten things you need to keep in mind when settling litigation, so you can do your best to make sure it's really over:

1. **Scope of the release—the claims.** The core of a settlement agreement is the release of claims, that is, the part that says the dispute over "Claim X" is resolved. The key is making sure that the release covers the claims you want it to cover. The first thing to consider is the scope of the claims to be released and whether you are agreeing to a specific or a general release. A "specific" release will resolve only the specific claim(s) at issue in the litigation. For example, if the defendant failed to pay you $500,000 under the contract, the specific

release would resolve that issue only. A general release is broader and is usually worded as "any and all claims" the plaintiff has against the defendant, whether alleged in the lawsuit or not. In our example, not only is the claim for $500,000 resolved but *any other* claims the plaintiff might have against the defendant are also released. Sometimes the language of a general release goes as far as to release any claims "known or unknown." Whether you want a specific or general release (known or unknown) depends on which side of the table you are sitting. Regardless of where you sit, the important thing is to know the difference and ensure that you work with your outside counsel to get the release you and the business want in place.

The second issue around scope of the claims released is whether the claims will just be dismissed or dismissed with "prejudice." If the claims are just dismissed, they can be filed again. If the claims are dismissed with prejudice, then they are completely extinguished and cannot be filed again by the plaintiff. Generally, the parties dismiss claims with prejudice in a settlement agreement because they want the dispute to be 100 percent over. Whether or not this happens depends on what the parties have negotiated, the consideration for the release, and other factors. Just be sure to think through which one you want and then ensure that's what the settlement agreement states.

2. **Scope of the release—the parties.** Once you figure out the scope of the claims you will release, you must state which parties are covered by the settlement/release. For example, if you are a defendant resolving a claim over a patent license, you may want to ensure that *all* of your affiliated companies are covered by the release, so they are not sued down the road by the same plaintiff over the same patent. On the other hand, if you are the patent owner, you may want more money to release all of the affiliated companies versus just the entity you sued. Corporations typically want to ensure that not only are they released, but also their officers, directors, employees, agents, affiliates, parent companies, and others are covered. Whether or not this is agreeable will depend on the circumstances. Sometimes the plaintiff will want a "mutual" release where the defendant releases any claims it might have against the plaintiff. While this makes perfect sense if there are counterclaims, it doesn't always make sense if the defendant has not filed or raised any claims of its own. To further complicate things, sometimes there is a need to consider releasing third parties, that is, parties unrelated to either the plaintiff or the defendant (e.g., codefendants such as alleged joint tortfeasors). Again, the key is to be sure to think through, with counsel, the "who" as much as the "what."

3. **Get the logistics right.** The other side to the litigation emails you and writes "We'll pay you $400,000 to settle." You respond back with "Sounds interesting, let me think about it." In your head you're thinking "This is a great offer. I

should just accept it." While you may think it's great, it's not for you to decide. From a common sense and ethics standpoint, you need the client to agree to accept the offer. For the in-house world, unless the business delegated the decision to you, the decision maker is either the business unit involved in the litigation or, if the stakes are high enough, the C-suite or even the board of directors. Regardless of who gets to make the decision to accept any settlement offers, you need to be sure you have a process in place to get the necessary input and approvals from all of the right people. If it's at the board of directors' level, that will mean some type of formal vote and delegation of signature authority—all of which you will need to properly document in the minutes book. Moreover, you may have a very hands-on C-suite or board, which means they might want to read the proposed settlement agreement and weigh in with comments or suggestions. Understand up-front whether this is the case and build in the necessary timing to allow this to happen without "surprising" anyone at the last moment with a ridiculously short turnaround time. And don't be afraid to ask the other side about the logistical process they need to go through. It will save you and the other side a lot of pain and worry if you both understand the process each needs to go through to get sign-off internally. To ensure a smooth ending, spend time thinking about all of the "process issues" and steps that you need to deal with to get from settlement authority to settlement signature.

4. **Contingencies.** In a perfect world, the parties sign the settlement agreement, the payment (or whatever consideration provided) occurs instantly, and everyone goes home happy—the process completely finished and done. As you can guess, that isn't the way it works 90 percent of the time. There are almost always contingencies that need to be dealt with, including having those contingencies clearly spelled out in the settlement agreement. The goal in a settlement agreement (and in settlement negotiations) is what some call "perfect communication." The closer you can get to that goal, the less problems you will have both before and after the settlement is signed. For example, if you are receiving $400,000 from the defendant to settle the litigation, is that in a lump sum or in installments? If a lump sum, how long does the defendant have to pay? What happens if they don't pay? What happens if the ninth and tenth installments are not paid? Your job (and that of outside counsel) is to think about all of the things in the settlement "deal" that need to happen so that each side gets the benefit of their bargain, especially your side. That means for each contingency there needs to be some type of consequence if the other side fails to execute, for example, if they don't make a payment what happens? Does the settlement become void? Is there a pre-signed consent judgment you can file? Among the easiest things you can do in a settlement agreement to prevent

problems is to include time frames for things to occur (i.e., don't leave critical steps open-ended that could leave you holding the bag). Think about what you are giving up and how can that be reversed if the other side defaults. The consequences then need to be set out clearly in the agreement. As I used to tell my business colleagues when we were doing a business deal, we need to plan for the divorce in the contract and hope it never happens. The same rule applies to settlement agreements.

5. **Confidentiality.** While the company may be very excited you settled the lawsuit, it may not want the entire world to know the terms of the deal. As you are working on the settlement, think about the terms you want to keep confidential (and be sure to bring the business into the analysis as you may miss something they are passionately concerned about). It's likely both sides will want to include a confidentiality provision. Even so, you will probably need to make some exceptions. For example, you'll want to be able to share the document with your outside attorneys, accountants, and auditors. If you're a publicly traded company, there may need to be some accommodation for you to disclose parts of the settlement in a Form 8K or in a quarterly filing. What you *want* to disclose and what you *must* disclose may not be the same thing, so keep that in mind and be sure the C-suite and board understand this as well (i.e., don't let them be surprised if terms of the settlement they thought were going to be confidential need to be disclosed). You may also need to disclose the settlement agreement to the court (and you may even need court approval, such as in a bankruptcy context). The court, in turn, may need to make the document public or perhaps a redacted version. Consider including a provision for a joint media statement with the parties agreeing in the settlement that this statement is the full extent of what either side will disclose to the media. Otherwise you and the other side may get tied up in an escalating game of each "spinning" the settlement as a victory.

6. **The insurance company/indemnitor.** If you have insurance that covers the claim and the insurance company has been providing a defense (or paying for a defense) and will be paying some or all of any cash settlement, then you will need to discuss the settlement with them before you finalize anything. However, if the insurance company has been stiffing you on its obligations (i.e., breaching the policy), not paying defense costs, and/or otherwise making it clear they do not think they are responsible, then it's probably not necessary to involve them as they have, by choice, not been involved to date and have waived any rights to be involved now. Likewise, if you sought indemnity from a third party for the litigation costs and the claim, you likely need to involve them in the decision to settle, especially if they have already acknowledged

responsibility and are paying the defense costs. The key is to anticipate who needs to be brought in to the process and when that needs to occur.

7. **Worry about the tax/accounting implications.** Stephen Hawking will tell you that everything in the universe comes down to one thing—gravity. Finance will tell you that it is crap—everything comes down to taxes. While taxes may not drive the entire universe, they certainly drive business decisions, and anything legal does that throws a company off course with respect to its tax strategy is most unwelcome and will make you very unpopular with the number crunchers. Money, products, or services changing hands through a settlement agreement can have an impact on taxes and on financial reporting (e.g., cash flow, profit, and loss) just like any other contract, and this is especially a concern for publicly traded companies. As you work through your settlement agreement terms, be sure to consult with finance early in the process, both the tax side *and* the accounting side. You want to make absolutely sure that any tax or accounting impacts are fully vetted and understood before there is an agreement. You may need to reword the agreement or recast the consideration given or received in a different manner in order to match up with the appropriate tax structure or accounting treatment. And don't be surprised if the other side asks for wording changes along these lines as well. Don't worry if your positions clash; that's just part of the normal craziness of settlement negotiations.

8. **Enforcing the settlement.** Part of "planning for the divorce" mentioned above is what to do if there is a breach of the settlement agreement, for example, the other side does not make the required payments. You need to have this covered in the document itself. Do you want the same court to keep jurisdiction of any disputes around the settlement or do you want a different court to handle it? Maybe you want confidential arbitration? Be sure to also consider choice of law, injunctive relief, attorneys' fees and costs, interest, and so forth. Just like any other contract, the parties can plan for how disputes will be handled. This is an area worth investing time on as you plan and negotiate the agreement.

9. **Create a "settlement team."** Here is one thing that always happens during settlement negotiations: you start to doubt the strength of your position and you start to rationalize why the other side's positions make sense—even if they didn't before you sat down at the table. If you happen to be in or beginning trial when the settlement discussions start, having to knock your own case is a bad place for your trial team to be mentally. The last thing you need is for your lead trial lawyer—on the eve of trial—to be coming up with reasons why your case sucks and a settlement makes sense. They need to be thinking like Vikings about to storm the shores of Northumberland—taking names and kicking butt. The solution is to create a separate "settlement team" to handle

the negotiations and documentation of the settlement, leaving the trial team "out of the loop," so they can focus all of their energies on winning the case. There will certainly be coordination with some of the trial team, but not much. Make it on a need to know basis only. Otherwise, your trial team members might start thinking about what they will be doing when they get home versus tearing someone up on cross-examination.

10. **"Accidental" settlement agreement.** If your response in point 3 above had been "Sounds like we have a deal" versus "Let me think about it," you may have accidently accepted a settlement offer that you (a) really did not mean to accept and (b) you did not have authority to accept. This means that you need to be *very* careful during settlement negotiations, especially when exchanging drafts or term sheets via email, to not somehow create a *binding* settlement agreement you did not otherwise mean to accept. Sometimes in the frenzy of trying to get to a resolution of your dispute, you can let your guard down and get lazy with language or not otherwise be clear about the conditions under which you will accept the core settlement proposal from the other side. For example, you may be happy with the $400,000 in cash, but you also need a dismissal with prejudice, an agreed media statement, a release that covers your affiliated companies, and payment by a certain date to make finance happy. If you end up with just the $400,000 and none of the other terms because you (or outside counsel) were too quick to write "agreed" without stating your conditions, just imagine the unpleasant conversation with the CEO/CFO or the board.

Remember to take some basics steps in any settlement negotiation to make it clear that nothing is final until you agree it's final. For example, if you get a term sheet from the other side proposing ten terms they are offering to settle, respond to each one. A court may find that the terms you did not specifically respond to were "accepted." When you do respond, include your own material terms that you need in order to agree to a settlement. Don't be shy. It's better to get everything on the table now versus seeing your settlement agreement blow up because the other side claims you sprung an unacceptable term on them well after the fact. The best thing to do is be maniacal in your written discussions of proposed settlement terms and consider including the following language in all material communications with the other side regarding the settlement:

All discussions and correspondence regarding a settlement are confidential, covered by FRE 408,[65] and are for negotiation purposes only. There is not

---

[65] Federal Rule of Evidence 408 regarding admissibility of settlement discussions, or use the state equivalent if you are in state court.

yet any authority to enter into a final, binding agreement on behalf of [the Company]. The execution of a separate, formal agreement is a material term of any settlement and there is no settlement without one. Other materials terms exist and [the Company] will not agree to any settlement without agreement on those terms as well.[66]

It may seem a little clunky (it is), but it is certainly better to overprotect yourself and the company from any claim that a settlement was reached before you intended.

*****

I wrote this from the standpoint of settling actual pending litigation. The principles above apply equally well to disputes that have not arisen to actual litigation but need to be resolved nonetheless. Likewise, while focused on the United States, most of these suggestions should work outside the United States as well (but it's worth researching the rules that apply where you practice). As excited as you may be to settle the case, especially those long-running, high-risk matters, always take a deep breath and be sure you methodically take all of the proper steps to ensure that not only are you getting the settlement you want but also you've taken all reasonable measures to ensure that when the agreement is signed, it is truly the end of the litigation.

March 31, 2016

---

66 *See* Robert H. Ellis, "Making Certain the Settlement You Intend Is the Settlement You Get," *Litigation* 42, no. 2 (Winter 2016).

Ten Things: Litigation Financing—A Primer for In-House Counsel

It is a common refrain in legal departments all around the globe: how do we get enough money to do the things we need to do to protect the company? There are always more matters clamoring for money than there is money available. This is especially true with litigation. If your company is being sued, you have little choice other than to spend the money needed to defend your interests (unless you feel a quick settlement is a better call). If the company has meritorious claims, then it often faces the difficult choice of whether to spend the money needed to proceed. If not, valuable claims may be lost. If yes, then money that could be spent on other parts of the business is rerouted to legal fees—and, unfortunately, under accounting rules money "invested" in a litigation claim is not treated the same as money invested in the business generally. To deal with this, in-house legal departments try a variety of measures to reduce legal expenses, from reduced hourly rates or fixed fees to contingency fees and blended rates or less expensive counsel. See my article on effectively managing legal spend.[67]

Over the past four or five years, another potential solution has emerged. Depending on which side of the table you are sitting, the solution is either a blessing or the manifestation of supreme evil. The solution is called "litigation financing," and it is something every in-house counsel should be aware of and thinking about. Below I will give you a ten-point outline of the basics around litigation financing:

1. **What is litigation financing?** In its most basic form, litigation financing means a third party agrees to finance your litigation (usually the plaintiff side, but it works for defense side as well) in exchange for a percentage of the recovery (settlement or posttrial) or some other agreed-upon return on investment. The financing is usually "without recourse," meaning that if you do not win your case, nothing is owed to the group financing the litigation; they take

---

[67] See page 115.

all the risk. This is very different from a contingency fee arrangement with a law firm. With litigation financing, your agreement is with a third party, not the law firm. Moreover, the financing can and does cover out-of-pocket costs in addition to legal fees, that is, depositions, travel, expert witnesses, copies, and so on.

2. **When can I use litigation financing?** The financing can occur at the beginning of the claim, in the middle, on appeal, and the like. It can cover legal fees, legal fees and costs, just costs, or half a dozen or so other ways of financing the lawsuit or paying your company for the value of the suit.

3. **How does it work?** There are a number of litigation financing companies (LFCs) operating in the United States (and elsewhere) today. Some of the largest are Gerchen Keller Capital, Burford Capital, Harbour Litigation Funding (UK), and Vinson Litigation Finance. These companies tend to manage a large pool of venture capital funding with the objective of investing in litigation. Like any investment company, a litigation financing venture uses a number of tools to analyze cases it may invest in. Some common aspects of due diligence include the following:

    - *The nature of the dispute* (contract, tort, antitrust, etc.)
    - *Plaintiff or defendant* (the plaintiff side is generally easier to fit in the litigation financing model)
    - *Where the case is pending* (the court, the judge, the country, the state and county—it does make a difference)
    - *The potential payout* (usually focused not on the "face amount" of the claim, but rather the likely amount that can be won at settlement or from a jury)
    - *The merits* (including key evidence such as emails and contracts)
    - *The budget* (cost in terms of legal fees, experts, and other expenses)
    - *The likely timeline for the case to get resolved and money changes hands* (including appeals)
    - *The lawyers representing both sides* (experience, reputation, results)
    - *Ability to recover the monies awarded* (e.g., is the defendant good for the money, how easy will it be to get paid or find and attach assets if necessary)

    Many LFCs use a sophisticated statistical model to analyze the above and other factors. The companies then take all of the information and match it up against their risk profile and other parameters. The key is that this is not an educated guess about which cases to take; it is a heavily data-driven exercise. The companies are not looking for frivolous lawsuits; they want lawsuits with merit and high potential recoveries.

4. **How do I make a deal for litigation financing?** Assuming the LFC is satisfied that the case meets its investment parameters, then the parties sit down and negotiate a detailed litigation funding contract, setting out the responsibilities

and obligations of both sides along with the percentage of the recovery the financing company gets if there is a win. All of which means there is a lot of thought that goes into defining "winning." How much of the recovery will go to the LFC versus your company ultimately comes down to how much risk there is in the merits of the case, that is, how solid is the chance of winning? The less favorable the odds, the higher the percentage of the recovery going to the LFC—the percentage return on investment is directly related to the risk of the investment.

5. **How does it work for defending lawsuits?** It is easy to see how litigation financing works for the plaintiff side of the equation, but it's harder to see how it works for a defendant. That said, it does work both ways and this is where litigation funding may have the most value to in-house counsel because it is likely that defending expensive litigation[68] is a bigger problem for companies than bringing litigation. One key to litigation financing of defense claims is the willingness of the company to pay a premium for success, but still generally paying less than cost of defense otherwise. Much like a law firm "success fee," this means that if certain parameters are met, the LFC gets a larger return on its investment. If there is no success, then the risk—in terms of the cost of defending the lawsuit—is borne by the LFC. In exchange, the company gets relief from funding the cost of the litigation while it's pending and, hopefully, a win at trial if it goes that far. Here are some ways where litigation financing can work in the defense context:

- *Funding an entire claim*—The LFC funds the entire defense cost in exchange for a multiplier or bonus in the event of a "successful" outcome (or hitting a certain level of "success"). Typically, this type of funding hinges on the analysis of "how weak is the claim against the company?" The success fee concept is usually based on a substantial discount up-front on legal fees, for example, 25–30 percent off standard rates. If the case is resolved at X, then the company pays the firm the amount held back. If the case is resolved at Y, then the company pays the firm the holdback plus a bonus/multiplier. This solves a problem with contingency fees whereby most law firms will not go below 70 percent off of their regular rates and that may simply not be enough of a discount for the company to proceed. The LFC can step in and fund the entire cost of defense, covering the law firm's risk (and the firm must still agree to a discount off its rates) as well as that of the company.
- *Portfolio funding*—The claim(s) for defense are part of a larger portfolio of claims that include claims as "plaintiff" so that the LFC's risk is diversified

---

68 http://www.burfordcapital.com/blog/litigation-finance-case-defense/.

across "good cases" and "bad cases." This means that companies need to think about litigation financing across multiple claims versus just a one-off claim.
- *Reverse contingency fees*—The financing company collects a fee that is a percentage of the difference between the amount a third party originally demands from a lawyer's client and the amount that client must ultimately pay the third party, whether by settlement or by judgment.

6. **What are the "pros" of litigation financing?** Like anything, there are good points and bad points that go with litigation funding. Taking the positive side first; here are several "pros" for litigation funding:
   - *The cost of the litigation becomes secondary.* As noted, the cost of litigation is becoming more and more problematic for in-house legal departments. Litigation funding can reduce or eliminate this problem. Rather than having to pay out of current cash flows and impacting current budgets, the LFC pays the costs of the litigation, and the company only pays when the litigation is over, either in terms of a share of the win or some type of success fee tied to defense of the claim. Any payments advanced by the LFC are typically "without recourse." This means a relatively risk-free reduction or elimination of what is typically the largest and most unpredictable cost in a legal department budget—litigation.
   - *The CFO will love it.* The added benefit of taking the cost of litigation off the company's books is that the company's earnings, cash flow, and other measures of financial success are not burdened or diminished by big, hard-to-predict legal fee payments. While a litigation claim is an "asset" of the company, just like any other receivable, it is not treated the same under the accounting rules. This means costs related to litigation are usually not capitalized; they are expensed—so they hit the bottom line as incurred. Moreover, the unpredictable nature of legal fees, especially in big litigation, can drive problems with earnings for publicly traded companies as even a difference of a penny or two off expectations due to unexpectedly high legal fees can negatively impact stock price in a material way. Litigation financing can remove a lot of these problems, keeping legal fees off of the P&L until there is a positive event to report.
   - *Lawyers of choice.* With litigation financing in place, your legal department has more flexibility with respect to choice of counsel as the cost/legal fees become a secondary issue. Your choice becomes more about which law firm you think is best for the case versus which law firm can do the job within a certain budget. It also removes the battle over how "low" can the law firm go on fees and still be incentivized to work for you or do its best work on your matter. For example, if the fees you are negotiating create a huge incentive

for the firm to utilize lower priced associates, then you may not get the right level of experience for some parts of the project. Litigation financing can better align the interests of the company, the law firm, and the LFC.
- *Getting paid.* Any "win" is useless if you cannot collect the money owed from the defendant. It can be even more complicated if the other side is a foreign company located outside the United States or if you are in arbitration and need to locate assets in countries that accept arbitration awards. An LFC usually specializes in locating assets and collecting damages. This can be a huge benefit to your company in terms of actually getting paid on a judgment or settlement.

7. **What are the cons of litigation financing?** Here are some of the negative issues associated with litigation financing:
   - *Champerty.* I remember this term from law school and never thought I'd ever get to write it in a sentence, but here we are talking about it.[69] Champerty is an old common law doctrine from Medieval England barring third parties from stirring up litigation and financing other party's claims. The concept actually goes back to the legal systems of the Greeks and Romans. The goal was/is to discourage frivolous litigation and to protect against harassment by wealthy backers of litigation. While the parameters have softened in the United States and the United Kingdom, the doctrine still exists, and as you can imagine, litigation financing appears to fall squarely within the doctrine. Yet, a number of states have relaxed prohibitions on third-party litigation financing. The Delaware Superior Court recently issued a decision upholding third-party financing of claims and finding its laws against champerty did not apply to the facts of the case.[70] The court found that there is no champerty if the following is true:
     - The financing agreement does not assign ownership of the claims to the financier;
     - The financier does not have any rights to direct or control the litigation; and
     - The plaintiff retains an unfettered right to settle the litigation at any time for any amount.

   Regardless, it is important as part of your research into whether litigation financing makes sense for your company to understand any legal limits, such as

---

69 http://www.duhaime.org/LegalDictionary/C/Champerty.aspx.
70 *Charge Injection Technologies, Inc. v. E.I. DuPont*, C.A. No. N07C-12-134-JRJ (Del. Super. Ct. March 9, 2016).

champerty, that may exist in your jurisdiction and that the LFC agreement be properly drafted to overcome any obstacles.
- *Attorney-client/work-product privilege.* Any time privileged information is shared with a third party, that is, anyone other than the law firm and the client, there is a risk of waiver of the privilege. See my article on the attorney-client privilege.[71] That risk certainly exists in the context of litigation funding where the LFC will want to get as much information as possible in order to evaluate your claim and set the "price" of the funding. The law in this is area is still very unsettled. In the *Carlyle Investment Management L.L.C. v. Moonmouth Company S.A.,* No. 7841-VCP, February 24, 2015, the Delaware Court of Chancery held that communications between a claimant and the LFC, and the claimant's attorneys and the LFC are protected by the work product doctrine. Regardless, since the law is unsettled[72] in this area, it is wise to take precautions with respect to any information you seek to share with the LFC, such as the following:
  - providing documents that are not privileged (e.g., pleadings);
  - providing what you expect to turn over to the other side through the discovery process; and
  - weighing risk of disclosure against the need for funding and provide privileged documents understanding *the risks*.

8. **What are the ethics issues?** Under the rules of legal ethics in the United States and the United Kingdom, your outside counsel owes a duty of loyalty and independence to you, the client. The funding relationship cannot interfere with that duty, and this must be made crystal clear up-front with your LFC. In fact, as noted in the *Charge Injection Technologies* case above, such a level of independence is necessary to prevent a successful claim of champerty. Three key points here:
   - You must retain the right to hire and fire counsel;
   - You retain the sole right to decide if to settle and for what amount; and
   - You and your counsel direct litigation strategy and decisions; the LFC is completely passive.

   While you should retain all of these key rights in managing your litigation, don't be surprised if the economic terms of the financing agreement encourage certain behaviors and decisions, that is, if you terminate counsel the LFC may retain the right to back out of the case, or if you settle for less than $X amount the LFC gets a certain payment, and so on.

---

71 See page 263.
72 http://www.non-competes.com/2014/02/trade-secrets-litigation-funding-and.html.

9. **What are my next steps?** You may be thinking that litigation financing sounds a little "sketchy" and not something you would necessarily be involved in. My thought is that every in-house counsel needs to investigate the issue further. The industry exceeds $1 billion and is growing rapidly. National firms like Bartlit Beck, Kirkland & Ellis, and Sidley Austin are already working with LFCs. If you have any material litigation spend (plaintiff or defense) or otherwise pass on (or not see through to completion) valuable claims because they are too expensive to prosecute, you owe it to your company to make an informed decision as to whether litigation financing makes sense or not. At a minimum, you should involve your CFO/finance team in the review as some of the most positive impacts come on the accounting/budget side of the equation, including preservation of/other uses for the company's capital. On the other hand, if you (or C-suite or board) are absolutely opposed to the concept and feel that your company's interests are harmed by the availability of such financing, then you should know that there are efforts under way in Congress to investigate the industry and potentially pass litigation regulating litigation financing.[73] You may wish to encourage Congress or state governments[74] to act. See my article on how to run an effective government affairs campaign.[75]

10. **Resources.** Here are some additional resources to help get you up to speed on litigation financing:
    - "Arms Race: Law Firms and the Litigation Funding Boom"[76] (Law.com)
    - ABA White Paper on Alternative Litigation Finance[77]
    - Gerchen Keller Capital[78]
    - Burford Capital[79]
    - "Who's Claim Is It Anyway"[80] Minnesota Law Review (2011)
    - Harbour Litigation Funding[81] (UK)

---

73 See August 27, 2015, *Wall Street Journal*, http://blogs.wsj.com/law/2015/08/27/senators-call-for-transparency-in-litigation-funding/.
74 http://cardozolawreview.com/content/36-3/SHANNON.36.3.pdf.
75 See page 271.
76 http://www.law.com/sites/articles/2015/12/30/arms-race-the-litigation-funding-boom/?slreturn=20160708212818.
77 http://www.americanbar.org/content/dam/aba/administrative/ethics_2020/20111019_draft_alf_white_paper_posting.authcheckdam.pdf.
78 http://www.gerchenkeller.com/.
79 http://www.burfordcapital.com/.
80 http://www.minnesotalawreview.org/wp-content/uploads/2012/03/Steinitz_PDF.pdf.
81 https://harbourlitigationfunding.com/.

- Vinson Litigation Finance[82]
- Six Virtues of Litigation Finance[83]
- Five Ethical Issues with Litigation Finance[84]

*****

Like it or not, it appears that litigation financing is here to stay and is only going to become more prevalent. As in-house counsel, you need to be up to speed on this issue and be able to provide guidance to the company and the senior management about whether it is something the company should explore further. At a minimum, you should get educated on the topic and have a discussion with your CFO/finance team to at least gauge their interest in whether to explore it further, or to be ready when the next "break the bank" piece of litigation comes into view.

August 12, 2016

---

82 https://www.vinres.com/.
83 http://abovethelaw.com/2015/11/6-virtues-of-litigation-finance/.
84 http://abovethelaw.com/2015/12/5-ethical-issues-with-litigation-finance/.

Contracts and Deals

Ten Things: Help Your Clients Get Their Contract Through Legal Quickly

A common complaint you will hear as in-house counsel is "why does it take so long for you guys to review my contract?" (second only to "why are our contracts so long?"). The answer, as you probably know, is complicated. Legal is a limited resource, typically a small team that reviews hundreds and possibly thousands of contracts in any given year. While a lot of contracts are fairly routine, many involve complicated provisions or transactions with millions of dollars on the line. Sometimes you have to create a contract from scratch, meaning you do not have a form or something to easily model from. Frequently, things like litigation or large M&A deals take up substantial amounts of lawyer time—time that cannot be spent on contracts. Finally, legal will generally prioritize contracts based on the strategic objectives of the business. Deals that better support the strategy/objectives get more attention more quickly.

From an administrative viewpoint, you have to make considerations when people are out on vacation or ill. Unfortunately, "giving it to somebody else" is difficult. A new attorney will not have the history or understanding of the business deal necessary to finish the contract quickly (and he or she would need to re-prioritize his or her own work load to handle the deal, meaning someone else's project will get less or no attention).

It's important that the business understand these issues. With this in mind, here are ten things I regularly shared and discussed with my business partners to help them understand the contracting process and how to give their contract the best chance of getting through the legal review process as quickly as possible. Feel free to cut and paste these (probably without my reader's tips) into your own talk points or email or however best you can get the word out at your company:

1. **Use the form agreement.** If one is available, use the company's form agreement and be willing to insist the other side do so. Nothing saves time like sticking with a well-vetted form agreement (and nothing adds time like drafting a custom contract or using the other side's procurement agreement that bears

no resemblance to the services the company is actually providing). *Tip: One thing we did that was very helpful was host contract "boot camps" where we met with a large group of clients and walked through one of the company's applicable form contracts section by section (and we gave all participants an annotated version of the contract). This was great for developing relationships and helped the business understand why the contract "is like it is" (e.g., "too long"). It also provided feedback to legal, helping us to shorten the contract, change terms, rewrite provisions in plain English, and—most importantly— give the business a form agreement customers would more easily accept.*

2. **Read and understand the business and deal terms of the contract.** Business folks negotiating contracts should understand the terms of their deal (and what the other side is proposing), especially if they are going to accept the other party's paper/form. Don't just ask legal "does this contract look okay to you?" and run off. Read the term sheet and contract drafts and understand your deal. Know how you make money and know how you could lose money under the deal—help us help you. *Tip: Another great opportunity here is to invest an hour or two with some of the clients you work most often with (lunch or a coffee) to help them understand the contract and negotiating process and why they are an important part of it. They will appreciate the attention and you will get paid back several times over as the clients become more savvy in their business dealings and use of the legal function.*

3. **Get the necessary business approvals/buy in.** Typically, the company's many different business units/staff groups need to sign off on a contract (e.g., finance, tax, HR, insurance, and tech development). The business should drive this process. You need to make sure all key groups are signed off on the agreement, especially when work is required by that group to fulfill the agreement. Don't assume legal is taking care of this legwork. *Tip: That said, legal adds value when it helps the business navigate this process and spots situations where the ball got dropped and moves to help fix it. Don't let the business process fail. When you spot issues, raise them and use these situations as teaching moments for the business and put the "counsel" into legal counsel.*

4. **Legal is a limited resource.** There is a lot of demand for legal services in most companies and there are only so many lawyers (*insert lawyer joke here*). The business needs to understand that legal has to balance the needs of many competing projects. Working on project A necessarily means less resource/time to work on project B and so on. Legal needs to constantly make judgment calls on what gets attention and when. If you disagree with how business has prioritized something, please discuss. *Tip: I was always willing to discuss with the business how we prioritized work in legal (and my team knew I had their back on this point). I was open to changing priorities based on these conversations.*

The key is to have and keep open communication with the various business leaders about what's important to the business. Once you know that, align with the business, get agreement, and focus your efforts on what they see as priorities.

5. **Get a nondisclosure agreement in place.** If you will be discussing or exchanging confidential information, make sure a nondisclosure agreement (NDA) is in place that covers your discussions. *Tip: Legal should have a short standard NDA form available to the business that can be used with little involvement of the legal team. In our company, the link to the NDA form was prominently displayed above the fold on our intranet site as it was probably the most frequently requested/used agreement. Ours was designed so that if used unaltered, all legal needed was a copy and we did not have to be involved any further.*

6. **Involve legal early.** Get legal involved *early* in the process to avoid fire drills. There is rarely such a thing as a "quick" legal review. Planning ahead minimizes pain for all involved. Build in time up-front to go over legal and business comments, recognizing additional changes may be needed before the next drafts goes out to the other side. If the other side sat on it for two weeks, it is not reasonable to expect legal to turn it in a few hours or overnight. *Tip: This last part is nice in theory but we all know that sometimes, regardless of how much time the other side took, you will need to turn the agreement quickly. But, if you speak with the business about this issue in advance they will tend to advocate for your team with the other side versus advocating for the time-frame set by the other side.*

7. **How much is the deal worth?** Decide in advance how much the deal is worth in terms of time and concessions. For example, if a party to a $25,000 contract sends back the agreement with massive redlining, tell the party to pick their top five issues and that's it (how much time and resource can the company spend on a $25,000 deal?). *Tip: I saw such problems frequently. To a frontline sales person, a $25,000 deal might be huge in terms of meeting his or her goals for the year. And, if the customer wanted to redline every page in the draft, the salesperson generally did not see why that was a problem and expected legal to simply fully engage. Obviously, for the company, this is not a smart use of legal resources. When such a situation arises, be sure to discuss the issue not only with the sales person but also with his or her supervisor in terms of why this is a problem, what the trade-offs are, and how the business and legal get better as a team going forward.*

8. **Provide legal with the deal history/term sheet/presentation materials.** When you request help with your deal, it's important to provide legal with all the core materials such as the term sheet and any presentations discussing the

parameters of the deal. Let the legal department know the history of the deal, what you're concerned about, and any important issues (good or bad) that may have arisen in the past with the other side or have arisen during the course of the negotiations. Legal will be able to move your contract along much faster, and draft a better agreement, if the issues are presented up-front instead of several drafts down the line. *Tip: I was continually surprised by how often business partners forgot to send key documents to legal up-front. Assuming you get over this problem, use your best judgment to determine when you can get what you need simply from "the paper" or if you need a call or a meeting. I encouraged my team to frequently stop by the businessperson's office/cube and get what they needed. The personal touch always pays off.*

9. **Don't draft the contract yourself.** While we know you want to be helpful, it's actually harder for legal when the businesspeople draft the contract themselves and then ask legal to "tweak it" to make it work. While you and your counterpart at the other company may think you've sped things up by "drafting" the contract, you have likely missed a lot of things that will need to be bolted on (e.g., limits of liability, warranties, and indemnities). The process will actually go faster if you come to a preliminary agreement on the high-level terms but let the lawyers draft the agreement. *Tip: One thing I did like to get from the business were examples of how different provisions were intended to work. I would often take those examples and turn them into exhibits to the contract so that both sides could easily see what was meant by a complicated or wordy provision.*

10. **Think about the endgame.** Everybody is excited when a deal is signed and the parties are getting under way with the contract. But how does the contract come to an end (term, breach, wind-down, other triggers)? Think about how you want to see the relationship end as, inevitably, it will. You will want to make sure things are clearly spelled out and that your business unit will not be unexpectedly impacted in a negative way when the agreement ends. Discuss how you can structure the deal to mitigate negative impacts. *Tip: Be sure you ask this question when working on* any *contract. The one thing you do not want to hear is someone say "How in the hell did we end up with a contract that ends like this?"*

*****

It's important to discuss your contracting process with the business and set expectations with them as to their role and what you need from them to make the process as painless as possible for everyone. It will take team work from both legal and the business to make the process work. If you have issues, do not underestimate the power of a short meeting or a phone call (versus firing off emails). You will find people much more reasonable when you have them on the phone or in a room and you are discussing how you can help them and how they can help you. If the business understands why there is a delay, or why the provisions of the contract are needed/or don't work, you will find they are less cranky and more willing to wait and to help you.

December 23, 2014

Ten Things: How to Negotiate—Practical Tips for In-House Counsel

One of the most valuable skills an in-house lawyer brings to a company is the ability to negotiate. In-house lawyers negotiate contracts, M&A transactions, litigation resolution, government/regulator inquiries, internal squabbles, and a host of other issues. While negotiation is an important skill, it is rarely—or poorly—taught in law school (certainly here in the United States), which means unless you were fortunate enough to learn negotiation skills while employed at a law firm (and I'd wager that it is hit-and-miss whether your law firm will truly spend time teaching negotiation skills), your ability to negotiate is largely self-taught. Some of us get by on instinct and natural ability; some of us flounder a good bit, sometimes doing a great job, and sometimes not.

I am a self-taught negotiator, picking up bits and pieces of good and bad advice along the way. I have negotiated a large number of contracts and settlements in many different countries and I supervised those that did as well (learning as much from that process as being in the room). One thing I learned for sure was that regardless of where you fall on the continuum of negotiation skills, there is always room for improvement. As usual, there are some core things you need to know and understand in order to develop or improve your skills in this area. Below are ten points regarding how to negotiate:

1. **Prepare (and prepare some more).** Preparation is the single most important factor for a successful negotiation. If you fail to take the time to properly prepare, you will almost surely get less than you could have otherwise gotten from the negotiation. The time you spend preparing should dwarf the time you spend negotiating with the other side. Here are some areas to focus on:
   - *Know your objectives*: What are you trying to accomplish? What issues are important to your client, and which ones are not? What is your "walk away" position?[85]

---

85   http://www.negotiations.com/articles/business-negotiation/.

- *Know your clients*: Who are the businesspeople you are paired with? What motivates them, what drives them, and what are they trying to accomplish with the negotiation (and does it match what's important to the company)? What do they need to get a successful "deal"? Equally important is to manage client expectations and keep them realistic under the circumstances. Sometimes the "internal" negotiation is the hardest.
- *Know the strengths and weaknesses of your position*: Where are your positions the strongest and the weakest? What issues/circumstances (e.g., home forum in litigation) run in your favor and which don't?
- *Know the other side*: Use every resource to get a handle on the people on the other side of the negotiation. What motivates them? How do they negotiate? Do you know anyone who has dealt with them in past? Scrub the Internet for firm bios, social media, LinkedIn profiles, and so on.[86] Are they young or old? Do they work in this area of the law regularly? Likewise, put yourself in their shoes and think about their objectives, how they might see the respective parties' strengths and weaknesses, what pressure points they are facing, and what do they need to get out of negotiation. Most importantly, do any of your objectives overlap with the objectives of the other side? If so, you already have an area of common ground.
- *Get information*: All of the above rests squarely on your ability to gather information. It may be as simple as asking "what do you want?" Ultimately, you need to understand several things about your and their positions: goals, needs, interests, and options. Your sources of information will include people internal to the company, people external who have dealt with the other side, and research from public sources (Internet, court filings, regulatory filings, etc.). Information is power in a negotiation and the side with better/more information is the side that usually comes out with the better result.

2. **Understand leverage.** A key part of preparation is understanding the leverage each party brings to bear in the negotiation. Leverage is simply the ability to influence the other side to move closer to your negotiating position. Typically, leverage comes down to some basic facts—facts that you need to dig out and think about before going into the negotiation. Knowledge = leverage. For example, how much does your side want or need the deal or the settlement? Same question for the other side. What are each side's alternatives in the event

---

86 https://lawyerist.com/92442/internet-tools-for-researching-opposing-counsel-judges-and-juries/?utm_source=Lawyerist+Insider&utm_campaign=1052e13314-2016_05_18_5_Random_Things_RE_Obstacles&utm_medium=email&utm_term=0_30d7a1f6e2-1052e13314-290847949&mc_cid=1052e13314&mc_eid=0c73e9e561.

no deal is reached? Who is facing time pressure (i.e., patience can be a highly effective negotiation tool). From a commercial perspective, where do you or the other side go for goods or services in the event you cannot strike a deal? If those "next best alternatives"[87] are not as good as the product or service being offered, then some of the commercial leverage will fall to the party offering the product or service. In litigation, a "decision tree"[88] chart showing the percentages of likely outcomes of the claims and damages can be very helpful in thinking through the question of leverage. Likewise, lack of confidentiality in legal proceedings may be a large incentive for one side to prefer settlement.

3. **Control the agenda/writing.** Resist letting the other side set a pace for negotiation that does not suit you or your team. This does not mean that everything will be done exactly on your timing, but it does mean you should not be a pushover and let the other side run roughshod over your side with respect to how the meeting(s) progresses and which issues get discussed when. If you need a break, take a break. If you want to go faster, push ahead. If you think the parties need to meet over the weekend to get a deal, set that out. If your side wants to discuss issue X or put issue Y in the "parking lot"[89] for a while, work on making that happen. If the other side wants a face-to-face and you think a telephone meeting is all that is needed at this point, stick to your guns. Similarly, once there is a deal in place, work hard to get control of the first draft of the agreement, the settlement, term sheet, order, or whatever. Even better, prepare the document in advance. It is always easier for your side when the other side is working off your draft. Volunteer to take the first cut. If that's not possible, then be sure to take your time going through any drafts presented to you by the other side. Make sure all of the issues and agreements are dealt with and fight for language you are comfortable with. Resist the urge to let down your guard based on the fact that you've an oral agreement on the basic terms. Don't let up until the document is drafted and signed.

4. **Have a written playbook.** For any negotiation of importance, invest the time to prepare a written playbook. This document will summarize the key issues you face in the negotiation and then go point by point with a summary of your position and the other side's position along with showing how those positions change over time (i.e., the "gives and the gets"). You will set out your preferred "landing zone" for each issue along with your "walkaway," that is, if you cannot get at least these terms or amount of value, then you are willing to

---

87 http://www.beyondintractability.org/essay/batna.

88 http://www.generalpatent.com/files/litigation_risk_analysis.pdf.

89 https://www.linkedin.com/pulse/key-benefits-negotiation-parking-lots-devon-smiley.

truly walk away from the deal. This last point is important. You must always be prepared to walk away from a bad deal.

In your playbook, you should rank the issues by importance, that is, those listed first are more important and core to the deal than those that come later. As to the latter, you may be willing to trade away to get those items higher on the list. This is part of your "offer and concession"[90] strategy, which is key to getting to a deal. Be sure you are building room for flexibility during the negotiation (i.e., "take it or leave it" attitude rarely works). The playbook should be regularly updated through each round of the negotiation. It is also a great tool to share with upper management or others on your side who have an interest in how the deal is progressing. A playbook will keep everyone on your side focused on what's important and will instill negotiating discipline, allowing you to maximize your leverage and strengths and focus on what's truly important to your side. Here is an example of what a small section of a simple playbook might look like after one round of negotiation:

Contract Issue	Our Position	Their Position	"Landing Zone"	"Walkaway"	Give/Get
Term of Agreement	10 years	3 years	5 years	5 years	Will give
Indemnity Cap	$5M	$20M	$10M	$15M	Need to get

5. **Nothing is done until it's all done.** Do not try to resolve your issues one point at a time. This will take forever and you will find yourself giving up things too early in the game. For example, of the first three issues in a contract negotiation, your side may truly care about only one of them. If you fully negotiate all three issues, when you come to issues 18 and 19—which both mean a lot to your side—you cannot trade issues 2 and 3 to get what you want for 18 and 19. Go through all of the issues once and understand generally each side's position, without fully negotiating each point. Most importantly, do not give something unless you get something for it. Ideally, present the other side with a draft document and let them mark it up with their changes. Don't be put off by a lot of red line[91] and comments; this is how you start to learn what issues are important to the other side, where there might be misunderstandings, and

---

90 http://strategicdynamicsfirm.com/concession-strategy-complex-negotiations-planning-give-take-part-1/.

91 http://www.webopedia.com/TERM/R/redlining.html.

where the other side is coming from in their thinking. Once you get the red line, you can go back and rank issues with your team. As you move forward, be clear that there is no deal until all issues are agreed to. This doesn't mean you cannot close out issues; just be sure to say "This seems agreeable. Let's see how the rest of the negotiation goes before we make anything final."

6. **Listen more than you talk.** In a negotiation, you want to get as much information as possible about what the other side is thinking and what they want, along with their motives, fears, concerns, and interests. The best way to do this is by listening to them versus talking. The rule of thumb here is to listen 70 percent of the time, and talk the other 30 percent. Ask the other side what it is they want and then listen hard to the answer. Not every meeting has to be a negotiation. Some of the most important meetings just involve listening to the other side explain what they want or why they made changes to the language in the draft agreement. It's a great time to probe and ask questions. Let them explain their point to you and then summarize back what you heard to make sure both sides are thinking about the point the same way. This doesn't mean you agree, but it will help you from missing each other (and the other side will feel that you are listening to them, which is helpful). Remember that 50 percent of communication is nonverbal,[92] so it's important to pay attention to body language and to facial reactions.[93] Odds are good that people in the room will try to wear a poker face throughout the negotiation but that is very difficult to keep up over time. At some point, everyone will give away what they are thinking or how they are feeling through body language, facial expressions, or other reactions to what you are saying.

7. **Build a rapport with the other side.** It is worth your time to try to build some type of relationship with the other side during your negotiations, even if it's just small talk about family, where you went to school, and the like. Some of this you will know from your research on the other side, but that should not stop you from taking time to be friendly. Sometimes during tough negotiations, I would invite my counterpart to step out of the session and grab a cup of coffee. We'd talk about the negotiations and things we could do to bring the sides together or just about sports or the weather or whatever and use the time to clear our heads. Usually we'd come back to the room with some new ideas or a renewed sense of purpose to get the deal done. There is a good article by Eric Barker where he interviews a former FBI crisis negotiation unit member

---

92 http://www.pon.harvard.edu/daily/negotiation-skills-daily/negotiation-techniques-and-body-language-body-language-negotiation-examples-in-real-life/.

93 https://www.mindtools.com/pages/article/Body_Language.htm.

who discusses negotiation strategy utilized by the bureau.[94] While the stakes are certainly not the same, the principles around effective negotiation are. The agent explained several techniques the FBI used—all of which fit perfectly into the world of business negotiations and for building a rapport with the other side. Some of the techniques from the article are as follows:

- *Ask open-ended questions*—encourage the other side to open up.
- *Use pauses*—use pauses for emphasis or to encourage the other side to keep talking.
- *Encourage the speaker*—simple phrases like "I see" or "Okay" make it clear to the speaker that you are listening to him or her and care about what he or she is saying.
- *Use mirroring*—rework the last sentence the other person used into your own sentence.
- *Paraphrase*—use your own words to repeat what the other person said.

8. **Take reasoned positions.** One of the most effective techniques in a negotiation is the ability to show why your position makes sense from a "reasoned" basis, that is, there is a reasonable, logical, and valid rationale for what you are asking and that what you are asking for is fair. For example, if you can show that the clause you want to insert around liability caps is "at market" and is fair based on the revenue stream of the contract, it is difficult for the other side to refuse to agree. They may have reasons, but those reasons will need to be based on why the provision is not fair or not at market or why the circumstances of your deal are different, thereby calling for a different result. But the focus of your negotiation should be built on reasoning and logic, and not emotion. Likewise, you need to listen to the other side as they lay out positions and understand whether those positions are market-based or are industry standard or are otherwise fair under the circumstances. If you disagree, bring facts to bear and not just "I don't want to do that." And, if you can, always try to show how what you are proposing works for them or their position. You may need to tweak language to get them over the hump, but if you are sure your proposal gives them what they are asking for, be prepared to explain why.

9. **It's not a war.** A frequent mistake people make heading into a negotiation is to think of it as a "war" where someone has to "win" the day. The basis of a good negotiation, however, is that everyone gets something, and if you can help the other side feel like they got things important to them (even if they're not important to you), it can go a long way to reaching a deal. If you want a war, that's what the courts are for. Each side will go into the negotiation with strong

---

94 http://theweek.com/articles/447394/6-hostage-negotiation-techniques-that-what-want.

points and weak points. Don't overestimate your strong points or underestimate those of the other side. Every once in a while you are part of a negotiation where one side simply has all the power. I have been on the "wrong" side of those types of negotiations and it's not fun. If you happen to be on the side with the leverage, my advice is that a little bit of humbleness goes a long way with the other side. You can get everything you want and need (because you have the commercial leverage) but do so in a way that does not leave the other side feeling crushed. Do you really need to win every point? Keep in mind that if it's a business contract, you're still going to need to work with the other side going forward. "Crushing" them in the negotiation is not going to make that easy and you can expect them to look for *every* angle to come back at you at some point. A little empathy goes a long way.

If you have purchased a copy of Donald Trump's ghostwritten *The Art of the Deal*, you may want to leave it on the shelf. While entertaining to read, those cartoon villain tactics rarely work (as evidenced by the number of unpaid debts, lawsuits, and bankruptcies). A recent *Harvard Business Review* article entitled "What Donald Trump Doesn't Understand about Negotiation"[95] looks at the "Trump" negotiation style and concludes that there are many problems with it — in particular, preconditions and ultimatums are usually bad ideas, and "they lose" does not equal "you win." If you do come across a "bully" negotiator,[96] don't make it personal. The best thing to do is let them rant and rave and then say either "are you through and can we start the negotiation now?" or "we'll come back when you can behave like an adult" and leave.

10. **Be ethical.** The one thing you have in your professional career is your reputation. If that gets tarnished, it is very hard to recover. People respect tough, hard negotiators. People despise liars and cheats and will look for the first of many opportunities to "stick it" to them down the road. If you have a reputation for being truthful, living up to your word, and doing what you say you will do, your negotiations will go much better and deals will be easier to reach because there is a level of trust between the parties. Breach that trust, and the relationship between the parties becomes contentious and unpleasant. How you and your side negotiate will become known and the other side will be looking into your reputation (just like you will theirs). This does not mean that usual gamesmanship of negotiation is off limits (e.g., it may not really be your

---

95 https://hbr.org/2016/04/what-donald-trump-doesnt-understand-about-negotiation?utm_source=twitter&utm_medium=social&utm_campaign=harvardbiz.

96 http://stevemehta.com/blog/handle-negotiator-bully/.

"final" offer), but misrepresenting material facts to gain an edge is. In sum, play hard, but play straight.

*****

There is a lot of information packed into the above and there is much more to negotiation than my high-level points. Here are a few additional resources I have found useful:
- *Effective Legal Negotiation and Settlement*[97]
- *Getting to Yes: Negotiating Agreement without Giving In*[98]
- Brodow.com[99]
- The Accidental Negotiator[100]
- The Harvard Program on Negotiation—Daily Blog[101]

While outside resources are nice, don't forget that there may be even more valuable resources close at hand, that is, your colleagues in the business or the legal department. If you know of an experienced negotiator within the company or department, ask her to coffee and pick her brain on how she negotiates (or refer someone on your team to her). Similarly, be willing to share what you know with others. Some companies offer negotiation training (live or online) to their sales teams. Little prevents in-house counsel from taking those same courses. Investigate all available resources and then be proactive and volunteer to set up a negotiation boot camp for your legal department. That's a good deal for everyone.

June 14, 2016

---

97 Craver, Charles B. *Effective legal negotiation and settlement*. 7th ed. New Providence, NJ: LexisNexis, 2012.

98 Fisher, Roger, William Ury, and Bruce Patton. *Getting to yes: negotiating agreement without giving in*. New York, NY: Penguin, 1991.

99 http://brodow.com/articles.html.

100 http://theaccidentalnegotiator.com/.

101 http://www.pon.harvard.edu/blog/.

Ten Things: Insurance Contract Basics for In-House Counsel

Looking back on my career, I realize I spent a good amount of time working on insurance-related issues as in-house counsel. Sometimes it was helping the insurance team figure out what types of coverage were needed; at other times, it was about filing a claim or trying to answer questions from senior management about how the policies worked, and—unfortunately—several times it involved litigation with the insurance carrier over its failure to pay claims. I was thinking about insurance issues because my good friend and noted insurance law guru Amy Stewart of Dallas, Texas, recently published a book entitled *Texas Insurance Coverage Litigation—The Litigator's Practice Guide* (2015).[102] Reading through the pages I recalled various issues I came across over the last 20-something years. Even though it's aimed at Texas law, the book has very useful general discussions on insurance law issues.

As in-house counsel you (or someone on your team) should have a solid understanding of basic insurance law issues. While hopefully your company will never need to make a claim against its insurance, if it does, the legal team's ability to spot issues and help guide the process can mean the difference between a quick payout or a long court battle with the insurer. You do not need to become an insurance law expert, but you should know the basics and know when you need to get help from outside counsel. This article will discuss ten things you should be familiar with regarding insurance contracts purchased by your company:

1. **The role of in-house counsel.** Many in-house legal departments view insurance as something "the other guy" needs to worry about, that is, usually someone in finance or risk management. While technically true, in-house attorneys ignore the insurance process and the company's policies at their risk (and risk to the company). While legal may not own the insurance process, you cannot

---

[102] http://www.lawjournalpress.com/player/eBook_329_Texas_Insurance_Coverage_Litigation_The_Litigator%E2%80%99s_Practice_Guide_2015.html.

stand off to the side and only get involved when a claim is filed. It is important that legal participates in the process from the beginning, understands the different policies, and knows what to do and how to proceed in the event a claim needs to be made or if a claim is denied by the insurer. In-house lawyers should be valued partners of the "other guys," including hosting regular meetings to discuss insurance coverage for the company, the procurement or renewal of policies, and how to deal with common problems. As you set goals for the legal department, be sure to include one or two around the issue of insurance, and ensure that someone in legal has the lead position with respect to insurance questions (and gets the training he or she needs to be successful in that role).

2. **Different types of insurance policies.** Start with understanding the different types of insurance coverage[103] a company typically has in place at any one time. There are many different types of policies, and, for a price, you can insure almost any type of risk. Here are some common policies and a short description of what they cover:

- *Commercial general liability (CGL)*[104] — This insurance provides broad insurance protection for claims against the policy holder alleging such things as bodily injury, property damage, advertising injury, and/or personal injury.
- *Directors and officers (D&O)*[105] — This insurance protects corporate officers and directors against claims alleging wrongful acts in their capacity as officers and directors.
- *Errors and omissions (E&O)*[106] — This insurance is designed to protect the company against claims that it was negligent in providing professional services.
- *Cyber and privacy liability (cyber risk)*[107] — This insurance protects data breaches, computer technology, privacy issues, computer virus transmission, and similar risks.
- *Environmental*[108] — This insurance covers claims related to environmental incidents, such as pollution spills and toxic cleanup. It can be important if CGL excludes pollution/environmental related claims.

---

103 http://www.insidecounsel.com/2015/02/27/insurance-for-business-litigation-risks-managing-m?slreturn=1467757775.

104 http://www.iii.org/article/commercial-general-liability-insurance.

105 http://www.iii.org/article/directors-and-officers-insurance.

106 http://www.iii.org/article/professional-liability-insurance.

107 http://www.iii.org/article/cyber-liability-risks.

108 http://www.iii.org/article/environmental-liability-insurance.

- *Excess and umbrella*[109]—This insurance kicks in once the primary insurance policy is exhausted (or limits paid out) or to fill in gaps in the primary insurance coverage of certain risks.
3. **Key terms.** There are several key terms you should know as part of any day-to-day understanding of how your insurance policies work:
    - *First party versus third party*—First-party insurance insures against loss of or damage to a policy holder's property, for example, business interruption insurance or fidelity/crime policies. Third-party insurance covers the policy holder's liability to another party, for example, CGL insurance or E&O insurance.
    - *Occurrence versus claims made*—For third-party insurance, it is important to understand whether you have an occurrence policy or a claims-made policy. Occurrence-based policies mean that the insurance in place at the time the injury occurred is the policy under which to make your claim. For example, if you are sued in 2015 for an injury that arose in 2012, the policy in effect in 2012 is the one to look to for coverage. Claims-made policies mean that you look to the insurance in place on the date the claim is made. Under these policies, pay close attention to any retroactive date, which limits how far back the policy will cover. For instance, a claims-made directors and officers policy in effect for 2015 with a retroactive date of 2011 will cover the company for lawsuits filed in 2015 even if the actions at issue took place in 2011 or later. If the actions took place in 2010 or earlier, the policy will not apply.
    - *Policy limits*—A policy limit is how much coverage you have and how it is calculated. If you have a $5 million overall limit policy, then you have $5 million of coverage regardless of how many claims are made against the policy, that is, if all claims exceed $5 million, you will exhaust the policy limit. If you have a $5 million limit per occurrence, then each occurrence arising during the policy period has a separate policy limit of $5 million regardless of the number of claims filed. Per occurrence provides a much greater level of coverage than an overall limit policy (but is likely more expensive). The company should understand which type of policy it has, so no one is under any misconceptions about the amount of insurance available in the event of multiple claims.
    - *Glossary*—The Insurance Information Institute has a helpful glossary of key insurance terms.[110]

---

109 http://definitions.uslegal.com/e/excess-liability-insurance/.
110 http://www.iii.org/services/glossary/a.

4. **Reading an insurance policy.** There is no substitute for reading your policies. This is the only way you can truly understand the nature and amount of insurance protection available. You will typically see the following in a basic CGL policy:[111]
    - *Insurance binder*—This is the initial document that summarizes the basic terms of the policy. When the policy is delivered, it should be checked against the binder to make sure they line up.
    - *Declarations*—The first section of the policy is the declarations page. This is a summary of the policy and includes the named insureds, the policy period, the policy limits/amount insured, the specific type of insurance purchased (e.g., CGL, E&O). If you do nothing else, check the named insureds and make sure it lines up with everyone's expectations around who's covered by the policy. This is important if the company has subsidiaries (or is a subsidiary).
    - *Policy form*—Next comes a standard document describing who or what is insured, the actual insurance agreement (and definitions), endorsements, exclusions, and any conditions. Most policies are based on standard forms with little customization. Read the policy form carefully, especially the endorsements (adding to the coverage), exclusions (what's not covered), and the conditions, all of which amend or impact the applicability of the insurance to any particular situation. When reading the exclusions, look for exceptions to the exclusion, which can provide insurance where it appeared such claims were excluded. Conditions are duties of the insurer and the policy holder, for example, the policy holder's duty to give notice of a claim.
    - *Generally*—When reading an insurance policy, read it quickly one time through to get familiar with the format, general provisions, and key terms, and then go back a second time for a slow read to truly understand the coverage and the obligations, especially those of the company. Legal should keep a full set of copies of all of the company's insurance policies (including old policies as those may—under an occurrence policy—still be important).
5. **Notice.** One of the most important provisions of the policy is the section that discusses how and when to give notice to the insurer of a claim. Insurance companies will often try to avoid responsibility under the policy by claiming that notice was deficient in some manner (e.g., it was late). Fortunately, most courts construe notice liberally in favor of the insured and require that the insurer provide evidence of material prejudice[112] from the imperfect notice before

---

111 https://tulip.ajgrms.com/Content/Policies/URMIA_TULIP_General_Liability_Policy.pdf.
112 http://www.duanemorris.com/articles/static/evans_abainsurance_0312.pdf.

allowing the insurer to escape responsibility. One key role in-house counsel can play regarding insurance coverage issues is to help with the preparation of the notice of a claim. Understand the requirements of the notice provision and, even then, give as broad notice as possible with respect to a potential claim, stating that you are making the claim under any and all applicable policies. Remember that with respect to a lawsuit, it's not necessarily the headings of the claims that matter; it's the specific facts alleged. You need to match the facts alleged in the lawsuit to your policy. If you restrict your thinking to just the name of the claim in the lawsuit, you may miss out on allegations that bring the lawsuit under your policy.

6. **Deductible versus retention.** A retention-based policy means that the insured needs to go out of pocket some amount before the insurance company has any obligations. A typical example is defense costs. If you have a $1 million retention policy, this means your company will need to pay the first $1 million out of pocket before any insurance will kick in. This can be painful, especially when it comes to attorneys' fees and costs. If you have a $1 million deductible policy, then the insurer's obligation to defend/resolve any claim is immediate, with the insured paying its deductible amount toward the costs or claim.

7. **Duties of the parties.** You should be aware of the respective duties of the parties under the policy. There are typically three parties to a business insurance policy: the insured, the insurer, and the broker. To keep things short, we'll skip the broker and focus on the key duties of the other two:
   - *Insured*—payment of premium, prompt notice of loss/claim, honesty when completing the applications for insurance (this is important), cooperation with insurer in defending a claim against the insured.
   - *Insurer*—collection of premium, payment of claims, issue the policy, duty to defend, duty to indemnify.

8. **Duty to defend versus duty to indemnify.** An insurer has two key duties. The duty to defend is the duty to pay the costs of defending a claim against the insured. This duty is broader than the duty to indemnify, which is the duty to pay out any damages owed by the insured to a third party. The duty to defend is broader because the insurer must provide a defense if *any* of the allegations in the lawsuit against the insured are covered by the policy and it must pay for the defense of all of the claims, even if one of the claims is otherwise excluded. The costs of defense are sometimes outside the policy limits, meaning they are unlimited. Some policies place the cost of defense within the policy limits, meaning defense costs could wipe out any insurance money left to pay out claims. This can be a big problem in the event of mass tort litigation. Consequently, it's important that in-house counsel understand which type of policy the company has or is considering and to ensure that the policy selected is the

one the company wants in place (and that everyone understands the potential issues if the cost of defense is placed within the policy limits).

9. **Reservation of rights.** Here's where things get messy. You've given notice of your claim to the insurance company and you get back a letter where the insurer accepts the claim subject to a reservation of rights. This is a reservation of rights letter (ROR). First, keep in mind that this is not a denial of coverage. It does mean that you may have a tough road ahead in terms of getting paid (e.g., defense costs). Second, the insurer may be teeing you up for a declaratory judgment claim—which it would file in a venue it thinks most favorable to itself, given the issues. Third, an ROR means there are several things you need to do:

- *Respond*—Always respond to an ROR, even if your response is simply "we do not agree with the insurance coverage positions set out by you in your letter of [date]." A better plan is a more detailed response. For this you will be well served to hire outside counsel that specializes in insurance coverage matters.

- *Cooperate (within reason)*—Even with an ROR in place, you will still have a duty of cooperation with the insurance company (e.g., provide copies of pleadings). However, with an ROR, you need to be careful that the insurer does not take the information you provide and use it to support its denial of coverage. This is likely when the ROR uses language from the plaintiff's complaint as a basis to potentially deny coverage (i.e., the insurer's defenses to your policy claims are similar to/same as the underlying plaintiff's allegations). If so, there is now an inherent conflict of interest between the insurer and the insured, and you need to be careful in what information you turn over to the insurer as you may waive privilege. Make sure you have a confidentiality agreement in place with the insurance company, preferably the same one the court entered in the case. The insurer may be satisfied with meetings with your outside counsel (vs. jeopardizing the privilege) or, at a minimum, ensuring that no one at the insurer involved in the coverage dispute has access to your confidential documents.

- *Control of the defense*—As noted, the ROR may tee up an inherent conflict between the insurer and the insured where their interests are not aligned. If so, most states acknowledge that the insured controls the defense and is no longer required to accept counsel that the insurer seeks to impose. Also, things like the insurer's outside counsel guidelines[113] will likely not apply to your choice of counsel. As the insurer is still paying for the cost of defense,

---

113 http://digital.todaysgeneralcounsel.com/?issueID=36&pageID=59.

you need to reasonably cooperate with the insurer but keep your inherent conflict top of mind. This is a tricky area and another reason why investing in experienced coverage counsel will be valuable.

10. **Litigation with the insurance company.** Sadly, not every encounter with your insurance company will be positive. Litigation may be the only way to protect the company's rights. Following are some things to keep in mind. First, if the relationship get contentious or if the ROR is particularly gruesome, or the insurance company utterly fails to live up to the agreement, consider being the first to file. The insurer is probably already thinking about a declaratory judgment. By filing first, you pick the venue, set the timing, and can send a message to the insurer that your company is not going take a breach lying down. Second, regardless whether you file first or not, know that the insurance company will be interested in three things: delay, delay, and more delay. It will try to keep pushing things out into the future, using every tactic at its disposal to be unresponsive, ask for additional time to respond, seek continuances, and so on. You must think like a plaintiff's lawyer. Be aggressive in terms of pushing things forward as quickly as possible toward trial. File for summary judgment on duty to defend as soon as possible. Don't fall for the "let's put the case on hold and mediate" line. You can mediate while the litigation goes forward. Third, keep your senior management (CEO, board of directors) up to date on how the case is progressing.[114] They will want to see quick action/results, and money coming in as soon as possible. Unfortunately, it does not always work that way. Make sure your CEO and CFO understand the litigation process and to expect the insurance company to do everything possible to delay the case, increase your cost to prosecute, and hope that ultimately you will accept substantially less than you are entitled to under the policy to settle the matter. Lastly, look at all possible causes of action including bad faith, breach of contract, statutory and punitive damages, interest (pre and post), any statutory penalties that might be available, and recovery of your attorney's fees for the litigation.

*****

I don't mean to imply here that all experiences with insurance companies will be bad. I had a number of positive experiences over the course of my career. In fact, many insurers offer programs to help you spot and minimize risk. Still, you must be vigilant to ensure that your company receives the benefits of the policies it paid for.

---

114 See page 53.

Hopefully, you'll never need to make a claim. But if you do, the insurer should live up to its end of the bargain. In-house counsel can play an important and helpful role around the procurement and utilization of insurance (and by retaining experienced coverage counsel). Insurance policies are valuable corporate assets. Spend some time thinking about how insurance works today at your company and whether legal is playing the right (or any) role in that process. If not, begin planning now and come up with an A–Z plan to ensure legal is engaged at all of the important points including obtaining the right insurance, working with the broker, and leading the process to make a claim and respond to any ROR.

September 9, 2015

Legal Department Operations

Ten Things: Setting Goals for the Legal Department

The beginning of any calendar year is always busy with key administrative tasks for an in-house legal department. One of the more daunting tasks (whether you are general counsel or not) is setting useful goals for the upcoming year. Legal departments do not always lend themselves to neatly setting goals like the business units, that is, it can be difficult to measure "success" in legal versus measuring profits and sales or setting key performance indicators.[115] That said, setting goals for the department or yourself is important and a fresh opportunity to take stock of many things. I always approached yearly goal setting as, among other things, an opportunity to market the department (i.e., all the great stuff we were doing), get a deeper understanding of what was important to the business, and gather feedback on how the department could improve in the upcoming year. Meaning, don't shirk the opportunity and think of goal setting as some type of pain-in-the-neck HR exercise you have to muddle through. Embrace the process as the more thought and effort you put into goal setting, the bigger the payoff. And, there will be a payoff for you and your team if done properly and with some enthusiasm.

Below I will set out ten things you can do to prepare/think through/implement goals and then I will set out a sample list of goals for the upcoming year. As for the sample goals, I used very similar goals over the course of my career for myself and for running different legal departments (feel free to use or adopt or modify any of the sample goals). I would start with my "big five" top-level goals, and then build specific goals underneath them. My big five were the following:

1. *Build and retain extraordinary team with exceptional people.*
2. *Meet budget targets in 20XX.*
3. *Prioritize and complete high revenue/cost saving and strategic commercial agreements.*

---

115 http://barnraisersllc.com/2012/02/experts-define-key-performance-indicators/.

4. *Deliver on strategic transactions and initiatives (mergers, joint ventures, acquisitions, and key deal activity).*
5. *Defend and protect the interests of the company (litigation, IP, government affairs, compliance).*

These five themes allowed me and everyone to develop precise goals underneath each item. This process worked well for the entire department (U.S. domestic and international employees) and was easily tailored by different sections of the legal department or by individual lawyers/staff members. The key is that everyone is rowing in the same direction under the big five. With that in mind, here's how to get started:

1. **Take a look at last year.** The best place to start is to go over how you did on last year's goals. Are there any goals worth repeating or that you left unfinished? Did you find a better way to measure success? What worked for you and your team and what did not? Look back to look forward.
2. **Talk to your clients.** Next talk to your business clients and find out what is important to them in the upcoming year (big deals, disputes, strategic initiatives, legislative concerns, or opportunities, etc.). This can be done at several layers, meaning talk with the folks at the top, the middle, and the front lines. The middle and lower layers will give you a more granular insight into what the business unit hopes to achieve. Then, match up the goals of the department (and those of individuals supporting that business unit) to what the business thinks is important. Additionally, think about all of the staff groups you interact with and what are they trying to accomplish in upcoming year and how the legal department can help them (e.g., HR, internal audit, investor relations, corporate communications, finance, technology). Alignment with other staff groups is good for the company and helps build teamwork across the organization.
3. **Talk to the boss.** As general counsel, I needed to make sure the goals of the department lined up with those of my boss, the CEO (and to get CEO buy in on the goals we were setting). Additionally, and with permission from the CEO, talk with members of the board of directors, especially the committee chairs (e.g., audit, governance, compensation). It's important to understand what the board is concerned about heading into the year. If you're not the general counsel, talk with your manager about what he or she thinks is important (and bring your own ideas to the table).
4. **Talk to your team.** Spend time with your team and pick their brains about what should be on the list. Who will know better about specific legal issues facing your department than your own lawyers? And, don't forget your staff members. You can uncover important issues by getting insight from paralegals or administrative staff (e.g., e-discovery issues, technology needs).

5. **What's in the hopper already?** Think about litigation or contracts that are ongoing (and worthy of being part of the goals) or other things you can see coming down the pike for the company. For example, as we were planning for a potential IPO, I knew to put that into my and the department's goals for the upcoming year even if we had not started on it (though be careful not to prematurely disclose confidential information if the fact of a potential IPO—or whatever—is not widely known).
6. **Be proactive/forward thinking.** Be aware of what's going on in the world around you. For example, some called 2014 the "Year of the Data Breach," given the number of high-profile data breaches that occurred during that year. This is good indication that data privacy or data breach planning should have been on your list for 2015. Stay up to date (websites, magazines, newspapers/trade press, trade associations,[116] etc.) on how the environment your company operates in is changing and evolving (both domestically and internationally). There are many sources to patch into here.
7. **Upgrade skills and talent.** Your most valuable asset is the people you already have working for you. How can you help them upgrade their existing skill sets, develop different skills, and become more efficient and productive? You should spend a good bit of time thinking about this one. It may be better or more Continuing Legal Education training, new technology, moving people into different roles, or adding responsibilities to existing people. And don't forget yourself. What can you work on? Everyone has something they can get better at or gain insight into.[117]
8. **Find ways to measure success.** This is one of the hardest things for legal to accomplish in the goal setting exercise. How do you measure success?[118] Maybe it's a percentage reduction in spending in some area or an increase in response time. It could be volume as in number of contracts completed over the course of the year. Every goal you set should have some type of measurement associated with it, even if it's just "complete review of data privacy policy by December 31."
9. **Go over the goals with your team.** Once you've set goals, you will need to sit down with your team and go over them, so everyone understands what's important and what they need to focus on and potentially add to their own goals—which are typically developed after the department-level goals are set. I did this at the department's January monthly meeting (and I shared all of the

---

116 http://libguides.rutgers.edu/c.php?g=336557&p=2266143.
117 https://www.theladders.com/career-advice/new-years-resolutions-of-successful-people/.
118 http://www.catalystlegal.com/Articles/Key_Performance_Indicators.htm.

goals with *everyone*, so we were all on the same page). You can and should do more focused discussions on goals during one-on-one meetings with your section heads or in direct reports. Make sure everyone on your team has a copy of the department's goals.

10. **Keep track of success (or failure).** If you wait until December to think back on how well you did versus your goals, you will probably find that you cannot remember everything you accomplished (especially earlier in the year). For example, I kept track weekly by creating a folder in Outlook and sending myself emails about different goals or achievements (my own or the department's). At the monthly department meeting I went through a dashboard that showed progress (green, yellow, red) on key goals for the year so everyone knew where we were versus our goals and "why." When midyear review or end-of-year review time came, I had most of the data in one spot. Also, it is unlikely that your goals will stay static over the course of the year. New issues and problems or deals will arise that will become "goal worthy." Be ready to update or alter goals as needed, and my big five were generally flexible enough that important new items easily fit underneath. If you are a manager, discuss progress toward the goals with your direct reports regularly (at least monthly). And you should always keep track yourself and update your boss regularly as well, even if not asked.

*****

Below is a set of sample goals for the year using my big five themes. The specific goals underneath are taken from several different sets of goals I developed over the years when I was general counsel. I have dumbed them down a bit for obvious reasons and some are simply statements about gathering the list yourself. I have left in some measurements where it made sense but (sorry) you're a bit on your own with that piece.

"Any Company Inc." Legal Department 20XX Goals

1. **Build and retain extraordinary team with exceptional people.**
   - Every manager has a career discussion with his or her directs, with more time dedicated to reviews and development. Fully utilize HR tools for the review and career development process. Create and distribute feedback form to clients regarding each attorney. Develop and distribute feedback form to attorneys to evaluate support staff.
   - Prepare/update a "who does what" document, explaining areas of concentration/skills of each attorney in the department and have everyone in

department prepare a one-page bio with photo and distribute both to all members of the department.
- Create and send out a client satisfaction survey and maintain or increase satisfaction rates on key metrics year over year.
- Recognize achievements of department members on regular basis (team meetings, one-off, etc.).
- Strive for work/life balance and appropriate level of flexibility for members of the department.
- Keep clients up to date on their matters, communicate frequently—ultra engage—know what the customers need and stay fully aligned and in touch/available. Respond to any email or phone call within 24 hours (even if just to acknowledge receipt).
- Everyone should "act like an owner"—solve problems as they arise and be able to give several examples.
- Share knowledge—with team, with department, with company (develop ways to do this regularly)—and be able to give examples.
- Innovate—what we do and how we do it. Apply better use of technology (online research, etc.).
- Stay trained and up-to-date in your area or expand skill set.
- Engage in team charitable event(s) and develop potential pro bono program.

2. **Meet budget targets in 20XX**
    - Find ways to maintain or reduce hourly effective rate for outside legal services.
    - Increase utilization of "niche law firms" by 15 percent of total spend (do not be wedded to any firm for any type of matter).
    - Use joint cost-sharing agreements and alternative billing arrangements where it makes sense.
    - Give clear instructions to outside counsel on every matter regarding spend limits/work product expectation.
    - Implement e-billing tool by December 31.
    - Forecast legal spend accurately. Hold monthly budget/spend meetings with team and finance.
    - Develop new or enhance existing form agreements to reduce legal work/churn.
    - Meet travel expense budget.
    - Reduce "waste" (money, time, etc.). Every team member should identify three things for the year they did to meet this goal, for example, better meetings and eliminating costs, etc.

3. **Prioritize and complete high-revenue/cost-saving and strategic commercial agreements.**
   - [Work with business to identify high priority contracts for coming year and list those—add to as year goes on]

4. **Deliver on strategic transactions and initiatives (mergers, joint ventures, acquisitions, and key deal activity).**
   - Implement data use initiatives. Help create a company-wide data use plan that is compliant with law, the company values, and is in alignment with the company's strategic objectives.
   - [If your company has a key charity, think of ways how legal could help the company advance that cause?]
   - [Work with business to build a list of key corporate development transactions (M&A, JVs, etc.)—add to the list as the year goes on]
   - Launch and complete IPO.

5. **Defend and protect the interests of the company (litigation, IP, government affairs, compliance).**
   - Win/settle key litigation/regulatory matters within or better than settlement parameters set by client.
   - Make compliance easy and second nature for the employees—update all training materials and review/update policies.
   - Update all data privacy policies and training.
   - Give presentations on legal topics to company employees on relevant topics designed to reduce risk or help employees be better users of legal services.
   - Develop a plan to enhance patent portfolio.
   - Review and update policies and training around trade secrets.
   - Take action on legislation important/harmful to the company.
   - Win on regulatory initiatives important to the company (e.g., patent reform).
   - Assist company with new market entry/development (via government relations, legal actions, etc.).
   - Identify three problem risk areas internally and fix them (e.g., record retention policy, visitor policies, media training).

*****

Good luck with your goal setting for this coming year. If you haven't set goals in the past, make this the year you and your team make this process an important part of how the legal department operates.

January 8, 2015

Ten Things: Simple Ways to Reward and Retain Your People

As I mentioned in the section regarding setting goals for the legal department,[119] I am going to dive deeper into some of the sample department goals I set out in that discussion. Here I will focus on this goal: **"Build and retain extraordinary team with exceptional people."** I always put my "people goal" first because I truly believe that nothing gets done in legal unless you have top talent who are motivated and happy in their jobs. How do you keep and reward people so they stick around? The obvious answer is pay them well, have a good performance bonus program in place, and let them share in equity plans. The problem is, for many reasons, it usually is not fully in your control to make any of these three things happen. For purposes of this section, I am going to assume that you are doing what you can for your team around salary, bonuses, and equity and, instead, focus on some low-cost ways you can reward/recognize employees.

Fortunately, there are many ways to reward and recognize that don't require you to break the bank. The goal is to find simple ways to show your employees that you and the company appreciate them and their work, and that you want to encourage their growth (or just make their job more interesting and fun). While money isn't everything, it can be if there isn't anything else keeping people happy working for you. If your employees have a job where they feel wanted and encouraged—and enjoy coming to work—they will be less likely to take a job offer for "more money." Here are ten simple things you can do to reward your people and build retention and a better work environment. These are all things that I did in my past jobs. They won't make everyone happy all of the time, but they do work:

1. **Remember birthdays and anniversaries.** I kept a list of everyone's birthday and anniversary (of starting work with the company). I would send a short personal note to people on their anniversary date thanking them for being with

---

[119] See page 103.

the company and for their hard work. On birthdays I would send out an email to the entire department wishing the particular employee a happy birthday and letting everyone know it was a special day. I also tried to include something fun in the email like a list of famous people born on the same day,[120] or what were the top five albums on this day,[121] and so on. Not only do people appreciate you remembering their birthday; the emails usually got people writing back and forth either with good wishes or sometimes commenting on the list I put in the email. This good-natured back-and-forth is important for team building, especially if you have an internationally based team like mine was. Finally, we always had a birthday card signed by the people in the department. All this cost me was a little time and a couple of dollars for a card.

2. **Create quick awards.** If someone was involved in a big litigation win or a big contract or deal, I liked to get a copy of the first page of the court's order or the agreement (or whatever) and stick it in a plain black frame they could hang on their wall. You can do more elaborate awards (custom framing or Lucite cases[122]), but I found a simple inexpensive frame worked just fine to show someone you were paying attention to his/her accomplishments. I would typically give the award to the person at the next department meeting and highlight for the full team what this person had accomplished.

3. **Pick a charity to support as a team.** Our company had a great program where it encouraged employees to get involved in the community. Every year, my team would pick a charity and spend half a day volunteering. If we were lucky, we could manage the event so people in the department from out of the headquarters region could visit and participate. Over the years we supported a botanical garden, a camp for disadvantaged children, an equestrian center for wounded soldiers, a food bank, and many others. The important thing was the event brought most of the team together, attorneys and staff, in a casual setting to do some good. Everyone got their hands dirty (painting, weeding, whatever) and everyone had a great time. Afterward, we'd go out for a group lunch or have lunch delivered to us. The charity got a bunch of free labor (and we always did way more than they ever expected a bunch of lawyers could ever accomplish!). The only cost was lunch and making the time to get away for the event (which is actually the most important part, that is, you making time to attend and participate with your team).

---

120 http://www.famousbirthdays.com/.
121 http://www.billboard.com/charts/billboard-200.
122 https://www.crownawards.com/StoreFront/ACL.Acrylic_Awards.cat.

4. **Play hooky.** Sometimes you just need to sneak away for a while. From time to time, I would surprise the team and we'd go see a movie together (late afternoon matinee). This type of sneak away was always a big hit. You have to spend some time thinking about the movie you will see because folks are sensitive to different things and you don't want anyone to feel uncomfortable. We also did a bowling sneak away, "whirly ball," and Dave & Busters. For my employees based internationally, I encouraged them to do their own version of the sneak away as it wasn't possible for them to join ours here in the United States. I also asked that they share pictures and stories with me and I would later share those with the whole department.

5. **Tout your team.** Praise is free. When big things happened in the department (or even little things that were nonetheless important for some reason, for example, getting a new certification), I would always reach out to the CEO or the head of the applicable business unit or staff group and let them know what happened, give credit to whomever on my team was involved, and note why the accomplishment was important. And I would copy the employee(s) on the email. Your team will greatly appreciate knowing that you are talking about them with senior management. And always be ready to and be sure to say "thank you." Everyone appreciates hearing "thank you"[123] and being told they did a good job. All it costs is the time to write it down or say it.

6. **Listen.** When you are the boss, sometimes the hardest thing to do is to simply stop talking and listen to the opinions and ideas of your team. Become a great listener. Tell people up-front to feel free to let you know if they disagree or see a different way to do something. And then be sure to walk the walk (if you tell someone to speak freely and then cut their knees off, you will have done way more harm than good). You may not ultimately agree with them or do what they suggest, but at least they know they were heard and were part of the discussion—part of the team. That counts for a lot with most people. And help others become good listeners as well. For example, make sure everyone has equal time and feels equally comfortable speaking up at meetings.[124] And if you are male, you may not want to hear this but stop the "mansplaining."[125]

7. **"Pick a book."** I constantly asked my team if there were any resources they needed to make their jobs easier. I love books and "old school" legal research,

---

123 http://www.ted.com/talks/laura_trice_suggests_we_all_say_thank_you?language=en.

124 http://www.nytimes.com/2015/01/11/opinion/sunday/speaking-while-female.html?hp&action=-click&pgtype=Homepage&module=c-column-top-span-region&region=c-column-top-span-region&WT.nav=c-column-top-span-region&_r=1.

125 http://articles.latimes.com/2008/apr/13/opinion/op-solnit13.

so I particularly liked to ask them if there was a hornbook, treatise, nutshell, or some other book that would be nice to have on their shelf for instant reference. Yes, everything is online these days, but there is something special about having a book in your hands to look something up and something special that you got to pick it out and the company picked up the tab to help make your job easier.

8. **Create a department award.** When I was with Travelocity, our symbol was the "Roaming Gnome." I grabbed one of the gnome statues we had lying around in marketing, spray-painted it gold, and created a monthly legal department award called the "Golden Gnome." Every month, I would award the Golden Gnome to one of the team members (it was a traveling trophy) along with a gift card for $25. At our monthly meeting, I was sure to explain why the person won (usually tying it to one of the department's goal or an outstanding accomplishment). I encouraged my team to send me nominations as well (but I was always looking for things to recognize people for—and you can always find something if you make the effort). The award and gift card could go to anyone, attorney, paralegal, admin, and others (and often we had multiple winners in a month, which meant I had to paint more gnomes). I gave the award to internationally based employees as well. Having the golden gnome statue on your desk for a month was a source of pride, and no matter who you are, you can find a use for a gift card!

9. **Spot bonuses.** If you have the budget, don't forget about the possibility of small spot bonuses. These can be $250, $500, $1,000, and the like bonuses paid out for something truly deserving of recognition. Sometimes the business units will have a budget for these type of small bonuses and will, if you ask them, consider kicking in to give a bonus to a lawyer or paralegal who really helped them out with an important deal or dispute. It doesn't take a lot of money to make someone feel special and appreciated through a spot bonus.

10. **Flexibility.** Giving your team members flexibility with their schedules can pay off handsomely as to retention and general happiness. Being able to work from home occasionally (or regularly if that fits within what the company and your department need) can be almost as important as money for some of your team. The same is true for flexibility of work hours, for example, knowing they can catch their child's third-grade play at 10:00 am in the morning, or make that special early evening family dinner. Two things are important when you think about flexibility. First, if you allow work from home (more than just occasionally), have a written policy on the expectations and the rules of the road, especially around the ability of you and clients being able to reach them. It may be that they need to be signed into the company's instant messenger program or that their desk phone is forwarded to their mobile phone while working from

home. Work from home does not mean "unavailable," and everyone needs to understand that they need to be available and they may need to come into the office on short notice on a work from home day if that's what's required. Second, you need to hire professionals and then trust them to do their jobs regardless of where they are sitting. In my experience, people working from home are working—just like team members in remote offices—and, in fact, often get more done in a day when they do not have to spend time commuting. However, if you do come across that rare instance of someone abusing the privilege, then you need to take action quickly to correct it. The important thing is to be consistent with everyone.

*****

These are just a few of the things that worked well for me (believe me, there are a lot more but then it would be "Fifty Things"). Be sure to ask others in your department or in your company for their thoughts. They will likely have some great ideas (and will appreciate you asking for their input). A simple online search will show you lots of resources with ideas about inexpensive ways to reward employees.[126] The key is to find things that will work well for your particular team and have some fun with it. It doesn't matter if you are the general counsel or run a small group within the department; any steps you take to show appreciation to your team (no matter how inexpensive) will pay off ten times over in retention and a happy workplace.

January 15, 2015

---

126 https://smallbusiness.americanexpress.com/ca/en/big-ideas-for-small-business/employee-retention-and-engagement/101-ways-to-reward-employees-without-giving-them-cash.

Ten Things: Effectively Managing Outside Counsel Fees

In this section, I want to focus on this legal department goal: "Meet Budget Target for 20XX." No in-house department is immune to cost pressure. After taking care of your team, nothing is more important than being able to successfully manage your outside counsel spend. As I have said before, the legal department is a cost center and the business is always looking to cut costs. That's why it is important for you to be on top of what you spend with outside counsel (or vendors). Being able to demonstrate that you are paying close attention to costs and that you are thoughtful in what you are spending and why will make conversations with finance (and the CEO) go much easier. In-house lawyers who run their matters, teams, or department like a business have more credibility at budget time—and during those really tough times when the business is looking for more difficult cost-cutting measures.

This section will focus on ten things you can do to reduce or better manage outside counsel spend. One thing you will want to do up-front is establish some metrics so you can measure success, for example, "reducing total outside counsel spend by a certain percentage" or having "all legal spend come in at an average hourly rate of $X." You can also use your own data for whatever metrics you set. For fee-based metrics, you can also pull it from court fee requests available on PACER or you can buy data about average hourly rates[127] by city by type of work from several sources.[128] With that background, here are some ideas:

1. **Use a monthly "budget tool" to forecast and predict (and control) spend.** If you have an e-billing system, this can usually be handled via features in that tool. You may have to modify a few things to get the information in the most useful format (and require your outside firms to include new or different information), but doing so should not be a showstopper. If you don't have

---

127 http://businessoflawblog.com/2014/08/law-firm-rates/.
128 http://www.wkelmsolutions.com/products/legalview-analytics-offerings.

an e-billing system (and we did not in my last job), you can create a simple spreadsheet that shows what was just spent in a month and the forecast for the next month. For example, at the beginning of May we would ask all of our outside counsel to tell us the following: (a) what did we spend in April (the preceding month) and (b) what do you forecast we'll spend in May? The Excel spreadsheet captured all of this data over the course of a 12-month period (with a running total showing how we were doing against budget overall). Additionally, in the middle of the month, we would go back out to our outside counsel and ask if anything changed in the forecasted spend. This gave us a very detailed (and accurate) look at spending. This is different than a project or case budget as those focus on the entire cost of that matter (which is important as well but not always useful in the short term). A monthly budget forecast gives you precision and allows you to exercise proactive reductions in spending if necessary. It also causes you to talk more with your outside counsel about what is driving costs. My experience has been that outside counsel are happy to discuss spend and ways to reduce it (they would rather have those proactive discussions versus an unhappy client).

2. **Agree with senior management what's included in the legal budget and what's not.** For example, the business may decide that M&A spend is not part of the regular legal budget and will be part of the project cost center and ROI on that deal. Likewise, you may want to charge trademark searches to the marketing department to help drive efficient behavior. You will still need to be on top of all legal spend (whether it hits your budget or not), but being clear on what hits your budget gives you better ability to actually manage the spend you will be measured against.

3. **Use alternative fee arrangements.** There are a number of ways you can go with this angle. Some of the ones I used include the following:
   - *Discounted rate cards* from firms for the lawyers you use most frequently.
   - *Discounts tied to the average hourly rate for your city*—you'll need data for this one (see above).
   - *Retainers* (i.e., a set amount paid monthly for a negotiated set of services from the firm).
   - *Blended rates*—one fixed rate that covers partners and associates.
   - *Fixed fees for specific projects* (contracts, litigation, patents, trademarks, etc.).
   - *A percentage contingency fee*—that is, the firm is paid by receiving a percentage of whatever is collected by your company in the lawsuit. But consider building in safeguards to limit the windfall effect; for example, have different percentages apply at different points in the case or have a cap of 2× or 3× of actual billed time.

- *Cost sharing with other companies* involved in your matter (joint defense, share expert costs, local counsel costs, translations, etc.).
- *Cap on rates*—rates cannot increase by more than X percent in any year or over the course of engagement (for example, in some agreements we had 0 percent rate increase for first 18 months, and the hourly rates could not go up by more than 3 percent thereafter in any given 12-month period).
- *Volume discounts*—discounts off the rate as you hit certain spend thresholds with the firm. If you can, get the discounts to apply back to the first dollar spent versus just the incremental spend over the threshold.
- *Get a number of free hours* per attorney for them to get up to speed on your new matter, for example, 15 to 20 hours of "up to speed time" on the firm's nickel.
- *Limit use of first-year lawyers*—I was a first-year lawyer once. One thing I remember pretty clearly: I didn't know much. Basically, I don't want/need first-year lawyers on my matter. If the firm thinks it needs first years, then either substantially discount the rate or, better yet, let the first year tag along for free. The flip side idea is to get free summer associate time for simple but time-consuming projects.

There are many more ideas here. You can mix and match the above or be more creative (and this will likely be a future "Ten Things" topic).

4. **Don't be afraid to move work to save significant costs.** Nothing gets you cost savings faster than being willing to move work. If you are unhappy with the firm (or simply made a mistake in terms of sending a low-value project to a high-dollar firm), move the work to a firm better suited for what you need and offering costs savings that justify the move. You may wish to give the current firm a chance to retain the work if it can match the cost savings. And, if you do move work, be sure to get free hours from new firm to get up to speed on the matter.

5. **Use less expensive firms for certain types of work.** Sounds pretty basic but you'd be surprised how often you or your team will send matters to certain firms without really thinking much about the match between cost and complexity or risk. Be sure you (and your team) are sensitive to which work goes where and why. There may be reasons other than cost as to why you want to use a certain firm or lawyer—and that's fine. Just be sure to have a discussion with your team about which firm should get the work. Not only will you make a better decision, but also you will start to train the next generation of department leaders about how and why to make such decisions. We created a list of quality niche firms and made an effort to push a certain percentage of our yearly legal spend to those firms. We created the list from our own experience or from speaking with colleagues at different in-house departments.

A niche firm is typically a smaller firm that specializes in a particular area of the law and is usually staffed with lawyers who moved away from the larger firms. One niche firm described itself as five-star lawyers for three-star price.

6. **Use (and try to stick to) outside counsel guidelines.** If you do not have an outside counsel billing policy, put one in place quickly. And be sure that you send it to counsel with every new matter and to counsel you use most frequently on a yearly basis. This policy will set out clearly, among other things, what you do and do not pay for. For example, the policies I created stated we did not pay for online research (e.g., Lexis or Westlaw), and we did not pay for car services or food unless someone from the company was present or it was cleared in advance. Also, we reserved the right to reject any bills we did not receive within three months of the work performed. Nothing kills budget planning like getting a bill in November for work performed back in January. A policy will also help you in the event you did not get an engagement letter for the project. You can find a number of sample policies online with a simple search.[129]

7. **Get request for proposal/engagement letters.** If you have the time, run a request for proposal (RFP) process where firms bid on the project. You will probably get better rates, and you usually get some free analysis of your legal problem as firms like to set out how they would attack the problem. You can find sample RFP[130] documents online.[131] Sometimes you can ask a firm you prefer to match the rates offered by a competing firm. There is not always time to go through an RFP process or you may have other reasons for not doing so. That is fine as everything depends on the circumstances at hand. Likewise, engagement letters are more important than you might think. Be sure to get one for every engagement (or at least have a master engagement letter with your preferred law firms). Your law firm will likely take the first cut at the engagement letter. Review it carefully and don't be afraid to mark it up. The letter should clearly spell out any discounts or alternative fee arrangements you bargained for, and be sure that your outside counsel policy trumps anything contradictory in the engagement letter unless otherwise agreed in writing.

8. **Get to mediation fast.** Ninety percent of litigation settles, why wait two years with your wallet hemorrhaging? Consider if it makes sense to see if you can get the other side to agree to mediate early. Another trick is to use the phone. I

---

129 http://apps.americanbar.org/buslaw/newsletter/0021/materials/ringmasters.pdf; http://news.acca.com/accnj/issues/2013-08-03/2.html.

130 www.lexmundi.com/Document.asp?DocID=671.

131 http://www.srtabus.com/wp-content/uploads/General-Counsel-RFP-FINAL.pdf.

can recall several times where there was a dispute pending and I simply picked up the phone and spoke with either an in-house lawyer or outside counsel on the other side and worked out a quick resolution. If you go this route, you can create some simple decision trees to help you analyze where you think a case may go if it goes to trial (including the cost of trying the case) and use that to help set your settlement authority for the mediation. Finance folks/business folks like decision trees because it gives them something concrete on which to make decisions (and it gives you a more reasoned basis for any recommendation you may make).[132]

9. **Set expectations up-front with outside lawyers.** Face it; if you tell outside counsel you want something, they will move heaven and earth for you to get the answer. Problem is, moving heaven and earth is pretty expensive. Sometimes you just need a little dirt shoveled. Set your expectations up-front with your outside lawyers. It can be a cap on the amount of money you are willing to spend (e.g., cap it at $5,000) or on the number of hours you are willing to pay for (e.g., no more than 20), or just making it clear you do not want a formal memo with the answer (an email or highlighted copy of the relevant case will suffice). Make it clear that you only want so many lawyers involved ("one riot, one ranger" as we say in Texas). Doing these things will provide clear guideposts for counsel. And, of course, encourage counsel to come back to you if they think you need to spend more or get more people involved, but make sure they know you expect them to justify why it is needed.

10. **Create a monthly (or quarterly report) showing savings.** At some point you will want to show the CFO[133] or CEO (or the general counsel) that your efforts at saving money are paying off. It will also keep you focused on the task at hand. Two easy things to do: (a) track on a monthly basis how you are doing against your budget or forecast (and if you are tracking "over" that tells you it's time to start cutting spend somewhere) and (b) create a short summary PowerPoint showing cost savings (monthly or quarterly is best). On this one you will need to be both creative and conservative. Meaning, turn over rocks to show you are saving money but don't go so far that you lose credibility with finance. Keep things simple and make sure you can reasonably support any assumptions or assertions you make in the report. The report can show things like the following:

---

[132] http://www.nortonrosefulbright.com/files/or_passport_fall08_decisiontree-pdf-882kb-49403.pdf.
[133] https://www.unitedlex.com/sites/default/files/2016-08/transform_legal_departments.pdf.

- Spend versus forecast/budget (hopefully running under, and if not, discuss your plan to get back to budget). We did this in the spreadsheet I mentioned above;
- Cost savings based on using lower-cost counsel or based on deals you struck to shave costs off standard hourly rates or savings on vendor costs;
- Costs avoided (legal), for example, cost savings because you won the case, settled a case quickly, or settled under settlement authority. Primary attorneys' fees;
- Costs avoided (business), for example, cost savings when management does not have to prepare and give a deposition or attend a hearing/trial because of things the legal department did. If the CEO does not have to spend 20 hours in depo prep, that is a huge cost savings;
- "Money in"—this was always my favorite because I got to highlight legal as a "revenue generator" versus a cost center, that is, if you win and the other side has to pay your company, or pay your attorneys' fees, or you were able to avoid paying a tax.

You can also get your outside counsel to help quantify savings (they will be happy to show you ways they are cutting costs!). I know a small innovative firm that is already creating reports like these for its clients—exactly the type of information general counsel would love to have. Also, get your team involved. If people get excited about the process of saving money, the entire process starts to snowball in a good way. Ask your team for their ideas—in terms of both cost-saving ideas and how to measure/report. Set up a big board or something to show costs saved (and if you hit a certain target, there is a small reward for the team such as a lunch out or an afternoon sneak away to the movies).

*****

I am only scratching the surface here. There are dozens of other ways to save costs, but I need to stop writing or else this will turn into a slog. Also, nothing is in stone. Not every situation lends itself to cost savings or easy management of outside counsel. Some cases or deals are just too complex, too important, and too risky. The circumstances will matter, so don't feel bad if you just have one of those deals or cases that don't fit.

January 22, 2015

Ten Things: Running an Effective Staff Meeting

Whether you run a small team of seven or you are in charge of a sprawling international-based 200+ lawyer legal department, you will need to have regular staff meetings. Unfortunately, staff meetings have an inherent tension. On the one hand, people in the legal department want to know what's going on in the department, the company, and the industry you operate in. On the other hand, people want another meeting about as much as they want a root canal. The tricky part is balancing these opposing views and running a staff meeting that is both informative and interesting (i.e., one that people actually look forward to attending).

I have run a lot of meetings in my day (and I have also attended a lot of meetings). Over the years, I learned a few things that help make for an informative and interesting staff meeting (as well as some things that make for uninformative and dull meetings). Below are ten ideas to help you run a great staff meeting (and these ideas will work for small group meetings as well):

1. **What is the purpose of the meeting?** You need to figure out *why* you want to have the staff meeting. Is it simply to pass information along to your team? Do you want to use it to bring your team together and increase cooperation/interaction? Is it an opportunity to teach new skills? Most likely it will be a combination of several things but it is important that you spend some time thinking about what you want to accomplish. It will also depend somewhat on who attends the meetings. My meetings included the entire department (lawyers, paralegals, admins, etc.). If you have an inclusive meeting, you need to think about the different skill sets and interests that will be in the room. Thinking out the *why* will help you structure your meeting and the agenda. Moreover, as you go forward, it is important that you tell your team what you want to accomplish with the meeting, that is, set the table so they understand why the meeting is important and why they are being asked to attend. Be sure new people joining the department know the purpose of the meeting as soon as they come onto the team.

2. **Meeting logistics.** Next, decide how often and when to have your meeting. I think once a month is best (but, it depends on your department/company culture somewhat as well). Use a fixed point, for example, the second Thursday of every month, so everyone knows the general rhythm of the meeting over the course of the year. When you set your date, be thoughtful about other meetings/activities that occur regularly that could conflict with yours (e.g., a company-wide "town hall," regular CLE sessions, business unit meetings that your attorneys may attend). Similarly, you don't want your staff meeting to be on the same day as another long mandatory meeting as then you basically cede most of the day to meetings versus getting stuff done. Mondays and Fridays are typically not great days to have a staff meeting, given the large number of conflicts that arise on those days. Pick a meeting room that is large enough to comfortably hold everyone and that has a good speaker phone and projector/screen. Be sure to reserve the room well in advance (for the full year) and have a standing calendar invite prepared and sent to everyone in the department with the room, time, links, and other meeting details. Use the same room every time if possible. Select a time for the meeting that makes sense for your department. We had a number of internationally based colleagues, so we held the meeting in morning (Central Time) which is mid-afternoon in Europe. Unfortunately, it was pretty late for our friends in Asia but that is something that cannot be helped. Do the best you can with the scheduling and shoot for what's best for the most people. Finally, figure out how long you want the meeting to be. An hour is ideal. Ninety minutes is okay. Anything over 90 minutes is not a good idea. We set ours for 90 minutes, and then I tried like mad to keep it to an hour. That way I have some flexibility if it ran long, but usually I was able to give people back some time (which is always appreciated!).
3. **Have an agenda.** Never freelance your staff meeting. Go in with a set written agenda that follows the same basic contours every time. This will keep your meeting focused, purposeful, and on schedule. At the end of this section, I set out the actual agenda (annotated) I typically used.
4. **Solicit ideas/topics/questions from your team in advance of the meeting.** A week or more before the meeting, ask your team what they would like to see covered (in addition to whatever items you already have teed up). Not only will it make the meeting more compelling because you will be addressing things your team wants to hear about, you will also gain insights into what's on their mind generally, which will make you a better manager. Also, be sure you have a way for people to ask questions anonymously in advance of the meeting; that is, if they are not comfortable asking a question during the meeting or sending a question directly to you, they can send it to one of your directs or

your admin with the knowledge that only the question (and not the ID of the sender) will be given to you to respond to during the meeting.
5. **Use technology.** The key to an engaging meeting is having an interesting presentation. If your meeting only consists of you reading off of a script to people sitting in the room, you have already lost. As technology developed, I incorporated it into our staff meetings. Some things worked, and some things did not—but we had fun trying.
   - *First* (if you have folks who are not in the office), have a good speaker phone and microphones. People need to be able to hear you or whoever is speaking. Bad speaker phone = bad meeting. Be sure that the people calling in mute their lines to limit background noise and be sure people in the room don't shuffle papers near the microphones.
   - *Second*, use PowerPoint (or equivalent) to present and track your agenda (and incorporate lots of pictures and/or other media). People like to follow along visually with the speaker. A well laid out and colorful PPT accomplishes this goal. There are dozens of preset themes and templates for PPT available for free either in the tool[134] itself or online.[135] Definitely use a theme or a template. Don't use black and white. If you're not sure how to use a theme or a template, ask around the department or the company to see if someone can help you. I tried to use the least amount of text possible and incorporate as many pictures, clip art, pdfs, photos, sound clips, movie clips, and the like. For one meeting I used only pictures and sound and had no text at all (I just spoke to the pictures). You can get great pictures and clip art, and other material for any topic or agenda item simply by typing in whatever it is you're looking for in Bing, Google, or Yahoo! and selecting images. YouTube has great stuff too. And you can convert just about any document you have (court order, intranet page, etc.) into a pdf that can be used in the PPT. Use your imagination and have some fun.
   - *Third*, use WebEx or LyncServer, or GoToMeeting to webcast your meeting and allow people working remotely to see your PPT presentation (way better than just listening to you talk on the phone). If you need a free webcast tool, try FreeConferenceCall.com (it costs nothing, works great, and has up to 1,000 attendees).
   - *Fourth*, use the live video feature of your webcasting tool, so people working remotely can see you as you talk (and you can see them if you have them

---

134 https://templates.office.com/?legRedir=true&CorrelationId=01427cb1-6ed5-4f8f-95ae-f6d-fa4887aed.
135 https://www.presentationmagazine.com/free_powerpoint_template.htm.

turn on their cameras—which is always interesting to do!). Adding video streaming is probably the best thing you can do to make a staff meeting engaging for those who are not able to attend it in person. When we did this at my old company, the team loved it.

6. **Think about who will speak.** Determine for each meeting who is going to do the presenting or talking. This depends on the purpose of your staff meeting, that is, what are you trying to accomplish? I think the most boring staff meeting is one where you go around the table and everyone tells everyone else what they are working on. It takes way too long, it's boring, and people tune out. The best meetings we had consisted of the main speaker (usually me as general counsel) and a guest speaker from the business (HR, CTO, CFO, etc.)—not all the time but several times a year, the heads of different groups within legal discussing one (or at most two) important item their teams were working on and then a short 5- to 10-minute presentation on a go deep topic of interest to the legal department (and alternating who presented from among the lawyers on the team). Having only one person speaking can get a bit monotonous, so try to have at least one other speaker during your meeting (and nothing wrong with calling on someone to speak during the meeting either).

7. **Test everything before the meeting.** Nothing kills your meeting faster than a technical glitch. I tried to set aside 30 minutes before the meeting to get everything set up: test the phone, test the projector, test the WebEx connection and video feed, get the room lighting and temperature to the right levels, and so on. When you are booking your room, be sure to book the extra time for getting the room set up correctly before the meeting starts (otherwise you are standing in the hallway while someone else's meeting winds down and then rushing to get your meeting up and running). Additionally, I had a backup of the PowerPoint on a flash drive in case my laptop crashed or locked up and my admin had her laptop ready to go if we needed to switch over because something happened to mine. You will not be able to eliminate all glitches every time (as I learned repeatedly), but you will generally have a smooth and seamless/professional meeting if you spend some time up-front getting the room and the technology ready (and anticipating problems).

8. **Solicit feedback about the meeting regularly.** Ask your team what's working with your meeting, what's not, what did they like, and what would they like to see changed or added. Is the technology working? Can everyone hear the speakers and see the video feed? I did this regularly after most meetings (and via a yearly survey to my team). I especially sought the input of those who were based outside the United States or worked in a remote office who had to listen over the phone and watch the video feed. Your team will appreciate you asking. One trick I used was for one meeting I had *everyone* dial in

and view the webcast (vs. anyone attending the meeting in person). I got a lot of really useful feedback and everyone who normally attended the meeting in person learned how difficult it can be to participate remotely (and were more sensitive to speaking clearly and avoided background noise when we went back to the regular meeting format).

9. **Evolve/Change the meeting over time.** Once you get the feedback, use it. My first staff meetings were pretty dull: lots of me simply reading from my notes, lots of go around the table. Over time, and from listening to my team, I received plenty of great ideas and I tried to incorporate those into the meeting, for example spending 60 seconds to highlight a new technology or app that would be of use/interest to the department or holding the meeting from a remote office when I was traveling. We tried a lot of different things in my staff meetings; some worked and some failed spectacularly. But, I was never afraid to try something new and add the stuff that worked and ditch the stuff that didn't or had gotten stale. And be sure to tell your team when you make changes based on their feedback, so they know you are listening and that their suggestions are important to you.

10. **Make the meeting important.** This is almost as important as creating an interesting presentation. You need to be sure that your staff meeting is important to you and your team. I used to say this is one time every month when we'd all come together as a team to discuss things and learn from each other. For that reason alone, it was an important meeting. Make sure as leader you stick to the schedule (and if you absolutely have to miss a meeting that you reschedule it vs. canceling it). Likewise, your team needs to understand that the meeting is not something they can blow off. Conflicts will arise but make sure your team understands that the meeting is important and attendance is not optional and can be missed only for good cause. They should not intentionally schedule other meetings or phone calls during the department meeting, and they should try to get meetings they are invited to set to a different time if the time of that meeting conflicts with the department meeting, if possible. Good meetings are meetings where people feel they need to be there because it's important (vs. just going through the motions and marking time). If you treat the meeting as important, it will rub off on your team.

*****

Meetings are a fact of life in the corporate world. There is no better way to communicate within your department and to gauge in real time the pulse and mood of your team. No matter how well run and informative your meetings are, people will gripe about having to attend. But, they will gripe louder if they feel left out of knowing what's going on in the company or the department or if they do not have a regular opportunity to engage with other members of the department. Your job is take the time and make the effort to create a meeting that is useful, informative, and interesting. The above is just a start, but if you give it the time it deserves, you will be able to create the right kind of staff meeting for your team.

January 30, 2015

Sample Legal Department Staff Meeting Agenda

Welcome

Review the company's high-level strategic goals for the current year, and go over legal's high-level strategic goals for the current year [keeps people aligned on what's important]

Administrative items
- Special announcements (babies, awards, etc.)
- Anniversaries and birthdays
- Upcoming events (in legal, at the company, etc.)
- Other miscellaneous items

[*when thinking about upcoming events, and the like—don't be U.S.-focused only, especially if you have an internationally based team*]

What's going on with the department [*briefly discuss several big deals, developments, lawsuits, etc.*]
- Direct reports speak (5 minutes each)

What's going on with the company [*important news, financial information, point people to intranet site, etc.*]

What's going on with the industry [*big news and developments outside the company that affect the company or the department*]

Recognition
- Team photos [*I asked my team to share photos of things they were doing—together, in their free time, at company events, and so on. It was a nice way of bringing the team together.*]
- Good jobs [*read emails I received from the business or from within legal recognizing people for doing a good job with something*].

- Announce monthly award winner(s) [*as discussed elsewhere, we had a monthly award called the Golden Gnome. I announced the winners—and what they did to win it—at the monthly staff meeting*]

Go deep topic 1 [*I would ask members of the department to present a few slides on a particular legal topic that would be of general interest to most of the team—for example, insider trading policy, a new deal in the Middle East, or big court win. Just high level*]

Go deep topic 2 [*optional—and be ready to roll it over to next meeting if time was running short*]

Technology minute [*quick 1- to 2-minute discussion of a neat website, app, or technology that would be of interest to the department, for example, a website that calculates deadlines. I would solicit team for their picks as well as my own*]

Q&A [*The questions can be collected from emails or from the participants at the meeting. Be sure to ask if there is anything you can do for anyone on the team/does anyone need anything*]

Close meeting

Ten Things: Increasing the Efficiency of the Legal Department Through Use of Technology

A goal of every legal department is to increase efficiency (and reduce costs). One of the easiest ways to do this is through the use of technology. This can mean anything from apps for your smartphone to sophisticated software programs running on servers at your company. For some, using technology can be daunting and frustrating. For others, it is as easy as falling off of a log. But to be a successful in-house lawyer or general counsel, you need to embrace technology and make sure your team does as well. So, if you are afraid of technology, you need to get past that.

One issue with using technology is that the choices are almost endless and it can be difficult to distill things down into a useful list. Here I take on the task of identifying some key technology that can help you increase your own efficiency as well as the efficiency of your team or the department overall. I am going to assume you know how to use Microsoft Office products (free and pay) and Google products (free), so those tools—certainly very useful—are not included. That said, if someone asked me to list my ten key technology tools for an in-house lawyer, here they are:

1. **Practical Law.** This is probably my favorite tool. Practical Law[136] gives you instant access to simple, useful articles, forms, checklists, practice notes, memoranda, and so on. For example, if someone in the business calls you and says "I need to know the ins and outs of insider trading in the next hour" you go to the Practical Law website, type in "insider trading," and you will instantly get back several articles discussing the topic in simple black and white along with checklists, sample insider trading polices, sample memos to the client, and other useful materials. It can save you hours of research and can save you the cost of contacting outside counsel on a myriad of issues. My team based

---

[136] http://us.practicallaw.com/.

in the United Kingdom first pointed out Practical Law to me (so there is an excellent European version) and raved about it. I contacted the U.S. offices and we had a CLE demo webcast set up. Then we had a free trial period. My team really liked the product, so we signed up. It was probably the most used and popular tool we ever purchased. It can be a bit pricey, but it's worth it.

2. **E-billing system.** Unless you only have a handful of outside counsel invoices every month, almost all in-house legal departments should have an e-billing system. It will save you time and money. In particular, you will get deep insights into your legal spend, average hourly rates, efficiency of law firms, projected spend, budgeting compliance, monthly accruals, hourly market rates in your area (or other locations), and usually some type of matter management system built in, all rolled into one. We had just begun to implement the Serengeti[137] e-billing system when I retired. Prior to implementing this system, we were doing everything by hand and spreadsheets. While that worked well when we had a handful of cases, as the number of legal matters grew, the cost in manpower spent cranking things out by hand, paying bills by hand, and the like grew as well, and we still did not have all the data we needed to really help us manage counsel spend down even further. This time and cost savings (and data analytics) went a long way to justifying the cost of the system with the finance team. You will have to do the ROI[138] yourself to see if adding a tool like this is worth it. There are other highly rated e-billing systems[139] available, including Lawtrac, Lexis CounselLink, and TyMetrix.

3. **E-discovery tool.** I am old enough to remember when document discovery meant sending a memo or email to a group of employees and asking them to go through their desk drawers, file cabinets and emails/computer files and let us know if they had any documents that dealt with "X." There is no way you can get away with a document search like that today without risking major sanctions. If you rarely deal with litigation, you can go with one-off document collection efforts by various third-party vendors to collect document in an appropriate manner. If you have a lot of litigation, then you will want to seriously consider investing in an e-discovery tool. We used MatterSpace.[140] MatterSpace provided us with litigation hold automation, document collection

---

137 http://www.serengetilaw.com/Pages/default.aspx. This product is now called "Legal Tracker."
138 http://ebillinghub.com/roi/.
139 http://www.mitratech.com/wp-content/uploads/HGPR_ELM-MarketView_2014_VendorView_Mitratech-Lawtrac.pdf.
140 http://www.businesswire.com/news/home/20090720005730/en/Microsoft-WorkProducts-Partner-Deliver-MatterSpace-ELM-eDiscovery%20-%20.VNF1MfnF9h4.

(where the only thing the client needed to do was give us access to their laptop or computer), cloud storage, and the ability to connect to multiple discovery management tools (e.g., Relativity, Summation). It saved us hours and hours of work, made the discovery process much easier for the business (i.e., how popular are you when you are asking the CFO to go through all of her emails for the past five years looking for relevant documents?), and gave us a defensible chain of custody/review in the event the other side ever questioned our document search or litigation hold practices.

4. **Getting the Deal Through.** This is a great website that contains a number of multijurisdictional guides for many legal areas, including merger control, labor and employment law, competition law, arbitration, telecoms and media, intellectual property, cyber security, and banking and finance. The guides are written by top lawyers and top law firms from various countries, are updated frequently, and, best of all, are free to in-house counsel. Do you need the down and dirty on merger control in Chile? Want to know about trademark protection in Mexico? Need to understand dispute resolution in India? Simply go to GettingTheDealThrough.com and sign up.

5. **Lexology.com.** This is a free daily newsfeed service providing access to hundreds articles, blogs, law firm publications, newspaper stories about legal issues. When you subscribe to Lexology.com, you set preferences regarding your geographic areas of interest (e.g., United States, Europe, and Asia) and legal areas of interest (e.g., litigation, finance law, employment law, and M&A), and you get a daily email chock-full of great content. I read this every day and almost always found at least one article that I would save and/or share with my team. Lexology is a service of the Association of Corporate Counsel[141] (ACC). If I had to pick one group to belong to as an in-house lawyer, it would be the ACC (either the U.S. or the European versions). Tons of great information, webinars, CLEs, forms, practice materials, message boards, and the like are available on its member website.

6. **SigFonts.** SigFonts[142] is a program that scans your signature and makes it available as a font in the font drop-down list in Word. You can then use it to sign and send documents directly from your computer (and it looks just like you actually signed it—none of the fuzziness of pasting in a pdf signature). You get signature options that include your full name, first name only, and initials as part of the package. This tool can save the day when something needs to be signed and sent and you are not near a fax machine or scanner. If you are

---

141 http://www.acc.com/.
142 http://www.sigfonts.com/.

interested in SigFont, you will probably also be interested in the technology to convert native files (e.g., Word) to pdf. If you or your company has Adobe Acrobat (not just Adobe Reader), you can convert Word documents, PowerPoint presentations, web pages, and the like into pdf documents (along with a host of other features). You or the company will have to pay for the Acrobat software, so buying it depends on a lot of different factors. If you are just interested in converting native files to pdf and looking for a free tool, I use CutePDF,[143] which works great (and it has pay options to add more functionality).

7. **TripCase.com.** I will first disclose that I worked for the company (Sabre Corporation) that developed TripCase. That bias aside, this is an awesome app (smartphone, tablet, laptop) that tracks your travel itinerary information from any travel source, that is, air, hotel, rental car, dinner reservations, limo, boat, and conference room. It's perfect for business or personal travel. Your admin can enter business trip information for you. It has several services, like notifications, weather, reserve parking, and a link to Uber. And most of your information can be added by simply forwarding your travel email confirmation directly to your TripCase account. Before using TripCase, my admin would type up all of my trip details, meetings, phone numbers, and other information and then I would make a copy for my wife. If I lost the piece of paper, I had to scramble to find my information. With TripCase, this is all done automatically and you can print it out if you want to, or simply add your spouse as someone who gets a copy of the trip details emailed to them. And the information is always with you on your smartphone, tablet, or laptop (or now your smartwatch too).

8. **Instant message (IM) program.** I don't care which one you use (Microsoft, Google, Skype, Yahoo!, etc.) but accessing and using an IM program to its full potential is a great tool for the in-house lawyer, especially with remote/international offices and work-from-home colleagues. While the instant part of IM is great, the more powerful tools are the ability to add a video stream by simply clicking a button (creating an instant video conference) and to share and collaborate together on documents (i.e., work on one version) as part of the IM session. My team used IM all the time, including for group meetings, for late night document drafting, and simply to stay in touch with colleagues. Of course, the same rules apply to writing IMs as drafting proper emails and other documents, that is, treat all IMs and sessions like professional business communications—and I have seen poorly drafted IMs come back to life as trial exhibits, so this is important.

---

143 http://www.cutepdf.com/.

9. **Copernic desktop search.** If you're like me, your laptop has basically become your file cabinet—a very, very large file cabinet (kind of like the big Twinkie in *Ghostbusters*[144]). This also means it can be very difficult to find things you need. You know you have that email, or memo, or PowerPoint somewhere on your computer but you just cannot remember where you stored it. While Microsoft Office has a decent search program, Copernic[145] is much better and more complete, and it's easier to navigate the results. There is a free version (perfectly good) and a pay-for version (even better).

10. **"TRACE."** This makes my list because there is simply no avoiding the increasing importance of compliance with the Foreign Corrupt Practices Act, the U.K. Anti-Bribery Act, and a host of other anticorruption laws. Every in-house lawyer should be thinking about how to best ensure compliance in this area of the law. One of my team members at Sabre came across this great resource. TRACE[146] provides anticorruption compliance tools (and many other things) including a slick due diligence tool called TRACEsort.[147] Given the risks to company reputation, to your board of directors and executive officers, and perhaps even to yourself, it is worth finding and investing in a top-notch anti-bribery compliance tool.

*****

There are so many more technology-related things I could have listed. Others near the top of my list are a free deadline calculator[148] (contract deadlines, court-filing deadlines, etc.), a free world meeting calculator[149] (helps you set meetings across multiple time zones), and handy smartphone apps to create pdf documents[150] using your phone's camera (another tool that comes in handy when you need a signed copy of something at 3:30 am with no fax machine or scanner in sight). The takeaway here is that there are many resources out there that can make you and your team or department more efficient (therefore driving down costs). If you've set a goal to better utilize technology in the coming year, now is the time to start identifying those tools and get them up and running. Some, like an e-billing system,

---

144 https://www.youtube.com/watch?v=pzaQjS1JstY.
145 http://www.copernic.com/en/products/desktop-search/.
146 http://www.traceinternational.org/.
147 http://www.traceinternational.org/risk-assessment/.
148 http://www.calculatorsoup.com/calculators/time/date-day.php.
149 http://www.timeanddate.com/worldclock/meeting.html.
150 http://www.bestfreewebresources.com/iphone-android-apps-scanning-documents.

will take a good amount of time to select and implement. Others, like SigFont or TripCase, can be up and running today or in a few days. And do not be afraid of technology. Have fun trying and testing different applications. You really cannot break anything, and you will likely find some really useful tools out there if you're willing to experiment a bit. And lastly, whatever you find that works, share it with others in your department, in your company, or with other in-house lawyers.

February 6, 2015

Ten Things: Creating a Client Satisfaction Survey

In an earlier section, I dealt with setting yearly goals for the legal department.[151] One of the goals was sending out a client satisfaction survey, that is, asking those in the business to weigh in on questions related to their satisfaction with the services provided by legal. There are a number of reasons why you would want to send out such a survey—primarily to gather helpful data and comments about how the legal department is performing and how it is perceived throughout the organization and the second being to use the survey as a tool to market and promote legal by reminding people that the department is there, that it provides valuable services to the company, and that you are directly seeking their input into improving the quality and value of the services the legal department provides.

Below I will walk you through the process of creating, distributing, and analyzing the results of a client satisfaction survey. Though the discussion deals with in-house counsel sending a survey to their internal business clients, the why and how apply equally to the relationship between outside and in-house counsel, and outside attorneys can easily use this guide to create a satisfaction survey to distribute to their in-house counsel clients. If you intend to put out a survey this calendar year, now is the time to get start creating it for distribution after the summer holidays.

1. **What is the purpose of your survey?** The first thing you need to do is spend some time thinking about what it is you want to know or capture with your survey. Typically, you will want the survey to give you insight into some measurable metrics showing how efficient or effective the department is, such as timeliness, quality of advice, accessibility of the lawyers, and the like. Likewise, you will probably want to get some general feedback on the department as a whole or about individual performers. In addition to your own thoughts, gather a cross section of your team and get their input on the survey as well.

---

151 See page 103.

Spending time up-front thinking about what you want to accomplish gives you an excellent road map to prepare the survey questions.

2. **What tools can I use to create my survey?** The easiest and best way to go is to use an online survey tool. This will allow you to create a professional looking survey, let your clients complete the survey online, and provide you with the ability to tabulate and slice and dice the results in a number of interesting ways. Check first to see if your company has its own internal survey generator. If it does, use that tool as it will give you the widest variety of options/analytics (and you'll probably have access to help and support in creating and managing your survey). If not, there are a number of tools available online, typically a free version (which usually provides all the tools you need) or a paid version (which gives you more questions and more powerful analytics/flexibility). Whether you use the free or paid version will depend on the purpose of your survey, the number of questions, and the level of information and detail you need. Four easy-to-use survey tools for you to consider are: Survey Monkey, Zoomerang, Survey Planet, and TypeForm. The WordStream blog has a list of additional survey tool options.[152] If you have the budget, you can also hire a professional consulting company to create a survey for you (e.g., Altman Weil). But, unless you believe you have some really complex issues to sort out, I am confident you can create a valuable and useful survey on your own using the tools and ideas set out here.

3. **Creating the questions.** Once you have selected your survey tool, it's time to prepare the questions. To start, don't make the survey too long or complicated. If you do that, people will not complete it. The maximum number of questions should be 20 or less. You will also want to mix up the type of questions you ask—that is, yes/no, rate on a scale, multiple choice, open-ended, and so on. Mixing up the types of questions keeps the survey interesting. Most of the online tools give you numerous templates to use to design your questions. Your survey should not take more than 15–20 minutes to complete. Additionally, before finalizing your questions, seek the input of your team. Let them propose questions or give feedback on your questions. Likewise, and more importantly, identify a group of clients and get their feedback on the types of questions they would like to be asked as well as on some of the questions you propose to use. This will help you draft questions that clients will want to answer. You should think about the order of the questions so your survey has a logical flow, and do your best to not build bias into the questions (another reason to have several folks review your questions). Instead of listing a bunch of potential questions

---

152 http://www.wordstream.com/blog/ws/2014/11/10/best-online-survey-tools.

for you to consider, I am providing links to sample surveys that you can use as guideposts in creating your own questions (or copy verbatim if you wish). I have posted a copy of a survey I created using Survey Monkey online at Issuu.com which you can use as a starting point for your own survey.[153] I used very similar questions in the surveys we circulated when I was general counsel at Sabre and Travelocity. You can find other sample surveys online, including one from the ACC[154] and one from the eHarmony legal department.[155] These will give you a selection of potential questions and different question formats you can use. If you want more ideas, type "law department client satisfaction survey" in your search engine and you will get other examples.

4. **Confidentiality of responses.** As you prepare your survey, you need to create a short introduction. You will see an example in the sample survey I created in footnote 153 above. Let the user know why you are seeking their feedback, why it is important that they participate, and how long the survey will take to complete (e.g., "15 minutes or so"), and, most importantly, let them know that their answers and feedback will be kept confidential and their identity will not be revealed or tied to any of the responses. Confidentiality is important so as to obtain maximum participation and to generate more honest responses. Still, one of the frustrating problems with an anonymous survey is that you have no ability to follow up with someone if they have particularly good or important feedback or ideas for the department. One way around this is to add a place near the end of the survey to allow users to give their name and email address/phone number if they are willing to disclose that information. You will see such a question at the end of my sample survey.

5. **Who gets the survey?/How often do you survey?** One critical question to answer before launching your survey is "who gets it"? This is important because you certainly want the survey to go to people who are frequent users of the department, but you do not want the survey only to go to fans of legal, as the results will be skewed and will not be useful. The first few surveys I sent out as general counsel were limited to vice presidents and above, along with some additional select employees. While this gave use a pretty useful sample, we realized that a large group of people who used the legal department regularly were left out. We then increased the survey distribution to include

---

153 https://issuu.com/tenthingslegal/docs/sample_legal_department_survey__ste_72b39808e51a83.
154 http://www.acc.com/advocacy/valuechallenge/toolkit/upload/Sample-Client-Satisfaction-Survey.pdf.
155 http://www.surveymonkey.com/r/?sm=%2fdzDcSLR8Jtp502dBtFN7UGHt1DZoK%2baNt6fsnX-1RW9q4Szwc0UOEXcrh5qU0uDQRE3DQRbPCQ30s05BHWPLXX0FFK5WiTc63Me6%2bVa-7ziU%3d.

two levels down from vice president. We got better results by doing this but it still seemed wrong to leave out anyone who wanted to take the survey. As a result, we began sending the survey to every employee in the company, around 10,000 people. We did not really add a significant amount of information by doing this (as many employees had very little, if any, interaction with the legal department), but I know the employee base felt better about the department because we included them and asked for their opinion—even if they did not complete the survey. That goodwill alone was valuable to me. Depending on your situation, my advice would be to just make sure you have a wide enough sample of people who will likely give both positive and negative feedback to the department–making for a much more useful survey.

Another question is how often should you send out a survey (and when should it go out to your clients). Any more than once a year is too much in my opinion and you will see response levels suffer from survey fatigue if you seek input more frequently than that (as employees get bombarded with company surveys all the time). Our surveys tended to go out about every 14 months or so. I found that a little bit longer than one year between surveys got the best overall response rates. As to when to send out the survey, be sure to avoid the summer (vacations) and the major holidays (e.g., in the United States, avoid November and December and March—spring break). In my experience, the best months are September and October because then you can use the results to plan for next year. Also, coordinate with other departments to make sure your survey does not clash with or overlap another major survey going out to employees. Keep the survey open for 30 days post launch and send out several email reminders during the time that the survey is open, noting that you greatly appreciate people taking 15 minutes to complete it. You can also promote the survey on your company's intranet, the legal department website, and company newsletter, and also at town hall meetings and on TV monitors around the facility. Ask your team to encourage their internal clients and colleagues to complete the survey.

6. **Weighing the responses.** Not all responses are created equal. In my experience the opinions and thoughts of the frequent users of the department and those of the senior management tend to carry more weight. The former is important because their frequent use means the feedback is generally more specific and useful; the latter because they control the purse strings and their perceptions of the legal department as an important and valuable part of the company (vs. a black hole cost center) are critical as to whether the legal department thrives and has a seat at the table or is constantly fighting for funding and a voice. One way to account for this is to weigh the responses from those who are frequent users or who are part of senior management a bit higher than other responses. For example, give a 1.25 weight to the former versus a

1.00 weight to the latter. To do this, you will need to ensure that you have the users identify themselves (generically) as frequent users of legal—however you want to define that—and/or as senior management (e.g., VP and above, or SVP and above). You will see an example of this on the first or second page of my sample survey in footnote 153 above.

7. **Create a "word cloud."** You've probably seen a number of word clouds on a day-to-day basis. These are charts that show different words at different sizes, shapes, and colors. Using the available data set, the words that appear most frequently are larger and brighter than the words used infrequently. In my sample survey, you will see a question that asks the user to list three words that they think best describe the legal department. I used this same question in my actual surveys, created a database of the words provided by the users, and then used a word cloud generator to create a word cloud. I included the word cloud chart in the survey results I shared with my team and with my CEO. It is a great way to visually capture a snapshot in time as to what your clients think of the department. You can see a list of word cloud generators at Edudemic .com.[156] I used Wordle.net to generate my word cloud. Here is the word cloud generated by my last survey:

---

156 http://www.edudemic.com/word-cloud-generators/.

Needless to say, we were pleased that Responsive, Helpful, and Knowledgeable were the three biggest, brightest words. If you look closely, you'll see that a couple of the words are not flattering (but hard to see in the black and white image). And that's okay. It is just part of the deal and something we could focus on trying to make better (but we were glad these were among the "smallest" and "darkest" words in the cloud).

8. **Analyzing the results.** Once your survey closes, it's time to analyze the results. There are a few things to understand about surveys. First, don't be disappointed if you do not get a 90 percent response rate. That would be amazing. You should more realistically expect anywhere from 5 to 10 percent of the people to respond (more if the survey pool is small). Second, you will tend to get more responses from people who are unhappy with legal. This is just human nature. Don't be put off by this. Accept the criticism as just something you and the team need to work on to fix. The fact that you asked for feedback has probably made some positive inroads with these unhappy clients. There will always be some people that no matter what you do, or how unreasonable their complaints, you will never satisfy—just a cold hard fact of in-house life. Hopefully, none of those people are part of senior management. If they are, that is a topic for another chapter down the road! Depending on the capabilities of your survey tool, you should be able to slice and dice the data in a number of different ways (e.g., by region, by line of business, by type of legal matter). This will give you a lot of insight into where things are going smoothly or where you need to put in some work. If you included the ability for people to write open-ended comments, there is a lot of great information you can extract. Look for patterns involving certain types of matters or certain groups or members of your team (good or bad). All of these are areas for improvement or enhancement. Prepare yourself for the odd curve ball, for example, someone complaining on the survey about things that are not part of legal's purview, such as procurement or IT system security. The simple fact is not everyone has a true understanding of what fits under legal and what falls outside of legal. Your word cloud will give you additional insights as well. Here is an example from one of my actual surveys showing the results regarding overall satisfaction with legal year over year. Given (like many in-house departments) we had budget and staff cuts leading into 2014, we were very pleased that 97 percent of our clients had the same or higher level of satisfaction with legal versus prior years:

8. As compared to prior years, my level of satisfaction with the Legal Department in 2014 is...

#	Answer	Bar	Response	%
1	Lower	▪	14	3%
2	The same	▬▬▬▬▬	318	76%
3	Higher	▬	86	21%
	Total		418	

9. **Sharing the results.** After you have been through the results yourself, it's time to share them. Most importantly, you will want to share them with your team. I would first share the results with my department leaders, and after they had a chance to digest everything, make the results available to everyone else. We would then go over the results in detail as a team at an offsite or during one of our monthly staff meetings (be sure to see my chapter on running effective staff meetings). Be sensitive about sharing the results with the full team if there are any extremely negative or unfair comments about any individual person set out in the comment sections. If this happened, I would edit out names of those people from any version I shared broadly (though either their manager or I would show them the comments and discuss the matter). After your team, you want to share the results with your CEO and senior management. When you do this, your cover email should list the top three positive and the top three things to improve, gleaned from the results. Be sure to note that you have plans in place or are making plans to address any particular shortcomings. Finally, share some of the key results with the company at large. You solicited feedback from a large group of people; let them see how the department fared (along with some general comments from you thanking them for their feedback and that you are putting into place action plans to work on issues identified through the survey). You can post this on the legal department web page or work with corporate communications for the right way to proceed.

10. **Create an action plan.** Lastly, you want to be sure to use the data and the comments to make changes. Develop a formal action plan to deal with the most important areas. You do not need to do this alone. Form a team with your department heads (and potentially others), and ask them to help develop plans for the department, themselves, and their teams. You should also solicit ideas generally from the entire department so they feel vested in the process. Ask everyone on your team (and don't forget yourself) to make the relevant sections of the action plan part of their development plans for next year. If users identified themselves for follow-up, be sure to follow up with them and get their thoughts and ideas and to show them that their feedback is important and valued. Finally, share your action plan with the CEO (especially during

any midyear or full-year review) and senior management to let them know you are moving forward with fixing any problems. Consider asking for a short meeting with your senior management peers to individually go over the key survey results and get their feedback on the action plan and/or the department in general. Even if they don't take you up on the invitation, they will greatly appreciate being asked for their input.

*****

Client satisfaction surveys are great tools for in-house counsel. You can easily create a useful survey in an hour or less, and you will get a large amount of useful and actionable information from your clients. The information will help you improve the delivery of legal services to the company and to build the brand of the legal department as a group that is constantly looking to improve, cares about what its clients think and need, is proactive and strategic, and is using cutting-edge technology (i.e., the online survey) to build a better department. However, don't rely solely on surveys to get feedback. Get out around the office and talk to your clients regularly. There is still no substitute for a face-to-face conversation.

July 28, 2015

Regulatory

Ten Things: All I Want for Christmas Is an FCPA/Anti-Bribery Health Check

Whenever you head into the holiday season, it is the perfect time to give your anti-bribery program a health check. For those in the United States, we tend to focus on the Foreign Corrupt Practices Act (FCPA)[157] when thinking about anti-bribery laws. However, if you work for a company that operates globally, you know that many countries have anti-bribery laws[158] and you need to be aware of those requirements as well. Enforcement of the FCPA/anti-bribery laws is not going away. In fact, in my opinion, it will get even more intense over the next few years. Given the level of fines and the reputational risk at stake, it's important to ensure you are taking the right steps to give your employees the tools they need to stay on the right side of the line. At my prior company, we typically used the advent of the holiday season as the time to take a number of steps relating to FCPA/anti-bribery compliance. Below are ten things you can do now to help ensure compliance with anti-bribery laws. In key spots, I have included links to articles or websites with additional information you might find helpful:

1. **Have an FCPA/anti-bribery policy.** You need to have a comprehensive anti-bribery policy. It can be separate or part of a larger business ethics policy (though the better practice is a separate policy). If you don't have one, now is the time to get one in place. Take time to customize your policy so it tracks to and resonates with your business. If you operate globally, you need your policy translated into the local languages of your employees outside the United States. It's difficult to explain to a regulator why you think a policy in English would be easily understood and followed by an employee whose first language is not English.

---

157 https://www.sec.gov/spotlight/fcpa/fcpa-resource-guide.pdf.
158 http://www.freshfields.com/en/insights/Bribery_Act_1_Year_On_Research/.

2. **Review/update your FCPA/anti-bribery policy.** If you have a policy, now is the perfect time to read through it; make sure it's up to date, clear, and easy to read. This last point is important. If you have a policy that is 15 pages of dense legal speak, it will be hard to get people to read it, let alone understand it. Keep it simple and straight forward, the key message being "we don't bribe people." One easy trick is to have a coffee or lunch with some business colleagues and get their feedback on the policy. You'll learn a lot about how clear your policy is to understand when you ask nonlawyers for their thoughts and suggestions.
3. **Identify countries of operation with a higher possibility of bribery issues.** If your company operates globally, you can create a "heat map"[159] of countries where your company should focus attention on bribery risks. If you do business in Russia, China, and Brazil, you will need to be more alert to bribery issues and focus extra training for and communications to employees working in those "hot" countries.
4. **Send an email reminder to all employees about your anti-bribery policy.** This is an easy and effective step. A short email communication to all of your employees several weeks before the holidays reminding them about the key points of your anti-bribery policy can prevent a misstep. It's easy for folks to get carried away on gifts or expensive dinners during this time of year, not realizing that they could land the company (and themselves) in hot water. For some, just a reminder as to which of your company's customers are potentially government officials can be very helpful as they may not realize that quasi-governmental entities are covered under these laws (e.g., airports, hospitals, and utility companies).
5. **Update your FCPA/anti-bribery training.** Review the materials and tools you use to train your employees about anti-bribery laws. Are they still fresh and relevant? Are they easy to follow and clear? Do you have special training tailored to those in sales or located in high-risk countries? Are the members of your legal team sensitive to spotting FCPA/anti-bribery issues? Some companies use computerized training,[160] but live teaching sessions (including webcasts) are highly effective too. Similarly, new training tools allow you to create apps and games to teach compliance and provide access over smartphones and tablets.[161] Keeping training fresh and cutting edge will help it "stick" with your employees.

---

159 http://www.fcpamap.com/.

160 http://lrn.com/.

161 https://elearningindustry.com/?s=Compliance+Online+Training.

6. **Create/update your FCPA/anti-bribery processes.** Do you have processes in place to deal with potential issues? What is your due diligence process for FCPA issues in M&A deals? Do you have a process to research and vet the background of potential sales agents or joint venture partners? There are a number of do it yourself[162] tools out there that make at least the first step in research easier and more comprehensive. Do you have a simple process for employees to report concerns or questions (e.g., a hot line or dedicated email address)? Do you remind employees regularly of the risks of violating anti-bribery laws? One thing we did at my former company was send a monthly email to all employees called "Ethics Every Day." These were short emails that focused on ethical issues arising from specific provisions of our business ethics policy and reminding employees about the rules of the road. We also used examples from current headlines where companies got into trouble or employees went to jail or faced heavy fines for engaging in forbidden activity. Short emails containing real examples of how people tripped up really bring the message home in an effective way.

7. **Review/update contract provisions.** Odds are your vendor contracts contain representations around bribery laws. If your company regularly engages sales agents in foreign countries, you should have agreements that require certain certifications and acknowledgments about compliance with anti-bribery laws. Now is the time to review those agreements[163] and update them as necessary (or get them in place if you do not have them). Be clear in your contracts about the importance of compliance with the FCPA, and other laws. Your agreements should have audit rights and the ability to terminate in the event your partner is in violation of anti-bribery laws. If a partner refuses to sign the agreement or include these provisions, that is a huge red flag to your company not to do business with that partner.

8. **Get executive team buy in.** The most important tool in your tool box is getting senior executive buy-in that compliance with FCPA/anti-bribery laws is paramount at your company. Not only will this set the tone from the top, it will also help you in your job in terms of obtaining completion of training, reporting concerns or questions, and gaining compliance with processes you set up to help ensure third parties are properly vetted before your company engages them. When we kicked off compliance training, it was the CEO who sent the message out to employees about the importance of the training and it was the executive team that generally completed the training first (which

---

162 http://www.traceinternational.org/.
163 http://media.mofo.com/files/Uploads/Images/110118-FCPA-White-Paper.pdf.

helped me address employees who later said they were "too busy" to complete the training).

9. **Consider an audit/assessment.** Consider teaming up with your internal audit team or an outside vendor to review your FCPA/anti-bribery program[164] and benchmark it against industry standard practices. If you decide to do this, be sure to confirm that the review is being done at the request of the legal department for the purpose of providing legal advice and be sure to take the necessary steps to preserve any applicable privileges.[165] This can be a big task, so do not rush into an audit/assessment[166] lightly, and it is smart to take advice from your outside counsel about such a project.

10. **Identify outside counsel.** I always told my team to "plan ahead for the divorce." That typically meant how does the contract deal with issues that arise when a business relationship ends badly. In the context of FCPA/anti-bribery law, you need to plan on how you deal with things when you have a real problem. Unless you are a particularly sophisticated in-house legal department, odds are that you will not have the expertise or experience to handle a serious FCPA/anti-bribery issue. Figure out whom you will call now, before there is a problem. When things blow up, you want to be ready to go as time will be of the essence most likely, and you will be glad to have experienced counsel guide you and your company through the process.

December 4, 2014

---

164 http://corporatecomplianceinsights.com/how-to-conduct-an-fcpa-assessment/.

165 http://corporatecomplianceinsights.com/preserving-confidentiality-in-compliance-processes-the-attorney-client-privilege-at-work/.

166 http://www.ey.com/Publication/vwLUAssets/EY-FIDS-Anti-corruption-internal-audits/$FILE/EY-FIDS-Anti-corruption-internal-audits.pdf.

Ten Things: Trade Associations and Antitrust Risk

One of the most interesting questions you can get as in-house counsel is this: "Hey, I am going to a meeting with some competitors tomorrow. Is there anything special I should do to make sure I don't get in trouble?" A question like this is like a good law school exam—there is almost too much to talk about! As most in-house counsel know, meetings between competitors can be tricky stuff and fraught with risk, both for the company and for the employee. Improper agreements between competitors (e.g., price fixing, bid rigging, dividing territory or customers) can lead to costly litigation, investigations, fines, damages (trebled), and even handcuffs and jail. The only 100 percent safe route is no communications with competitors ever. A restriction like that, however, is unlikely to win the legal department any friends at the company and is unnecessary as there are a number of situations where conversations between competitors are needed and completely appropriate. The key is making sure the employees at your company, from the CEO downward, have a basic understand of the rules of the road for interacting with competitors and know when to contact the legal department for guidance.

One of the most likely scenarios where competitors interact is at a trade association meeting (in person or over the phone). Trade associations can (and do) serve a number of procompetitive purposes, including lobbying the government on behalf of its members, educating the public about the services and value its members bring to the table, and sponsoring standards setting exercises that encourage growth, interoperability, and innovation. On the other hand, it's important to understand that any time competitors interact—a trade association meeting, lunch, email conversation—there is always a chance that a perfectly innocent conversation or document will be misconstrued or taken out of context and unfairly presented as some type of nefarious, "smoke-filled" room agreement designed to thwart competition between the parties. Here are ten steps you can take as in-house counsel to help educate and keep your business colleagues on the right side of line and out of trouble:

1. **Have a written antitrust policy for your company.** Before you worry about creating or joining a trade association, you need to focus inward and make sure you are doing the right things to train your employees on antitrust issues generally and with regard to competitor interactions specifically. A written policy[167] sets out clear guidance and expectations for employees in this complicated area of the law. Additionally, it will be helpful if your company ever gets crosswise with the U.S. government as having a written antitrust policy that is part of a vigorous compliance program can be a mitigating factor under the sentencing guidelines. Your policy should cover the antitrust basics (e.g., no price fixing or bid rigging), and contain a specific section on interactions with competitors (with an example or two relevant to your industry). Make sure your policy states that before any competitor contact takes place, the purpose of the meeting and the agenda should be cleared with the legal department in advance. Once the policy is in place, be sure to do regular training and reminders about antitrust issues for your company's employees. One helpful thing to do is to periodically send out an "all-hands" email if you see a news article[168] on an executive getting into trouble over antitrust issues, explaining what happened and reinforcing the importance of compliance. For a good summary of setting up an antitrust compliance program, see "Clear Expectations: DOJ Outlines Tenets of an Effective Antitrust Compliance Program."[169]
2. **Prepare a concise statement regarding the trade association's purpose and mission.** Once you have your own house in order, you can turn your focus to ensuring your trade association is set up to succeed and operates in a manner compliant with the law. Note that all of the points in this article also apply to an informal association (i.e., a coalition) of competitors—usually put together to address a single issue.[170] Start with ensuring the association

---

167 http://www02.abb.com/global/abbzh/abbzh252.nsf/0/b750f9a433cca8b4c12579eb004cae2b/$file/antitrust+guidance+note_trade+associations.pdf.

168 http://www.bloomberg.com/news/articles/2010-10-22/ex-british-airways-manager-bets-his-prison-tales-will-scare-price-fixers.

169 https://www.bakerlaw.com/alerts/clear-expectations-doj-outlines-tenets-of-an-effective-antitrust-compliance-program.

170 For a great example of trade associations and competitor coalitions at work see http://aviationblog.dallasnews.com/2015/04/u-s-travel-association-adds-more-fuel-to-the-debate-over-whether-gulf-airline-subsidies-are-unfair.html/ discussing the lobbying here in the United States over Middle Eastern airlines and subsidies. You can almost guarantee that the members of each group have been counseled on the parameters of antitrust compliance with respect to the goals and actions of their associations and the discussions between participants.

(or coalition) has a clear written statement of its purpose and mission. It may seem a little silly but it can pay off in the event anyone challenges why a group of competitors were meeting in the first place. Additionally, it sets the boundaries for the group and provides guidance on the types of matters and issues the association will deal with.

3. **Use a written agenda.** All trade association meetings should follow an agenda sent out in advance to the participants and approved by counsel. Once you have an agenda, you need to stick to it. The agenda should be clear and concise and leave no wiggle room for misinterpretation over what is being discussed. The sensitivity about what was discussed stems from the fact that agreement with a competitor does not need to be in writing. An agreement can be oral and informal, including what is commonly referred to as a "wink and a nod" among competitors sitting around the table. Having a clear agenda (that you stick with) can minimize the risk of bad behavior or misinterpretation/miscasting of what occurred at a meeting.

4. **Take minutes.** Have minutes taken of each meeting that accurately reflect what occurred and have those minutes prepared or (at a minimum) reviewed by counsel prior to finalizing. Promptly distribute the approved minutes to all of the participants and keep a copy in case it is needed down the road. The final approved minutes should be the only minutes of the meeting. Members should not keep their own minutes.

5. **Have counsel present.** In a perfect world, you would be able to have counsel at every trade association meeting or call. That is not always possible or practical. Assuming not, the trade association staff should be well trained on competition law issues and beginning each meeting with an antitrust ground rules reminder is a good idea. Further, any meeting where the agenda contemplates discussing competitively sensitive information should have counsel at the meeting or on the phone. If you're not sure whether your meeting involves competitively sensitive information, that is a sign to check in with counsel before proceeding with that item.

6. **Know how to stop inappropriate conversations.** As the Federal Trade Commission notes,[171] the fact that you are participating in a trade association does not in any way transform inappropriate behavior into sanctioned behavior. This point should be emphasized strongly with your business team and with all members of the trade association. Clear problem areas include discussing current or future prices, costs, output levels, business and R&D plans, and

---

171 https://www.ftc.gov/tips-advice/competition-guidance/guide-antitrust-laws/dealings-competitors/spotlight-trade.

forecasts. If for some reason an improper topic is raised during the meeting, your trade association staff and members need to know in advance to shut those conversations down immediately (and if there is a question about whether the discussion is appropriate, the right course of action is to stop and only return to the topic after consulting counsel). If the discussion continues, you may need to shut the entire meeting down or, at a minimum, leave the room and get your exit noted in the minutes (and report what happened to legal counsel). These same rules apply outside of the formal trade association meetings (e.g., at dinner, on the golf course). Basically, every interaction between competitors is subject to scrutiny and therefore extra caution is required to ensure staying on the right side of the line.

7. **Understand the limits on key trade association activities.** In addition to promotion of their industry, there are several core matters most trade associations deal with, including (a) lobbying, (b) data exchanges, and (c) standard setting. If done properly, all three can be valuable and procompetitive. But care needs to be taken as there is no blank check for any activity of a trade association. If you cannot do it outside the trade association, then you cannot do it as part of a trade association. For example, lobbying[172] activity needs to be reasonably necessary to the goal and not a sham. If there will be data exchanges[173] between association members (e.g., for benchmarking or trade association marketing purposes), be sure that sensitive information is properly anonymized, aggregated, and historical. No current or future pricing/forecast information should be exchanged. Ideally, any such data should be submitted to and compiled by a third party. Also, any data-sharing plan should be cleared with counsel *in advance* of handing over the data as you will want to avoid any appearance that the process is being used to somehow fix prices. Standard setting[174] can be a very procompetitive action on the part of a trade association, especially if it spurs innovation and reduces costs. That said, before a trade association engages in a standard setting, the process and goals should be vetted with legal counsel. Standards must be based on objective criteria and reasonably related to the goals the parties are trying to achieve. They should generally be voluntary in that there is no agreement to compel compliance with the standards.

---

172 https://www.asaecenter.org/resources/associations-now.

173 https://www.ftc.gov/sites/default/files/attachments/us-submissions-oecd-and-other-international-competition-fora/1010informationexchanges.pdf.

174 http://www.weil.com/~/media/Files/PDFs/Standard-Setting%20and%20Antitrust%20-%20TPL%20Feb%202010.pdf.

8. **Make membership criteria objective and standardized.** It's no fun to not get invited to the party. So, keep in mind that competitors who are not allowed to join a trade association can be the source of an antitrust complaint. Even so, legitimate criteria for refusing membership is not an antitrust violation. Be sure your trade association's membership requirements are objective, transparent, and nondiscriminatory. Similarly, if there is a process to expel a member, that process needs to be carefully vetted with counsel as well. The operation and governance of the association are important too. Ideally, there should be one vote per member (i.e., no weighted voting that would give large competitors a disproportionate say in how the association operates). Election to the board of directors should be simple, transparent, and straightforward. Establishing membership criteria should be done in conjunction with the advice of counsel at the creation of the trade association and should be reviewed regularly to keep it current with the marketplace and the law.
9. **Train the trade association staff/attendees.** Your trade association should have its own antitrust policy, and all of the association staff should have regular training in the area of antitrust. If for some reason counsel is not present at a meeting, your next best line of defense may well be your well-trained professional staff. Likewise, the businesspeople who regularly attend trade association meetings should receive regular antitrust training. It is also a good idea to go over some simple basic antitrust ground rules at the beginning of each meeting. Every year the trade association should have a "health check" and work with counsel to ensure compliance with its policies and determine if anything needs to be changed or updated. You should also meet regularly with your own internal clients to stay abreast of what is going on at the trade association meetings and make sure your internal clients are trained and understand that they need to contact the legal department if they have any questions regarding the activities of the trade association. They need to own it just as much as the legal department.
10. **Know the rules about document creation.** Nothing new here. As Joe Friday said on "Dragnet," "Everything you say (or write) can be and will be used against you." Everyone—from the association's board of directors, to the staff, to the members—needs to understand that poorly drafted documents (email, memoranda, minutes, agenda, handwritten notes, reports, studies, etc.) can land the association, the company members, and even individuals in hot water over antitrust issues. Treat every document involving the trade association like a business document (e.g., professional in tone and language). Teach the company members to pretend like every trade association document, email, or report begins with "Dear People Suing Us ..." Thinking about it in this light

will help ensure people take time to draft truthfully, accurately, and in a business-like manner.

*****

Since antitrust law is complex and fact-specific, it is very difficult to cover all of the potential areas where problems can arise (and you should seek advice of counsel for any specific situation). Moreover, even if you do all of the things noted above, there is no guarantee that your trade association or any of its members will not get sued by a determined plaintiff, regardless of the merits (or lack thereof) of the claim. All meetings with competitors can create risk. That said, there is nothing inherently bad about competitors meeting and talking, so long as the guidelines above are followed and those attending the meeting are thoughtful and well trained about the risk areas. There are a number of additional sources available free online through a simple search engine search. The American Bar Association has a helpful book you can buy called *Antitrust and Associations Handbook*.[175] The Department of Justice and the Federal Trade Commission have produced free guidelines[176] dealing with a wide range of competitor collaborations and they are worth reading. These guidelines underscore the point that the rules around competitor interaction are the same regardless of whether there is a trade association involved or not. Finally, this is another area where experienced outside counsel can provide value at many different phases and where you can demonstrate a proactive approach to managing your company's risk profile.

April 16, 2015

---

175 http://shop.americanbar.org/eBus/Store/ProductDetails.aspx?productId=213788.

176 https://www.ftc.gov/sites/default/files/documents/public_events/joint-venture-hearings-antitrust-guidelines-collaboration-among-competitors/ftcdojguidelines-2.pdf.

Ten Things: Data Privacy—The Essentials

As in-house counsel, you have probably been asked the following question by a panicked (or at least pretty stressed-out) CEO or CFO: "What are we doing about data privacy? Are we okay?" You likely have a good answer, or at least the start of one. Still, your answer may be as open-ended as the question and you can feel overwhelmed by the sheer amount of information on the topic. I know that you want read another article about data privacy as much as you'd like to have a safe dropped on your head. But, don't stop reading. This will not be an overly detailed discussion about all of the nuances of the issue or a list of regulations and laws of multiple countries (though those discussions are valuable). Here I will set out the ten essential things you need to know about data privacy—key points that you can focus on as you work through or oversee data issues for your company.

I have worked on data privacy issues since the mid-1990s, before there even was an EU Privacy Directive (or as my daughters say, before I "fell off my dinosaur"). One thing I have learned is that data privacy is actually pretty straightforward, commonsense stuff. I'll go into some specific areas below but the key thing to keep in mind is this: tell people what you are doing with their personal data, and then do only what you told them you would do. If you and your company do this, you will likely solve 90 percent of any serious data privacy issues.

Below are some areas of data privacy laws that will help you stay on top of the issues and be able to add intelligently to the conversation where you work:

1. **Take a data inventory.** The first thing to do is to take a data inventory: (a) what types of personal data[177] does your company collect, (b) from whom, (c) how are they collected, (d) where and how are they stored and secured, (e) how are they used (including potential future uses), and (f) when and how will they be discarded? Since a data inventory is the linchpin of data privacy, take

---

177 http://searchfinancialsecurity.techtarget.com/definition/personally-identifiable-information.

your time to get it right—meaning ask lots of questions of lots of people across the business and always cross-check the answers to be sure everything lines up. As you go along, build a "data map" based on the answers and be sure to update it regularly, at least once or twice a year. Don't forget that the data you collect about your own employees count as well.

2. **Special data require special protection.** If you are collecting personal data that are sensitive (e.g., health information, information from children, political affiliation, sexual orientation, and viewing and reading habits), you need to take special precautions to protect the data and to obtain the correct permissions from the individual about how you may use such data, if at all. Treat sensitive data of your customers or website users the same way you would want sensitive data about yourself treated. One way companies are starting to take risk out of a potential data breach is to encrypt the data.[178] If encrypted data are lost or stolen (and the key is not taken too), most (but not all) data breach notice statutes do not require any notice as the encrypted data are otherwise considered safe. Depending on your company's business, this option is worth exploring with your IT team.

3. **Figure out which laws/rules apply.** Next, you need to know which data privacy laws apply to your collection and use of the data. Typically, it's a function of three things: (a) where are the personal data collected from, (b) where that data are sent, and (c) how are that data used. In the United States, you have a mix of state and federal laws. State laws are usually enforced by the state attorneys general and typically deal with things like notification requirements[179] in the event of a data breach. Federal laws tend to be sector specific, for example, Graham-Leach Bliley[180] (financial companies), HIPAA[181] (health information), COPPA[182] (protection for children), and Fair Credit Reporting Act[183] (credit agencies, employers). The Federal Trade Commission (FTC)[184] is the main, but not the only, federal-level privacy

---

178 https://www.eiseverywhere.com/file_uploads/4982c29aa16310269434b49b0ac62eed_EricHibbard_Data-Breach-Encryption-Safe-Harbor_Final.pdf.
179 https://oag.ca.gov/sites/all/files/agweb/pdfs/cybersecurity/making_your_privacy_practices_public.pdf.
180 https://www.ftc.gov/tips-advice/business-center/privacy-and-security/gramm-leach-bliley-act.
181 http://www.hhs.gov/hipaa/for-professionals/covered-entities/index.html.
182 https://www.ftc.gov/tips-advice/business-center/guidance/complying-coppa-frequently-asked-questions.
183 http://searchcompliance.techtarget.com/definition/Fair-Credit-Reporting-Act-FCRA.
184 https://www.ftc.gov/news-events/media-resources/protecting-consumer-privacy.

regulator and has wide powers under Section 5 of the FTC Act (prohibiting unfair or deceptive trade practices). Outside the United States, privacy laws tend to be comprehensive, applying broadly across all business and data uses, and are enforced by a central agency usually called a "Data Privacy Authority." In the European Union, for example, there is a minimum level of data privacy protection under the EU Data Privacy Directive that each member state must implement. Each member state, however, is free to pass more restrictive laws. The European Union recently overhauled its data privacy law with the new General Data Privacy Regulation that will go into effect in May 2018.[185]

4. **Create good/accurate privacy policies and notices.** A privacy policy is a policy internal to your company, that is, what the company tells its employees about the collection and use of personal data. A privacy notice is the policy the company shares with the outside world (usually via a small link at the bottom of the website marked "Privacy Policy"). Regardless of what you call it, the policy and the notice need to line up. You cannot tell consumers one thing and do something different internally. Your internal privacy policy should be a comprehensive set of rules your employees can follow and that tells them how they can collect and use personal data. You need to keep the policy current (e.g., catch any new uses for the data), which will entail several meetings every year with the employees in charge of or dealing with data. You also need a training program to educate all your employees about the policy. Inadvertent or deliberate data breaches by employees constitute a large portion of data breaches over the past several years. On the other hand, a privacy notice is required any place you are gathering personal data from the public (website, mobile phones,[186] etc.) and needs to set out five core things: (a) what data are collected, (b) how are they used and secured, (c) with whom are the data shared, (d) whom do you contact if you have an issue, and (e) information about the use of tracking software and cookies. It is critical that you live up to all promises made in your privacy notice. If there are changes around the use of data, be sure to update your privacy policy and privacy notice as soon as possible. Remember that changes to the notice will not apply retroactively, that is, you'll need to treat data collected in the past under the terms of the privacy notice in place at the time of collection. As to tracking and cookies, just remember to fully disclose what you are tracking and how, and give users

---

185 See page 171 for a discussion of the GDPR.

186 https://www.mwe.com/en/thought-leadership/publications/2013/02/ftc-recommends-privacy-practices-for-mobile-apps.

a way to turn off cookies if they want to. Finally, be sure to have a working opt-out[187] link on your website and as part of every email sent in a marketing campaign. If the consumer can simply tell you to "stop sending me stuff" and you respect that request, you will have much fewer problems.

5. **Stay on top of vendors.** Your company may be a model of best practices with respect to data collection and data privacy. But, if you use vendors to process any of the data (e.g., the cloud,[188] call centers, and outsourcing), you are still responsible and your company will be the one left holding the bag in the event of problems. Accordingly, your vendor contracts should require several things: (a) your vendors must follow the same data privacy practices as you do with respect to the data you are providing them, (b) vendors should provide you the right to audit around data issues, (c) your vendors should notify you immediately in the event of a data incident, and (d) your vendors should indemnify your company in the event of problems they cause. Try to stick with well-known and responsible vendors if possible. There are several companies that rank vendor security, for example, Bitsight Technologies and Security Scorecard, and produce ratings of vendors based on how *securely* the vendors operate. The Jordan Lawrence company has an automated vendor risk analysis tool available as well.

6. **Get cyber risk insurance.** A data breach can explode very quickly and the costs to your company can be very high (anywhere from $10 to $200 per record lost). If your company deals with personal data in a significant manner, you should look into whether your current insurance policies (e.g., commercial general liability or errors and omissions) cover a data breach and, if not, obtain a specific data breach policy. Your insurance department or insurance broker can be helpful here. One thing you'll need to figure out is how much insurance you need. You have probably seen recent data breach settlements and related costs of tens, if not hundreds, of millions of dollars (e.g., Target, Home Depot). Things you need to think about include how much personal data does the company process, what would be the harm of a data breach to the company's reputation, what is a reasonable cost per record lost, what if the business is materially interrupted in the event of a breach, what

---

[187] https://www.ftc.gov/tips-advice/business-center/guidance/can-spam-act-compliance-guide-business.

[188] http://www.lexology.com/library/detail.aspx?g=df65d227-3923-4db4-a785-607b8d3c7aef&utm_source=Lexology+Daily+Newsfeed&utm_medium=HTML+email+-+Body+-+Federal+section&utm_campaign=ACC+Newsstand+subscriber+daily+feed&utm_content=Lexology+Daily+Newsfeed+2015-04-29&utm_term=.

will consumers expect the company to do in the event of a breach (e.g., credit monitoring), and so on. Your insurance company may also be able to help you understand and implement best practices regarding data security, so do not leave that resource untapped.

7. **Make sure you can transfer the data.** The question here is whether or not you can legally transfer personal data from one country to another. For example, under the EU Privacy Directive, you can freely transfer personal data within the European Union but you cannot transfer the data of a citizen of the European Union (including that of your own employees)[189] outside of the European Union unless it is being transferred to a country with an adequate level of data privacy laws. According to the EU, the United States does not have adequate laws. This has caused some real problems for U.S. businesses. There are several exceptions[190] to the restriction (e.g., binding corporate rules, use of model clauses, explicit consent, the transfer is necessary to perform the contract), but you need to be sure to fall safely within one of the exceptions which Data Protection Authorities have narrowly construed. Prior to October 2015,[191] U.S. companies could avail themselves to the so-called Safe Harbor agreement to ensure the ability to transfer data out of the European Union to the United States. Since October 2015, U.S. companies have needed to rely on an exception to the prohibition against transfer out of the European Union or model contracts, and so on. However, the United States and the European Union have implemented a new data transfer agreement called "Privacy Shield"[192] which is designed to correct the problems that led to the down fall of Safe Harbor.[193] It is very likely that there will be legal challenges to the Privacy Shield and equally likely that the Privacy Shield will be amended in the future to deal with the GDPR once it is implemented in May 2018.

8. **Create a data breach response plan and practice it.** If you've heard from a law firm lately about data privacy issues, odds are good that it is about creating a data breach response plan. If you happen to have a killer response plan

---

189 http://www.friedfrank.com/siteFiles/Publications/FINAL%20-%209.25.2013%20-%20TOC%20Memo%20-%20Transfer%20of%20Employee%20Personal%20Data%20between%20the%20EU%20and%20the%20US1.pdf.

190 http://ec.europa.eu/justice/policies/privacy/docs/international_transfers_faq/international_transfers_faq.pdf.

191 https://epic.org/privacy/intl/schrems/.

192 http://ec.europa.eu/justice/data-protection/files/factsheets/factsheet_eu-us_privacy_shield_en.pdf.

193 http://www.wsj.com/articles/u-s-eu-agree-final-adjustments-to-data-privacy-shield-1466764267.

already prepared, you're in good shape. If you're like most companies, your plan probably needs some work. Meaning, it may be a good idea to take up one of the law firm offers to help you with a plan. A few important things to think about as you develop or update your plan are as follows:

- *Someone needs to be in charge of data privacy.* If you're serious about data privacy, then you need to have someone in charge of the issue—a data honcho. They can come from legal or from the business. But it needs to be someone senior enough to command respect and resources in the event of a crisis.
- *Know the difference between a "data incident" and "data breach."* Just because the problem involves data does not mean there is a breach. It's important not to prematurely label what has happened as a "breach." If you declare a data breach, you have a lot of obligations to fulfill and you are probably headed toward litigation. Start with calling it an "incident" until you are sure. Be sure that the appropriate people in the legal department and the business understand the distinction, especially at the beginning of an incident when the emails and the documents are flying fast and furious, and you will have to live with whatever people write down.
- *Identify your core team.* Set out in advance who will be sitting around the table if there is an incident. Some key people will be the head of data privacy, legal, HR, corporate communications, system security/CIO, outside counsel, outside communications team, forensic team, applicable vendors, and insurance.
- *Engage legal counsel at the beginning.* If there is a data breach, you will want to make sure the investigation is conducted at the direction of counsel (in-house or external) so that any appropriate legal privileges will apply.
- *Prepare for the notice process.* If there is a data breach, you will likely need to notify the impacted persons. Your outside law firm or insurance company should be helpful here. Your insurance company may even have a turnkey vendor who can handle the notice issues and processing. I recommend you download a copy of the Weil Gotshal security breach notification survey.[194] It is a comprehensive look at notification requirements by state in the United States.

9. **Read these core four documents.** There is an incredible number of articles and books about data privacy and data breaches. It is an overwhelming amount

---

194 http://www.weil.com/~/media/files/pdfs/1600811_security_breach_notification_broch_eng_digital_v1.pdf?la=en.

of information for any in-house lawyer to try to digest. I have read a lot of privacy-related material, and if I could have only a handful of documents to read and keep nearby, this would be my list:

- *The EU Data Privacy Directive*[195] and "Cookie" Directive.[196] If you can read and follow the requirements of the EU Privacy Directive and the companion Cookie Directive, then odds are high that you are in compliance with most any general data privacy protection law in the world. The directive is in effect until May 2018. In the interim, you should be studying the text of the new General Data Privacy Regulation.[197]
- *The National Institute of Standards and Technology—Framework for Cyber Security*.[198] This is quickly becoming the *de facto* standard for implementing data security. While data privacy and data security are two separate things, you cannot have appropriate data privacy without solid data security practices.
- *The 2016 Verizon Data Breach Investigations Report*.[199] This is a free resource full of great information and data about data breach issues.
- *A Sample Data Privacy Notice*. A great example of a state-of-the-art privacy notice is that of Microsoft.[200] The Microsoft privacy notice covers multiple Microsoft businesses in a one clean, user-friendly document. I would keep this on hand as model to emulate and monitor it for changes as those changes are likely changes I would need to consider making to my own notice.

10. **Keep public disclosures current and complete.** Given the growing importance of data and the material harm a breach can cause, you need to be aware of any obligations to discuss or disclose risks relating to data privacy and data security. If you work for a publicly traded company in the United States, risks around a data breach need to be appropriately disclosed in your quarterly and annual reports. The SEC has issued guidance[201] on such disclosures and its interest in the topic is growing. Failure to make appropriate disclosures can

---

195 http://eur-lex.europa.eu/legal-content/EN/TXT/PDF/?uri=CELEX:31995L0046&from=en.
196 https://www.cookielaw.org/the-cookie-law/.
197 http://data.consilium.europa.eu/doc/document/ST-5419-2016-INIT/en/pdf.
198 http://www.nist.gov/cyberframework/upload/cybersecurity-framework-021214.pdf.
199 http://www.verizonenterprise.com/verizon-insights-lab/dbir/2016/.
200 https://privacy.microsoft.com/en-us/privacystatement.
201 https://www.sec.gov/divisions/corpfin/guidance/cfguidance-topic2.htm.

also lead to shareholder litigation/class actions. Likewise, in the event of data breach, you may need to issue an 8K describing the event.[202]

*****

Is there more? Definitely, yes. There is a lot more. For now, just know that the legal issues surrounding data privacy are here to stay and are getting more risky and complex. Data privacy is a hot topic and it is well worth the time of all in-house lawyers to have a basic understanding of the law in this area. Your job is not necessarily to master every detail of data privacy but to be sure you understand when you need to herd the cats and get people into the proper positions and armed with the proper tools so that if (when) there is a data breach your company will be ready. This is how you can best add value to the company.

April 30, 2015

---

202 https://www.insideprivacy.com/data-security/cybersecurity/when-are-public-companies-required-to-disclose-that-they-have-experienced-a-material-data-security-b/.

Ten Things: Record Retention—Programs, Policies, and More…

The beginning of the year is a great time to think about reducing clutter. Many of us start the New Year with a personal plan to get organized, to throw out stuff that no longer matters, and to accumulate less junk going forward. It's a nice plan—and it usually falls apart by mid-February. Still, the idea of getting organized and reducing clutter is also a goal of many companies. One way to do this is by implementing or updating a record retention program.[203] For companies without a program already in place, this means starting from scratch. For companies with a program, it means a serious soup to nuts review and how (not if) the program needs to be updated.

The benefits of a well thought-out record retention program cut across every part of the business, including all staff groups, and especially within the legal department, which usually takes the lead in record retention issues. Whether you are based in the United States or a different country, whether you are a generalist or specialize in litigation, M&A, commercial agreements, compliance, intellectual property, corporate secretary, or employment law, a good record retention program can make your job much easier and reduce risk to the company. Here are ten basics of what is needed to put a record retention program into place or update an existing one:

1. **Why have a program?** There is no requirement that you have a record retention program. Other than regulatory requirements or litigation holds, a company is free to keep or dispose of whatever records it wants, whenever it wants to. Despite this, I think all companies should have a record retention program in place, regardless of size. Small companies may need only a relatively simple program, while large companies will need more complicated policies tied to the complexity of their business. Here are just a few benefits of a record retention program:

---

203 http://www.acc.com/legalresources/quickcounsel/rr.cfm.

- Reduces storage costs (e.g., storing data, emails, and paper costs money).
- Reduces litigation/regulatory costs and risk, including a process to implement a litigation hold, as well as a road map showing where to find things when disputes arise or when discovery requests come in.
- Mitigates risks from a data breach, that is, getting rid of personal data as soon as possible and knowing where the data are that you need to protect.
- Improves speed/accuracy of record retrieval, including locating documents for tax purposes, M&A deals, contract management, and corporate governance.

2. **Customize your program.** Unless your business is pretty simple, you cannot create an effective record retention program by simply downloading schedules off the Internet (though those schedules can be useful benchmarks). You need to customize your program to the particular needs of your company. For example, understanding the type of businesses your company is involved in, where the company operates, the company's culture, the types of technology used throughout the company, and the different regulatory environments it operates in will all be part of creating the program. The best way to start the process is to recruit a cross-functional team from the different parts of the business to help you answer these questions and develop the program. You must speak with employees in numerous parts of the business to understand record creation, storage, how records are used, and risks, all on a country-by-country basis. Limiting your focus to just the United States, for example, will make you miss many important things and your program will not be relevant to employees working outside the country. You also need to win over two key parts of the company to create a successful program: the IT department and the C-suite. The IT group will be invaluable in terms of where records are kept, how they are accessed, and how they can best be managed. The C-suite must buy in to the importance of having (and enforcing) a records retention program. If they do not, then the program will just be another piece of paper. Two things will help you in your effort to win these groups over: the ability to lower costs and the ability to lower risk. Repeat these often.

3. **Figure out what you have and where you keep it.** This is the most crucial task in creating your program, and you and the team should spend the bulk of your up-front time understanding and identifying the following:
    - *The types of records created by your company.* Remember, not everything is electronic—don't forget the paper! Signed documents, handwritten notes, calendars, policies, HR files, marketing materials, memos, correspondence, presentations, corporate minutes, and board of director meeting materials,

all need to be accounted for. You will be surprised by how much paper is generated by your company.
- *Where the records are located.* You need to really dig out all the places where company records are stored. The IT department can help you here. Be sure to consider computers (office/home/laptops), servers, backup tapes, document management systems, shared drives, email (server and local files), company web pages (external and intranet), social media accounts, CD ROMs, flash drives, instant messaging, audio and video recordings, off-site storage, corporate secretary, and so on.
- *Your vendors.* If your company uses outside vendors (e.g., consultants, accounting, legal, call center), you must ensure that your record retention program accounts for your records held/created by these vendors.

4. **Records you *want* to keep/Records you *have* to keep.** Once you have identified the types of records your company has and where they are located, you need to figure out what to keep and for how long. There are two categories here: (a) records you *want* to keep and (b) records you *have* to keep. Records you want to keep are records with no legal obligation to keep but are important to how your company runs its business. These are records with long-term business value, such as emails or presentations that memorialize important decisions and activities, explain contracts, discuss future strategic activities, and so forth. These may be documents that, from a cultural standpoint, your company expects to have access to several years after they are created. The only way to identify these types of records is to ask lots of questions across the entire business. Records you have to keep are records subject to legal or regulatory requirements. Almost every country has requirements about keeping tax records (e.g., IRS), employment records (e.g., Department of Labor), compliance records (e.g., Sarbanes-Oxley), safety records (e.g., OSHA), environmental records (e.g., Clean Water Act), and other statutory/regulatory requirements. And don't forget that some legal requirements call for your company to *get rid* of records after a certain time (e.g., EU Data Privacy Directive and the new General Data Privacy Regulation). Getting this right requires research on your part as you need to identify and understand the different legal and regulatory requirements applicable to your company's business and the record retention requirements under each. This is an area where outside counsel can add a lot of value.

5. **Prepare your written policy/schedules.** After identifying the types of records your company has, and any applicable retention periods, it's time to start drafting (or updating) your record retention policy. Your policy needs to be realistic and driven by business needs. A policy that fails to account for either of these is destined to fail. For example, if your company is small with a simple

business, the policy and schedules need to be short and straightforward.[204] A complicated, overly long policy is not necessary and is unlikely to get much traction with the business. Likewise, if your company has 100,000 employees, operating several heavily regulated businesses located in 75 countries, you're probably not going to be able to get away with a five-page policy. Even so, regardless of how complicated your business may be, focus on preparing a policy that is as simple to read and understand as possible under the circumstances. Use plain language and avoid legalese to the extent possible. Start with a good summary of the policy, explaining what the company is trying to accomplish and why and set out some basic record retention guidelines for the most common records and documents right up-front (i.e., a quick start guide). Make the document easy to find (intranet site) and easy to navigate (hyperlinks, definitions, good topic index, searchable, etc.). If you have employees operating in foreign countries, take extra care to ensure the policy makes sense to them. Use focus groups of employees if needed. Prepare schedules covering different types of records with easy-to-follow charts setting out the type or category of record, along with how long the record should be kept (and if applicable, the maximum amount of time the record can be kept). Finally, be sure to document how the policy was created or amended as this may be important in litigation. If the other side challenges your policy, you'll want a solid record of why your policy is the way it is, how it was created, and how it was rolled-out, enforced, and updated.

6. **Roll it out properly.** A successful record retention policy or update needs to be rolled out to the company in proper fashion. A successful roll-out requires that the senior executives of the company buy in to the need and value of having such a policy. If they view it as important, this tone from the top will cascade down and compliance by the rank and file will go up substantially. If the senior executives don't buy in, then compliance will be spotty. Identify a "champion" from each business unit and staff group whose tasks are to (a) help roll out and "evangelize" the policy and its importance to their coworkers, (b) help enforce the policy, and (c) be part of the team that provides feedback and regularly reviews the policy for revisions. You also need to create or update training programs, ensuring they explain the purpose of the policy, how each employee can help ensure success, key obligations under the policy, and where to go with questions or concerns. This training can be live, online, or a mix of both (e.g., a webcast). The policy should become part of the on-boarding process for new employees. When I was general counsel, we had an annual record

---

204 http://www.ckrh.org/pdf/recordretentionpolicy.pdf.

retention week to remind all employees and management about the policy and encourage compliance. Finally, it is a good idea to test the policy with one group first to see what works and what doesn't, and then make decisions about how best to roll it out to the entire company (e.g., knife-edge and phased).

7. **Litigation hold process.** Ironically, the most important part of your record retention program is knowing when and how to suspend it. Devising and implementing a proper litigation hold[205] process must be a priority. In the United States, once you anticipate a reasonable chance of litigation,[206] you have a duty to preserve records relevant to the dispute. Typically, this occurs when you receive a lawsuit or subpoena, but the obligation can attach earlier under the right circumstances, for example, a letter from a customer raising a substantial dispute and stating that a lawsuit is likely if the matter is not resolved. If you know you are going to file a lawsuit in two weeks, then the process is likely triggered on your side, even if the other side has no idea a lawsuit is coming. Failure to put a hold into place can lead to claims of spoliation of evidence and, at worst, to fines, sanctions, and even an instruction to the jury that they can infer that you destroyed records because they were "bad" for your side. All of this means you need to create a reasonable process to do the following:[207]

- Know when a litigation hold attaches.
- Give notice to the right employees to stop deleting or destroying any records relating to the dispute along with some type of acknowledgment from each such employee that they understand and will comply.
- Send regular reminders to those employees (each requiring an additional acknowledgment).
- Have a conversation with the IT team about the affected systems and ensuring any regular deletion is suspended.
- Set a process for dealing with records belonging to employees who leave the company and ensuring their files and laptop hard drive are not deleted or wiped clean.

What goes into a proper litigation hold process can take up an entire chapter, so for now just note that whatever process you put into place, it will have to pass the "giggle" test with the judge and the other side, that is, the process must be reasonable, enforceable, trackable, and implemented in a timely manner when the obligation to preserve is triggered. Telling the judge "well, we

---

205 http://www.insidecounsel.com/2013/08/22/litigation-litigation-hold-101.
206 http://www.btlg.us/News_and_Press/articles/Litigation%20Hold.
207 http://files.www.lawyersmutualnc.com/risk-management-resources/risk-management-handouts/e-discovery-what-litigation-lawyers-need-to-know/eDiscovery.pdf.

sent everyone an email telling them not to delete stuff" is not going to cut it. In fact, the better process now is to have a tool to automate the hold process.[208]

8. **Email.** If you deal with record retention, you know that one of the biggest problem areas is email.[209] I use to tell folks that if an atomic war broke out on earth the only things left would be cockroaches and every stupid email anyone at your company ever wrote. There are two key problems with email with respect to record retention: (a) if employees can save emails to their hard drive, then whatever retention process you put into place regarding the server will not reach those emails, and (b) people treat email like a fleeting private conversation and not like a potentially public business communication, which is what it is—meaning they often don't write exactly what they mean to say or they say it in a way that is not professional in quality or tone. Both (a) and (b) are challenges for the in-house lawyer. With respect to the latter, frequent training of your fellow employees in "writing smart" emails, presentations, instant messages, and the like should be standard procedure.[210] Employees need to know that email is a business document and the company expects employees to prepare them with that in mind. With respect to the former, I admit that I could never come up with a great solution. I suspect that technology is probably starting to catch up with the email storage problem, meaning better and more flexible email archiving tools, the ability to require that employees only use the server for storing emails (and not their hard drives), and tools to flag old emails for determination whether the email needs to be retained or deleted under the policy. Your record retention policy should have a section dedicated to email management. This is definitely an area where speaking with outside vendors might be useful.

9. **Enforce it/Review it.** If your company does not enforce its record retention policy, numerous problems arise, including failing to take advantage of cost savings, risk reduction, and increased efficiency in locating records. You need a set process to enforce the policy. Determine who is responsible for (a) following up on the policy with the different business and staff groups on a regular basis, (b) ensuring data are destroyed when it is time, (c) managing litigation holds, (d) working with the IT department, (e) ensuring new people step up to help manage the policy when others step away or leave the company, (f) publicizing the policy, (g) answering questions, and (h) ensuring that when

---

208 https://www.symantec.com/content/en/us/enterprise/fact_sheets/b-DS_legal_hold_module.en-us.pdf.

209 http://www.ca.com/us/~/media/files/whitepapers/10-steps-email-retention-wp-us_198118.aspx.

210 See page 45.

problems are uncovered they are quickly fixed and appropriate discipline (if any) is meted out. Additionally, legal should work with Internal Audit to periodically audit different groups and parts of the policy to determine what is and what is not working. Lastly, no policy remains relevant in all situations. Establish a process to review the policy annually (with the cross-function team) and discuss whether any changes are needed in the policy (e.g., new government regulation affects a retention period), in the training, in the enforcement, and the like. Feedback from employees (especially those outside the home country) is crucial here, as are the results of any audits. Once again, the culture of your company along with its day-to-day business needs will help you fine-tune the policy. For example, if your company has an expectation that marketing presentations from the last five years need to be available to the business, then it makes no sense to have a policy that requires the destruction of marketing presentations that are more than three years old.

10. **Additional resources**. Record retention is a complex and challenging process. There are sources available to help you prepare and manage your policies. Here are a few:
    - Sedona Conference—Guidelines for Managing Records (and more)[211]
    - ARMA Recordkeeping Principles[212]
    - International Organization for Standardization[213]
    - Outside counsel
    - American Bar Association resources[214]
    - Association of Corporate Counsel (U.S. and International divisions)[215]
    - Colleagues at other companies (or search the Internet for sample policies)
    - Vendors specializing in record retention programs (evaluation, implementation, etc.)

*****

A well-prepared and thought-out record retention policy can be a very helpful tool for the company and for legal. There is no one-size-fits-all policy. If your company is small enough, you may decide no policy is needed other than compliance with

---

[211] http://www.ned.uscourts.gov/internetDocs/cle/2011-01/TSC%20Publications%20Handout.pdf.

[212] http://www.arma.org/r2/standards-amp-best-practices.

[213] http://www.iso.org/iso/home.html.

[214] http://www.americanbar.org/groups/departments_offices/legal_technology_resources/resources/charts_fyis/rm.html.

[215] http://www.acc.com/legalresources/quickcounsel/rr.cfm.

any government or regulatory requirements. That's fine. Don't make your life harder than you have to. Where it is clear a company will benefit from a record retention policy, it is an area where legal can show value, strategic thinking, and leadership. Put updating or creating a policy on your to do list for this year.[216] Stay flexible and focused on what can really work given how your company operates. Don't be deaf to concerns from the business about the policy. Build an inclusive group to help you create and manage the policy—and remember the needs of your business and/or employees located outside the home country. Finally, be sure that your policy is defensible as prudent and reasonable. A good record retention policy can pay big dividends for your company.

January 18, 2016

---

216 See page 295.

Ten Things: Europe's New Data Privacy Law— What You Really Need to Know

You have probably been bombarded with articles, questions, and concerns regarding data privacy and the European Union. Given the sheer volume of material on the topic, it is difficult to figure out what you really need to know about the current state of data privacy and data protection in Europe. We saw the European Court of Justice strike-down the U.S.-EU Safe Harbor agreement in October 2015 (which has been replaced with the new Privacy Shield agreement).[217] We know that the EU approved a new EU-wide data privacy law to go into effect in 2018. The hard part, however, is figuring out what it all means. I will try to sum things up in a useful way so when those questions and concerns come across your desk, you have some ready answers and a road map for the next steps you and your company need to take to ensure compliance with all of the changes in EU data privacy law:

What Happened?

On December 15, 2015, the "powers that be"[218] within the various parts of the government of the EU agreed on the terms of a new data privacy law. The new General Data Protection Regulation[219] will replace the existing EU Data Privacy Directive,[220] adopted back in 1995. Below I will discuss some of the key new provisions but one of the biggest differences between the two pieces of legislation is that the 1995 "Directive" was a "floor," that is, each EU member state[221] was required to implement its own data privacy law with protections *at least* as strong as

---

217 http://www.alstonprivacy.com/faqs-privacy-shield/.
218 http://europa.eu/about-eu/institutions-bodies/.
219 http://data.consilium.europa.eu/doc/document/ST-5419-2016-INIT/en/pdf.
220 http://eur-lex.europa.eu/legal-content/EN/TXT/PDF/?uri=CELEX:31995L0046&from=en.
221 http://europa.eu/about-eu/countries/member-countries/index_en.htm.

set out in the Directive. The member states were free to (and many did) implement stronger protections, leading to a lot of inconsistency across borders. The Regulation, however, is designed to provide a uniform data privacy law that will go into effect across the entire European Union. It will not require action on the part of the member states and it will supersede the Directive (and any member state versions thereof).

May 25, 2018

On May 5, 2016 the Regulation was published in its final form. Under EU law, it will go into effect 2 years and 20 days later, that is, May 25, 2018. In the meanwhile, the 1995 Directive (as implemented by each member state) will still control data privacy in the EU. This means you must continue to comply with the law as set out under the Directive while planning out how to comply with the changes coming under the Regulation, effective in May 2018. Not an easy task.

Time to Get Moving

While two years may seem like an eternity, there are enough substantial changes and new obligations in the Regulation (vs. the Directive) that there is really no time to lose in terms of preparing. If your company processes personal data of EU citizens (or processes personal data in the EU), you need to get moving now. This is a great opportunity for legal to take the lead and help guide the company forward, in particular in terms of analysis of and preparation for the new requirements.

Ten Key Provisions

The Regulation is over 250 pages long, so I am only able to summarize some of the key provisions I think you need to be most concerned with at this point. There will be further guidance provided by the EU (in particular from the Article 29 Working Party) as to what is required under specific provisions. It will be important to stay tuned in to that guidance moving forward:

1. **Who's covered?** Any company processing personal data within the EU and any company that processes the personal data of EU citizens is covered by the Regulation—regardless of where the company or its equipment is located. For example, a company in Canada offering goods and services to EU citizens, for example, via a French language site with euro currency is captured by the new

law. This applies to both data controllers and data processors.[222] This broad sweep of coverage is a huge change from the Directive.

2. **Enforcement.** On its face, there are substantial fines that the EU or relevant Data Protection Authority (DPA) can levy against any company that breaches the provisions of the Regulation. The fines can be up to the greater of €20M or 4 percent of global gross revenue. Likewise, companies will need to cooperate with DPA investigations, including on-site visits. Individuals can bring legal actions against companies in the member state where the individual resides (even if the company is not based in the EU). There is now the possibility of joint and several liability of the controller and the processor; that is, you can be responsible for the actions of other companies you work with regarding the processing of personal data. At a minimum, this means you will need to be keenly aware of your third-party vendors' privacy and data security programs, and you will need to review your contracts with them and ensure that there is complete alignment on obligations and responsibilities.[223] On the positive side, a welcomed change under the Regulation is that it will provide companies with the ability to deal primarily with one DPA in the EU country where the data controller has its main business establishment. Under the Directive, a controller had to deal with multiple DPAs if it processed personal data in more than one EU country.

3. **Data privacy officer.** All companies where data processing is a core activity and all companies processing sensitive data on a large scale will need to formally appoint a data privacy officer (DPO). This applies to both a controller and a processor. A family of companies can have one DPO to act on behalf of the group. The DPO does not have to be an employee of the organization, that is, the DPO can be a third party such as an outside lawyer. DPOs will be responsible for ensuring that their companies properly train their employees on data privacy issues and for ensuring that their company regularly tests, assesses, and evaluates the effectiveness of its data security processes. The quality of such training and testing/evaluation will bear directly on the amount of any fine in the event of a data breach. Employee training is probably the single most effective thing you can do to prevent data breaches or the improper use of personal data.

---

[222] https://ico.org.uk/media/for-organisations/documents/1546/data-controllers-and-data-processors-dp-guidance.pdf.

[223] https://www.linkedin.com/pulse/vendor-risk-managementwhat-you-dont-know-can-hurt-chris-zoladz.

4. **"Right to be forgotten"/access.** You have probably heard of the decision against Google in Spain requiring Google to honor an individual's request that certain data and information about him or her be deleted.[224] This "right to be forgotten" concept is now enshrined in the Regulation and will become an obligation of all companies subject to the law. Surprisingly, the law will require that the company immediately take down the questioned information while it is deciding if the request for permanent deletion is warranted under the law. Similarly, individuals will be able to obtain a copy of their data from you, including the ability to transfer that data to another controller.

5. **Notification of breach.** In the event of a data breach involving personal, unencrypted data, the breach must be reported to the applicable DPA within 72 hours (if feasible), and the company must notify the affected individuals without undue delay when the breach is likely to result in a high risk to the rights and freedoms of those individuals. Processors must notify controllers of data breaches. Bottom line is, if you don't already, you will need to have a plan in place to report data breaches in the EU.

6. **Obligations on data processors.** Data processors (i.e., a party processing data on behalf of a data controller) are now directly regulated under the Regulation. Further, a data processor may not subcontract any of the processing work without the prior specific or general written consent of the data controller. These are big changes from the Directive. Unlike the Directive, the Regulation will place direct liability for violations (with limits) on all data processors and not just the data controller. The Regulation also contains numerous specific contractual obligations that data controllers must impose on their data processors and any subprocessors (and which must be included in any contracts between the parties), as well as new obligations owed by data processors to data controllers (e.g., confidentiality, requests for assistance with responding to data subject rights, notice of breach, detailed descriptions of the processing, privacy impact assessments, demonstrating accountability via record keeping, audits, and return of data postcontract).[225]

7. **Consent.** Where the basis for processing personal data is consent of the individual, such consent must be "freely given, specific, informed, and unambiguous" and "expressed affirmatively." This likely means no burying the "I consent" language deep within the user agreement or relying on preticked boxes. You will need to set up a process to obtain specific consent for any and each use of the personal data. Meaning, aside from collecting and using personal

---

224 http://ec.europa.eu/justice/data-protection/files/factsheets/factsheet_data_protection_en.pdf.
225 http://www.hldataprotection.com/files/2016/03/Hordern-Art-16WDPR02.pdf.

data for the initial stated purpose, any repurposing of the personal data collected will be difficult unless affirmative consent was or is obtained for that repurpose. Furthermore, consent can be withdrawn at any time. Children under the age of 16 require parental permission in order to give consent (though member states may set different ages for this provision, for example, 13 years old in the United Kingdom). All of this will require a new level of detail and transparency with respect to privacy notices on company websites (yes, privacy notices will become even longer and more complicated). Given the issues with consent, it will probably be far easier to rely on other provisions of the Regulation for the legal basis of processing personal data. For example, under Article 6(b), processing is permitted if it is necessary to fulfill the purpose of a contract to which the data subject is a party. If so, processing the personal data of a data subject using an online travel site to book an airline ticket is permitted, so long as the information collected is necessary to complete the transaction. If the online travel company wishes to use the personal information for other purposes, then the data subject would need to affirmatively consent to that other purpose.

8. **Transfers of data outside the EU.** There will still be a prohibition against the transfer of personal data outside of the EU unless (a) there is explicit consent, (b) the transfer is necessary to complete the contract, (c) the destination country provides an "adequate level of data security" (which must be essentially equivalent to the EU framework), (d) the EU model contract clauses are in effect (the use of which no longer need be notified under the Regulation), (e) binding corporate rules (BCRs) are in place (the Regulation explicitly recognizes BCRs), or (f) one of several other new exceptions apply such as approved industry codes of conduct (e.g., a trade association program) or a certification issued by an approved certification body (private or governmental). Note that legal requirements of third countries will not be a valid reason/basis for transfer of data.

The new Privacy Shield agreement provides another legal basis to transfer personal data from the EU to the United States.[226] Unfortunately, there will almost certainly be a legal challenge filed against it, similar to that made against the Safe Harbor agreement leading to the *Schrems*[227] decision last October

---

226 http://www.hldataprotection.com/2016/07/articles/international-eu-privacy/eu-data-transfers-to-the-u-s-considering-your-options-after-privacy-shield/?utm_source=feedburner&utm_medium=-feed&utm_campaign=Feed%3A+ChronicleOfDataProtection+%28HL+Chronicle+of+Data+Protection%29.

227 http://www.nytimes.com/2015/10/07/technology/european-union-us-data-collection.html?_r=0.

(though in my view it is likely that the European Commission took the *Schrems* requirements into account in its review of the Privacy Shield, making it much less likely that a court will strike down the new agreement). During the post-*Schrems* uncertainty, many U.S. companies that previously relied on the Safe Harbor agreement to transfer personal data out of the EU began to utilize other mechanisms to comply with the Directive.[228] The best interim alternative for most has been the "model contract clauses."[229] Given the expected challenge to the Privacy Shield, you should consider having a backup plan in place in the event a legal challenge is successful (but note that even the model clauses are subject to legal challenge as well).[230] And you may decide that living with the model clauses is easier than the enhanced requirements under the Privacy Shield. Finally, while all of the focus is on the United States/European Union, it is difficult to see how personal data transfers from the European Union to Russia, China, India, and other countries will be (are) permitted without massive changes in the laws of those countries to achieve some "essential equivalence" to the Regulation. Stay tuned on that fascinating issue.

9. **Data privacy impact assessments.** Where data controllers or data processors utilize new technologies and there is high risk of data privacy issues, they must conduct a data privacy impact assessment of the new/planned technology, and document their processing operations and information systems. Such documentation must then be available for inspection by a relevant DPA. On a side note, it may simply be a good idea to develop a data privacy impact assessment process regardless.

10. **Obligations around the collection of personal data.** A number of other new principles/obligations will apply to the collection of personal data under the Regulation versus the Directive. In particular, personal data my only be collected for a "specified, explicit and legitimate" purpose and companies will need to enact plans to ensure "data minimization," "privacy by design," "accuracy," "storage limitation," "accountability," "integrity," "pseudonymization/encryption" (where appropriate), and "confidentiality" of personal data. Moreover, there are new restrictions/obligations around using personal data to profile individuals, for example, interests or personal preferences. Finally, the Regulation contains a number of new obligations around the information

---

228 https://www.dataprivacymonitor.com/enforcement/safe-harbor-is-dead-long-live-standard-contractual-clauses/.
229 http://ec.europa.eu/justice/data-protection/international-transfers/transfer/index_en.htm.
230 https://www.privacylaws.com/Publications/enews/International-E-news/Dates/2016/5/Ireland-to-challenge-model-clauses-as-basis-for-international-transfers/.

a controller must provide to an individual before collecting personal data, including the purpose of the processing, the period of time the data will be stored, the identity of any recipients of the data, and the right to a copy and of redress/correction. All of these will add significant operational burdens on companies.

*****

There is a lot more to the Regulation than the provisions summarized above. As you can already see, there will be many places where different officials may interpret the meaning of certain words differently (e.g., "high risk" and "if feasible" in the breach notification section). While it will be a uniform law, there will undoubtedly be "nuance" in how the Regulation is enforced by different DPAs over time, just like under the Directive. Overall the key will be to act in good faith and diligently in terms of trying to comply. It will not be a perfect defense if there are problems, but in my experience regulators recognize when companies try to do the right thing and fail versus those that simply do not try or care at all. It's far better to be in the former category than the latter.

Next Steps

Regardless of whether you agree with it or not, think it is great or think it is the worst kind of government overreaching, the Regulation is here, the Europeans are serious about data privacy and data rights, and the penalties for failing to comply can be substantial. My suggestions are the following steps:

- **Read it.** There is no substitute for reading the Regulation cover to cover. If you deal with data privacy issues, you should have a well-worn, dog-eared, and heavily highlighted copy of the Regulation near your desk.
- **Brief it.** If you haven't already done so, it's time to begin preparing the business (including senior management) for what's coming. Take your time here and be sure you understand what is being proposed and how it will impact your company. Going in to a meeting half-cocked and not understanding the impacts is not a good idea.
- **Follow it.** There will be a lot written about the Regulation over the next two years. Work hard to stay up to date on the latest developments. The International Association of Privacy Professionals has an excellent website and resources that can help you understand the Regulation and the intent behind certain provisions. *See* iapp.org.[231] The European Commission and the new European Data

---

231 https://iapp.org/ (membership may be required to access some of the resources).

Protection Board[232] (along with the existing Article 29 Working Party[233]) will provide guidance, FAQs, and so on as the process moves forward. Finally, many law firms and privacy professionals will be writing and blogging about the Regulation as well.

- **Plan it.** Lastly, you should create a project plan based on your review of the final Regulation and the different requirements as they map to your company's data privacy practices. You (and a cross-company team) will need to focus your efforts first on the gaps. Nothing fancy or complicated is required; a simple matrix (see example below) can keep you—and the business—focused on what needs to be done over the next 18–24 months, and give your C-suite and board of directors comfort that there is a plan in place and you are executing the plan.

ABC company GDPR 18-Month Plan

GDPR $	Summary of Requirements	"TO DO" Steps	Owner	Target Date for Completion	Status/ Completed	Notes

Additional Resources

Here are some additional resources that can provide important information and guidance about the Regulation over the next two years:

Websites
- International Association of Privacy Professionals[234]
- Nymity[235]

---

232 http://www.dataprotectionreport.com/2016/02/2861/.

233 http://ec.europa.eu/justice/data-protection/article-29/index_en.htm.

234 https://iapp.org/.

235 https://www.nymity.com/.

- European Union—Data Protection[236]
- Article 29 Working Party (EU)[237]
- Federal Trade Commission—Privacy and Security[238]

Blogs
- *Chronicle of Data Protection*[239]
- *Privacy Matters*[240]
- *Privacy and Data Security*[241]
- *Data Privacy Monitor*[242]
- *Privacy Law Blog*[243]

May 13, 2016

---

236 http://ec.europa.eu/justice/data-protection/.
237 http://ec.europa.eu/justice/data-protection/article-29/index_en.htm.
238 https://www.ftc.gov/tips-advice/business-center/privacy-and-security.
239 http://www.hldataprotection.com/.
240 http://blogs.dlapiper.com/privacymatters/.
241 http://www.alstonprivacy.com/.
242 https://www.dataprivacymonitor.com/.
243 http://privacylaw.proskauer.com/.

Intellectual Property/Employment

Ten Things: Trade Secrets and Protecting Your Company

How's this for a nightmare scenario: You get a call from the company's chief operating officer informing you that Ms. Smith is leaving the company to go to work for a competitor. You're told she has knowledge and copies of many confidential projects and strategies, including key marketing strategy presentations. The COO wants to know what can be done to protect the company. You tell him not to worry because Ms. Smith signed a confidentiality agreement when she joined the company and therefore everything will be fine. A few days later you need to go back to the COO and tell him everything might not be fine regarding Ms. Smith and, in fact, according to outside counsel, the company has likely failed to do a number of things necessary to protect some of its trade secrets, meaning there may be little that can be done to stop Ms. Smith from divulging those items to her new employer—your competitor.

Pretty awful, right? But, this is exactly the scenario you can find yourself in if the company and the legal department have not been on top of how to best secure trade secrets. Failing to have the right agreements, policies, training, and plans in place could mean a very rough day in the office. While there is never any 100 percent guarantee, there are a number of things you can do as in-house counsel to increase the company's ability to protect itself. Below are ten practical tips for you to put together an action plan to help ensure your trade secrets protection program works:

1. **What is a trade secret?** You bosses probably think everything the company does is a trade secret. Unfortunately, that is not the case. A trade secret is typically (a) something not generally known to the public, (b) where reasonable efforts are made to keep it confidential, and (c) confers some type of economic value to the holder by the information not being known by another party. What exactly constitutes a trade secret can vary by state (in the United States) or by country. Here is a good shorthand for what constitutes a trade secret: any information you would not want your competitors to have. For an excellent discussion of what is (or is not) a trade secret, see Thad Felton's "What Is a

Trade Secret."[244] Some examples of likely trade secrets include new business models, customer and supplier information (especially around price), marketing strategy, processes and formulae, and other confidential business information.

2. **Keep it secret—every day.** Even if you have plans or processes or formulae that you don't want your competitors to have, if the company doesn't take appropriate steps to keep that information confidential, it can lose the ability to claim such items are trade secrets. In the example above, if the company has handed out copies of its future marketing plans to customers without any type of nondisclosure agreement in place or failing to label the plans as "confidential," there may not be any way to keep Ms. Smith from handing those plans over to her new employer. Courts will generally look at the following factors to determine if something is a trade secret: (a) the extent to which the information is known outside of the company, (b) the measures taken to guard the secrecy of the information, (c) the value of the information to competitors, (d) the extent to which the information is known throughout the company's employee base and others involved in the business, and (e) money or effort spent by the company to develop the information and how easy would it be for others to duplicate the information.

3. **Catalogue your trade secrets.** The first thing to do is to inventory all of the company's trade secrets. This does not mean a list of patents or trademarks. While such assets are protected by law, they are publicly disclosed and therefore not confidential. You should interview key company employees and executives around what they believe are trade secrets (you should also talk with your in-house legal team as they will have input as well) and match that against the definition above. By creating an inventory of what is considered a trade secret you can (a) identify what steps are needed to keep those specific items confidential and protected, and (b) be clear with the business what items are not considered trade secrets (i.e., set expectations so there are fewer painful discussions about what the COO *thought* was a trade secret versus what actually *is* a trade secret). For a great discussion around how to inventory trade secrets, economic impact of theft, and likely threats, see the 2014 PwC report entitled "Economic Impact of Trade Secret Theft."[245]

4. **Have the right agreements in place.** Core to any strategy to maintain trade secrets is ensuring you have several key agreements in place and that you regularly review and update those documents as circumstances warrant. First,

---

244 http://documents.lexology.com/c48908c7-c18a-4a8a-9198-321e0b6dc6f3.pdf.
245 http://www.pwc.com/us/en/forensic-services/publications/assets/economic-impact.pdf.

courts will want to see such agreements in place as part of its analysis of whether the company took the proper steps to maintain confidentiality. Second, provisions drafted ten years ago probably do not cover new situations and circumstances such as social media or smartphones. Now is a good time to review and refresh your contractual protections (and don't forget to consider having the agreements available in foreign languages to increase your ability to enforce the provisions outside your home country). The core agreements include (a) noncompete agreements (to prevent key employees from working for a competitor), (b) non-solicitation agreements (to prevent former employees from cherry-picking company employees with offers of a new job), (c) nondisclosure/confidentiality agreements (both internal and for use with third parties), and (d) work from home or telecommuting agreements (ensuring the employees are aware of expectations around confidentiality when they work remotely).

In the example above, if the company has a valid noncompete in place, it is unlikely Ms. Smith is heading out the door to work for a competitor in the first place.

As you review your existing agreements or create new ones, keep in mind that the enforceability of these types of agreements (especially noncompetes) can vary wildly depending on the jurisdiction. You can try a one-size-fits-all approach, but you should not take comfort that an agreement that is, for example, perfectly enforceable in Texas will be enforceable in North Dakota (which prohibits most noncompetes) or in Latin America, Europe, and other countries. It would be wise to spend a few dollars with outside counsel as part of the update process to best ensure that each of the agreements you are putting in place is state of the art and is enforceable in the most locations/jurisdictions you care most about. Moreover, now that the United States has implemented the new "Defend Trade Secrets Act,"[246] there are additional obligations on businesses around language in employee and vendor contracts, where those contracts deal with trade secrets. If the "magic" language is not present, the full benefits of the "DTSA" are not available.[247]

5. **Have the right policies in place.** The next step is to ensure that you have the right policies in place to educate employees and prevent leaks of your trade secrets and to best ensure you can convince a court that the company was taking

---

246 https://www.linkedin.com/pulse/guide-comparing-new-us-trade-secrets-law-eu-directive-sterling-miller?trk=mp-author-card.

247 https://www.linkedin.com/pulse/notifying-your-employees-under-new-defense-trade-secrets-miller?trk=mp-author-card.

the right steps to keep its trade secrets "secret." Proper policies should include discussions on the following:
- Proper marking of documents and materials deemed confidential.
- Social media (e.g., what employees should not discuss about the company's plans on social media).
- Limiting disclosures to those with a need to know.
- Visitors to the office (including the need for escorts and sign-in agreements whereby the visitor acknowledges obligations around confidentiality).
- "Clean desk" policies and policies around proper storage/disposal of confidential material.
- Password and information security (including the potential disabling of USB ports).
- The removal of confidential information from the premises.
- Security cameras and building access control.
- Work from home (including use of VPN networks, firewalls, passwords, etc.) policies.
- Email use/use of company computers (and companies' right of access to all emails).
- Bring your own device procedures and requirements around security of information (including smart phones).
- Procedures for providing confidential information to third parties (including need for a nondisclosure agreement).
- Procedures around on-boarding/off-boarding employees.

This is another area where spending money with outside counsel regarding your company's policies would be a worthwhile investment.

6. **Training.** It's one thing to have the right agreements and policies in place, but if your employees are not taught how to protect trade secrets nor regularly reminded about protecting company secrets, you may not be taking the steps necessary to convince a court that you are investing enough to protect your trade secrets. Putting in place a comprehensive training program around confidentiality, information security, and trade secrets will go far in convincing a court that your company is serious about its confidential information. The best training will include examples of things your company believes are trade secrets. Training should be conducted for all new hires and yearly for other employees. You can conduct most training via an online program. Better yet, add several live training events every year (including webcasts) where members of the legal department discuss trade secrets and confidentiality directly with employees. There are a number of third-party vendors who can help you set up an online training program. Likewise, regular company-wide email reminders from the legal department about trade secrets and confidentiality will

be helpful as well (and be sure to require that employees acknowledge they got the message and understand its contents). You and your team should be on the lookout for potential problem areas, including giving reminders—gentle at first—to colleagues who trip up (e.g., forget to mark confidential documents properly). View these as teaching moments and an opportunity to provide additional value to the company. Your ultimate goal should be to develop a strong company-wide culture around confidentiality and protecting trade secrets.

7. **Mark confidential documents as "Confidential."** One of the easiest ways to help ensure that confidential documents and materials will be treated as such is to develop a process whereby employees clearly mark such materials as "Confidential" or "Contains Trade Secrets" or some other moniker that will make it absolutely clear that the materials should be treated as a trade secret and extra care is needed in terms of distribution and storage of these materials. Similarly, if there are meetings where confidential information is going to be discussed, a reminder at the beginning of the meeting about the nature of the information is helpful, along with picking up and properly disposing of any confidential materials handed out at the meeting (assuming they are not otherwise needed by the attendees).

8. **Warning signs.** Managers, legal, HR, and others should receive basic training on "red flags" to look for in terms of determining whether an employee[248] (or visitor) is a risk to take or disclose company trade secrets. Unhappy employees are among the biggest risks. For example, employees who have received layoff notices, were passed over for promotion, refuse exit interviews, or are required to follow a performance improvement plan may warrant closer observation. You should prepare a checklist of things to look for. The FBI has produced a helpful publication on this topic called "Insider Threat: An Introduction to Detecting and Deterring an Insider Spy."[249] Here are some of warning signs the FBI notes with respect to an employee possibly stealing secrets from the company:
    - *Without need or authorization, takes proprietary or other material home via documents, thumb drives, computer disks, or email; inappropriately seeks or obtains proprietary or classified information on subjects not related to their work duties.*
    - *Interest in matters outside the scope of their duties, particularly those of interest to foreign entities or business competitors.*

---

248 https://www.linkedin.com/pulse/steps-protect-your-trade-secrets-from-theft-sterling-miller?trk=mp-author-card.

249 https://www.fbi.gov/about-us/investigate/counterintelligence/the-insider-threat.

- *Unnecessarily copies material, especially if it is proprietary or classified.*
- *Disregards company computer policies on installing personal software or hardware, accessing restricted websites, conducting unauthorized searches, or downloading confidential information.*
- *Works odd hours without authorization; notable enthusiasm for overtime work, weekend work, or unusual schedules when clandestine activities could be more easily conducted.*
- *Unreported foreign contacts (particularly with foreign government officials or intelligence officials) or unreported overseas travel.*
- *Short trips to foreign countries for unexplained or strange reasons; unexplained affluence; buys things that they cannot afford on their household income.*
- *Engages in suspicious personal contacts, such as with competitors, business partners, or other unauthorized individuals.*
- *Overwhelmed by life crises or career disappointments.*
- *Concern that they are being investigated; leaves traps to detect searches of their work area or home; searches for listening devices or cameras.*

9. **Exit interviews.** It is very important to have a proper exit interview process in place as departing employees constitute one of your biggest risks in the area of trade secrets. You should work with the HR team to develop a checklist that ensures the following:
   - Departing employees receive a copy of any confidentiality agreement, non-compete, non-solicitation agreement, and any other important agreements that they signed during their employment with the company along with the company's trade secret policy. The employee should sign a document acknowledging any ongoing obligations.
   - Reminders about obligations of the employee around trade secrets and confidentiality postemployment.
   - Determining whether the employee has any company information at home (hard copy or soft) or stored on any cloud system.
   - Determining whether the employee is going to work at a competitor and plans on engaging in any competitive activity (if so, that should trigger several additional steps, such as, noncompete enforcement). If you know the employee is going to work at a competitor (and there is no noncompete in place), you should consider a short, nonhostile business letter to the competitor's legal and HR departments explaining that the departing employee has confidentiality obligations and you expect their help in ensuring the employee honors those obligations and will take steps to ensure the employee does not breach any obligations owed to your company in their new job. Most companies will respect such a letter and take steps to ensure compliance

- Employee surrenders all company property including smartphone, laptop, documents, files, materials, and others (and signs an acknowledgment that he/she has returned all such items and has not kept copies or provided copies to anyone).
- Termination (immediately) of all passwords, access to information systems/email, identification badge/access to buildings, parking cards, and the like.
- If there is reason to suspect the employee is a risk of potential misappropriation of company trade secrets, a search of his/her email, hard-drive, computer files, and voice mail for any improper activity.

10. **Have a plan.** You have your new agreements, state-of-the-art policies, and a well-trained work force, but it's all for naught unless you have a plan for what to do when your trade secrets are threatened. Here are some things to consider to plan for when trouble hits:
    - A strong relationship with HR, information security, and internal audit is very helpful. Legal should work in concert with these other groups to ensure plenty of communication in the event they see, feel, or hear of trouble (e.g., via an exit interview, investigation, or "water cooler talk"). Getting this group together in advance to map out in writing what to do and how everyone will work together if there is a trade secrets breach is job one.
    - Have your outside counsel advisors lined up in advance. Know whom you will call in the event you need immediate legal action (e.g., a temporary restraining order) or advice. Ideally, it will be a firm you have already partnered with in terms of preparing and updating the agreements and policies discussed above. Don't forget counsel in foreign countries.
    - Have a good system in place to gather necessary agreements signed by the breaching employee, applicable policies, and so on. Counsel will need this for numerous reasons.
    - Work out in advance with information security whom to call to terminate system access and revoke passwords and building access. Also, know whom to speak with if you need to preserve hard drives or have email searched. Time will likely be of the essence in the event of a trade secret breach. Be sure to have backup numbers.
    - Think through your potential legal claims (especially by what is available by geography), so when you are asked "what can we do," you have some parameters you've already investigated. This doesn't mean they will all be available as you gather the facts, but it will be a lot better than saying "we'll need to look into that and get back to you" given that management will be somewhat frantic if they think trade secrets are walking out the door.

Potential claims include Defend Trade Secrets Act,[250] breach of trade secrets statute/law or unfair competition law (e.g., the Lanham Act or the Uniform Trade Secrets Act, which has been adopted by 46 states in the United States), misappropriation of trade secrets[251] (tort), breach of contract,[252] breach of fiduciary duty, tortious interference with business relations, unjust enrichment, inevitable disclosure (which is losing steam as a valid claim), criminal claims, etc. You should have a good idea of your options in your principal business locations.

- Be ready to contact the party that received your confidential information and ask that your trade secrets be returned immediately and/or destroyed, along with an acknowledgment that they have done so. This can be especially effective if the disclosure is inadvertent.
- Know whom to contact at local law enforcement and the FBI in the event of a computer crime or theft of trade secrets.
- Revisit your trade secret program at least once a year and update as necessary.

*****

Being prepared for a trade secret breach should be one of your key goals for the year. Prevention is key because once a trade secret is revealed, it may be too late to undo the harm. If you or your team haven't thought about this issue in a while, now is the perfect time to dust things off. This is a tricky area of the law, so experienced outside counsel can add a lot of value to your efforts.

March 19, 2015

---

250 http://www.ipwatchdog.com/2016/05/23/defend-trade-secrets-act-2016-creates-federal-jurisdiction-trade-secret-litigation/id=69245/.
251 http://www.dmlp.org/legal-guide/basics-trade-secret-claim.
252 http://www.ndasforfree.com/4StepstoTake.html.

Ten Things: Protecting Your Company's Reputation and Brand

It's a nice spring Friday morning. You arrived at the office earlier than usual and are settling into your chair with a big cup of coffee. You are expecting a slow day and want to catch up on some legal articles and other administrative items and then hopefully leave early to get a head start on a peaceful weekend. Then the phone rings. It's the CEO and she is very upset. Someone has posted very negative and untrue things about the company on a consumer complaint website and she wants you to do something about it. Now. Then your instant messenger box pops up. It's the head of HR and she's asking you to call her immediately because an employee has just tweeted something "really stupid" on the company's Twitter account, and it's about to blow up in the media and she needs your advice as soon as possible. At the same time you glance at your email and see "Urgent—someone's illegally using our trademarks!" in the subject line of an email from Bart in marketing. You put your coffee mug down, rub your face, and realize you are not going to be heading out early or catching up on any articles today.

While the early morning "perfect storm" scenario described above is unlikely to occur, things can go sideways very quickly when someone launches attacks on your company's reputation and brand. This is especially true in these days of 24/7 media and the "Wild West" of the Internet and social media. One of the most important jobs in-house counsel has is to protect your company's reputation and brand. Why? Because customers won't buy from a company they don't like, investors do not invest in companies that have bad reputations or cannot protect their brands, and employees do not want to work for a company they don't feel good about. If it's bad enough, a hit to the brand or reputation can cost the company multimillions of dollars. Here are ten steps you can take now to prepare for and defend against attacks on your company's brand and reputation:

1. **Set the right tone at the top.** You're probably tired of hearing this but it's true: Everything about reputation and brand starts at the top. How the C-suite behaves and acts will roll through the entire organization. If your executives

do not cut corners and do not play loose with the rules, odds are very good that the organization generally will not do so either. This means counseling senior management to take every opportunity (town halls, staff meetings, emails) to communicate and emphasize to employees how important it is to act ethically and to be vigilant as to how their behavior can negatively impact the company's reputation and brand. You don't need to be "preachy" about it, but the legal department should help lead the way here both with respect to coaching senior management and with respect to helping employees understand the rules of the road via messaging, training, and real-life examples of how company reputations can be damaged quickly (see, e.g., the New England Patriots and "Inflate-gate"). As the quote goes "It takes 20 years to build a reputation and five minutes to ruin it."

2. **Protect your company via trademarks, copyrights, and domain names.** There are many ways to protect the intellectual property of the company (e.g., patents and trade secrets). But, when it comes to brands (names, marks, or content), the two most important are trademarks and copyrights.[253] You should have a solid strategy[254] in place to apply for and maintain both. The same is true for licensing[255] any of your marks. With respect to trademarks, it is important you ensure that your employees (and licensees) are using the marks properly. A failure to do so[256] can result in your company losing the mark as diluted[257] or as generic or abandoned.[258] Regarding domain names and company websites, watch out for cyber-squatters[259] and spoofing.[260] In addition to taking various avenues of legal action,[261] consider buying up the variations and common misspellings of the company's domain names so those cannot be used by a competitor or someone looking to harm the company. Recently, many companies have begun buying the domain name extension ".sucks" so as to prevent third parties from using it to create a website featuring negative

---

253 http://www.lawmart.com/forms/difference.htm.
254 http://www.inta.org/TrademarkBasics/FactSheets/Pages/TrademarkPortfolioManagementStrategies.aspx.
255 https://ribbs.usps.gov/forms/documents/tech_guides/GUIDELINES_TO_TRADEMARK_USE.PDF.
256 http://www.ggmark.com/guide.html.
257 http://www.inta.org/TrademarkBasics/FactSheets/Pages/TrademarkDilution.aspx.
258 http://www.inta.org/TrademarkBasics/FactSheets/Pages/LossofTrademarkRightsFactSheet.aspx.
259 http://www.nolo.com/legal-encyclopedia/cybersquatting-what-what-can-be-29778.html.
260 http://www.phishing.org/resources/phishing-spoofing/.
261 http://www.nolo.com/legal-encyclopedia/cybersquatting-what-what-can-be-29778.html.

comments and stories about the company. Similarly, if someone is spoofing your website or email, you need to move quickly to stop it, including working with law enforcement, contacting the domain registrars and ISP providers immediately, and putting a notice on your actual website (and other channels) to warn customers about the fraud. You should have your process (e.g., whom to contact) to stop cyber-squatters and website spoofing already laid out in advance of any problems.

3. **Have a robust social media policy.** Today every company should have a social media policy[262] and make sure its executives and employees are trained on its provisions. At a minimum, you need to set out the rules for your employees using social media on behalf of the company or using their own personal accounts to discuss issues related to the company. A social media policy should cover, among many other things, expectations around posting content that can be misconstrued. Enthusiasm is great, but undirected it can cause major headaches. As an example, some of you may recall a Tweet from a Houston Rockets employee (using the official Houston Rockets Twitter account) as the Rockets closed out its 2015 opening round NBA playoff series against Dallas. The Tweet featured a picture of a horse with a picture of a gun aimed at its head with the words:

"Shhhhh. Just close your eyes. It will all be over soon."

While it was done as a ribbing of the Dallas Mavericks (and I am a huge Mavericks fan who took it exactly that way), it was not well received by the general public. The employee was fired,[263] and many lessons were once again learned about how humor does not always translate well outside the walls of the company. There are many other examples out there that you can use to train and remind your own employees about the risks of a poorly worded or poorly thought-out Tweet. Remember, however, that your social media policy must make exceptions and be clear around what employees may write on their personal social media accounts about the company so as to comply with recent guidance[264] from the National Labor Relations Board. Take a look

---

262 http://www.ccsstrategies.com/userfiles/files/Legal%20Considerations%20with%20Social%20Media.pdf.

263 http://www.al.com/sports/index.ssf/2015/04/houston_rockets_social_media_m.html.

264 http://www.natlawreview.com/article/nlrb-continues-aggressive-crackdown-social-media-policies.

at "5 Terrific Examples of Company Social Media Policies" for examples of top-notch social media policies.[265]

4. **Monitor the Internet and social media.** Having a social media policy is great, but in order to protect your company, you need to develop a systematic way to monitor the Internet and social media for attacks. This can be done in legal or in marketing or in corporate communications. The key is to have someone responsible for checking the Internet and social media every day and making sure that all employees know where to go in the event they see something on the Internet or social media that is potentially damaging to the company. One easy (and free) way to monitor things is to go online and create a Google Alert, Bing Alert, Yahoo! Alert, or Twitter Alert and put your company's name or a particular product or whatever it is that you want to monitor as the keyword that trips an alert being emailed to you.

5. **Be aggressive in defending your reputation and brands (part I).** If you do see your brand or reputation being attacked, it is important to not sit back and let things play out. You need to take some action immediately. Being aggressive, however, does not mean you have to be in attack dog mode from the get go. Most in-house lawyers have gotten a "nasty gram" from another company's legal department or law firm complaining about this or that. Often you think "if they had just called me and been nice we could have solved this in five minutes." Instead, a nasty letter or email usually results in an equally nasty or snarky response. And then it can be off to the races before cooler heads prevail. A great example of a company that was aggressive in terms of being proactive but also thoughtful about how its actions may be portrayed in the media/publicly is the Jack Daniel's company. In 2012 the company saw an author using something very similar to their distinctive trademarked "Old No. 7" label on the cover of his book.[266] Instead of blasting off a legal bazooka, the in-house attorney stole a line from the movie *Road House* and was "nice."

Not only did the nice letter solve the problem without further effort or expenditure by the company, it also helped foster the brand[267] of Jack Daniel's in a positive manner. It is also a reminder that whatever "cease and desist" letter

---

265 http://blog.hirerabbit.com/5-terrific-examples-of-company-social-media-policies/.
266 http://www.huffingtonpost.com/2012/07/23/jack-daniels-book-cover_n_1696453.html.
267 www.businessinsider.com/jack-daniels-wrote-what-has-to-be-the-nicest-cease-and-desist-order-of-all-time-2012-7.

you send out will likely find its way online. And sometimes that is not a good thing. In fact, you may make to the trademarks' "Hall of Shame."[268]

July 12, 2012

VIA EMAIL ONLY

Mr. Patrick Wensink
Louisville, KY
patrickwensink@gmail.com

Re: Mark: **JACK DANIEL'S**
    Subject: Use of Trademarks

Dear Mr. Wensink:

I am an attorney at Jack Daniel's Properties, Inc. ("JDPI") in California. JDPI is the owner of the JACK DANIEL'S trademarks (the "Marks") which have been used extensively and for many years in connection with our well-known Tennessee whiskey product and a wide variety of consumer merchandise.

It has recently come to our attention that the cover of your book *Broken Piano for President*, bears a design that closely mimics the style and distinctive elements of the JACK DANIEL'S trademarks. An image of the cover is set forth below for ease of reference.

We are certainly flattered by your affection for the brand, but while we can appreciate the pop culture appeal of Jack Daniel's, we also have to be diligent to ensure that the Jack Daniel's trademarks are used correctly. Given the brand's popularity, it will probably come as no surprise that we come across designs like this on a regular basis. What may not be so apparent, however, is that if we allow uses like this one, we run the very real risk that our trademark will be weakened. As a fan of the brand, I'm sure that is not something you intended or would want to see happen.

As an author, you can certainly understand our position and the need to contact you. You may even have run into similar problems with your own intellectual property.

In order to resolve this matter, because you are both a Louisville "neighbor" and a fan of the brand, we simply request that you change the cover design when the book is re-printed. If you would be willing to change the design sooner than that (including on the digital version), we would be willing to contribute a reasonable amount towards the costs of doing so. By taking this step, you will help us to ensure that the Jack Daniel's brand will mean as much to future generations as it does today.

We wish you continued success with your writing and we look forward to hearing from you at your earliest convenience. A response by **July 23, 2012** would be appreciated, if possible. In the meantime, if you have any questions or concerns, please do not hesitate to contact me.

Sincerely,

Christy Susman
Senior Attorney - Trademarks

JACK DANIEL'S PROPERTIES, INC.
4040 CIVIC CENTER DRIVE • SUITE 528 • SAN RAFAEL, CALIFORNIA 94903
TELEPHONE: (415) 446-5225 • FAX (415) 446-5230

6. **Be aggressive in defending your reputation and brands (part II).** Sometimes, as Patrick Swayze said in the movie *Road House*, you can't be nice. And when those times arrive you need to look for the best way to quickly and efficiently solve the issue involving your reputation and brands. You can, of

---

268 http://www.tabberone.com/Trademarks/HallOfShame/HallOfShame.shtml.

course, file a lawsuit[269] alleging some type of defamation, Lanham Act violation, or actions for trademark or copyright infringement. There are, however, other options out there that you may not be aware of. If a competitor of yours engages in some type of advertising comparing their product or service directly to yours, and does so in a manner you think is unfair or not truthful, consider filing a complaint with the National Advertising Division (NAD)[270] of the Better Business Bureau rather than filing a lawsuit. The NAD offers review by experienced attorneys who apply precedent to determine whether the advertising claims are truthful and non-misleading. The parties submit briefs and there may or may not be a hearing. There is no discovery process, which greatly reduces costs and shortens the time to resolution. You can appeal and you can file a counter claim. A press release is issued with all decisions but neither party may use the proceedings for publicity during or after the case. Compliance is optional (which sounds like a big hole) but advertisers generally comply, and if not, the NAD may forward the case to the Federal Trade Commission for action (something you should really avoid). Another avenue is asking the site to take down the offending post or material. If it involves the improper use of one of your copyrights, you can send a takedown notice under the Digital Millennium Copyright Act.[271] Additionally, most sites and search engines have a process to at least request that material be taken down. For example a false and/or defamatory consumer review may be removed from "Pissed Consumer"[272] if you can provide[273] either a court order (e.g., a temporary restraining order) or if the author submits a notarized letter asking to have the content removed. Similarly, Google has a process[274] to ask it to take down certain content. While it's unlikely to work in most cases, start with reviewing the website's terms of use and understand the process to make a complaint and try to get the content removed.

---

269 http://www.americanbar.org/content/dam/aba/events/entertainment_sports/2012/10/forum_on_the_entertainmentsportsindustries2012annualmeeting/lmbd/when_bad_things_happen_to_good_brands_2.authcheckdam.pdf.

270 http://www.bbb.org/council/the-national-partner-program/national-advertising-review-services/national-advertising-division/.

271 http://www.thelawtog.com/the-dmca-takedown-how-to-protect-your-copyright/.

272 http://www.pissedconsumer.com/.

273 http://www.pissedconsumer.com/static/publications/pissed-consumer-questions-and-answers-faq-2.html.

274 https://support.google.com/legal/answer/3110420?hl=en.

7. **Escalate problems and follow through solving them.** In your role as in-house counsel, you will be in a unique position to see things (programs, ideas, actions, investigations, etc.) that could turn into something very bad for your company's reputation and brand. Generally, you will not need to depend on your legal training to spot these issues. Your degree from the "College of Common Sense" will tell you when something needs to be explored more deeply and when you need to escalate a problem. Once you escalate a serious problem, follow through to make sure something has been done to solve the problem (or if not, why not). One of the best recent examples of this (and one you can use as an example of why you need to follow up on problems) is the controversy involving General Motors ("GM") and cars with faulty ignition switches,[275] which has led to numerous deaths, a billion dollars in recalls, over $35 million in fines, an as-of-yet unknown amount of civil damages from dozens of lawsuits, and a very dark black eye on one of the most respected and revered American companies. There is a lot to the story and many points of failure, but to keep it simple here is the part I found most disturbing: the lawyers in the GM legal department knew about the problems in 2004. No one told the general counsel about the problems until 2013. If you are the general counsel, you must train your team and foster an atmosphere where serious problems (e.g., deaths of customers) make it to your desk immediately. Had the general counsel known of the problems back in 2004, the investigation or remedial steps taken may have been different and more timely and GM's reputation (and economic health) could have taken a much smaller hit.

8. **Build a "reputation" response team.** You cannot do any of this alone, either as an individual attorney or as the legal department. It takes a broad group of individuals and cross section of business teams and staff groups to handle a serious problem with respect to reputation and brand. As always, you should be proactive and thinking ahead as to what the response team should look like, who should be on it, and what its charter should be, *before* there is a problem. If you try to create the team on the fly during a crisis, you will find yourself seriously behind the curve. Your response team should include senior business leaders, legal, corporate communications, investor relations (if publicly traded), marketing, and HR (in case the problem involves actions of an employee). All of these folks should be identified in advance and trained before there is ever a need to use the group. From the outside, you will likely want to identify

---

275 http://www.insidecounsel.com/2015/05/11/lessons-counsel-should-learn-from-the-gm-ignition?eNL=5550aa39150ba03f6222c5b3&utm_source=ic&utm_medium=email&utm_campaign=icscoopenews&_LID=173517506&slreturn=1467433680.

a reputation management expert[276] and outside counsel you would use in case of a serious problem. Create and maintain a list of everyone and their various contact information and distribute it to team members. All of the C-suite should be briefed on the response team and know whom to contact if there is an issue. The board of directors may need to be briefed on the response team and its function as well.

9. **Institutionalize your social media accounts.** You must ensure that the company owns and controls *all* of its social media accounts and has a process in place to ensure transition of responsibilities, passwords, list of accounts, and so on as employees come and go into roles involving the use of these accounts. Given the relative newness of social media, many company social media accounts are in the name of the individual who set them up and/or is in charge of social media marketing. There are many stories[277] regarding employees leaving a company and taking the Twitter or Facebook accounts (dedicated to promoting the company) with them. Ask yourself this: does legal know who owns all of the company's social media accounts? If the answer is "no," it's time to take action. Be sure your social media policy[278] clearly states that all such accounts are the property of the company and that the employee must turn over the account, passwords, and other key information when departing the company.

10. **Know when to speak out/when to keep quiet.** All companies need to know when it's time to speak out to defend their brand and reputation, and when it's time to stay silent. This is more art than a science. Still, if there is major negative publicity about your company, you need to say something. It is important, however, to know when to stay quiet or not overplay your hand. First, you do not want to get ahead of the facts. For example, in 2015 Blue Bell Creameries dealt with several fits and starts as the facts trickled out about *Listeria* in its ice cream, with each day adding to new revelations about what Blue Bell knew and when did it know it. Similarly, if a customer or blogger has unfairly attacked your company, do not engage in a give-and-take with that person as that will only keep the story alive and, most likely, increase the ranking of the story in search engines. Instead, there are several things you should and should

---

276 http://www.elixirinteractive.com/media/pdf/whitepapers/ElixirInteractiveDigitalStrategyandTacticsforBrandReputationManagement.pdf.

277 http://inthemix.on-premise.com/2013/10/who-owns-your-social-media-account-and-followers-when-your-employee-leaves/.

278 http://hr.blr.com/HR-news/HR-Administration/Employee-Privacy/Who-really-owns-your-companys-social-media-account.

not do[279] including the following: (a) Posting your side of the story on your own website—this will allow you to control your story, including making corrections or additions as needed, and will not help increase the ranking of the negative comments in search engines. (b) Contacting the website about taking down the false complaint or at least allow you to dispute it on the site. If the latter, keep your rebuttal short and do not raise to the bait if the complainer posts a response. (c) If the complaint is showing up in the top 10 to 20 search results about your company, consider pushing out or creating more positive content about your company (stories, press releases, announcements, customer testimonials) so that search engines pick up that side of the equation and you potentially push the defamatory material lower in the search results. Your corporate communications team will be invaluable here.

*****

We've only scratched the surface regarding ways to protect your company's brand and reputation. As always a big part of what you should be doing now is planning in advance of a problem. Legal should take the lead in getting the process under way or, if there is such a process in place already, ensuring that it works as planned and that time is spent every year keeping it current. If you do that, you may just be able to enjoy that Friday morning cup of coffee!

May 15, 2015

---

[279] http://www.elixirinteractivecomplaints.com/online-reputation-management-best-practices/.

Ten Things: Website User Agreements

You're reading through some notes for your meeting with the CEO later today when you get an email from your head of litigation: the company has just been sued for $25 million in a class action in another state's defendant "hellhole" over some products it sells on its website. The email says, "don't worry, we should be in good shape because we have a strong user agreement that protects the company in a number of ways from lawsuits like these." You're relieved to read this but then you start thinking—you've never really read your company's user agreement and you have literally no idea what it says, how it works or, more importantly, whether it is enforceable. If this describes you, you're not alone but don't worry. Below I will discuss website user agreements and ten things you can do to understand them and make them as protective and bulletproof as possible.

Almost every company of significant size has a website. If your company operates a website, then you probably have a user agreement (also called "terms of use," "conditions of use," "terms of service," or "legal"). If you're not sure, go to your company's website and scroll to the very, very bottom (i.e., the "Siberia" of the web page). You should see some tiny hyperlinks across the page. One of those links will probably say "user agreement" or something similar. If you don't see one, it's time to get one in place. If you do see one, click on it and read on! As you read through your user agreement or consider creating one, here are some key things to keep top of mind:

1. **Do we need a user agreement?** If your company sells goods and services over the Internet, collects data from users, provides a forum for users to post content or buy and sell goods and services, or otherwise engages in commerce online, you need a user agreement. A user agreement defines the rights of the user and the website owner (i.e., your company), protects the interests of the website owner, limits legal obligations of the owner, sets out how disputes will be handled and where and under what law, provides for indemnity to the company, and governs IP rights and acceptable use of the site, and a host of

other important things. If your company's website is *solely* for purposes of providing information and is not for transacting any business nor gathering any data, then you can probably go forward without a user agreement but the better course of action for any business is to have some statement of the conditions of use of their website.

2. **Where do I begin?** First, grab a cup of coffee or a Diet Coke, get comfortable, and read your company's user agreement—start to finish. When was the last time it was updated? Does it still address the key elements of your business? Is it clear and easy to understand (could your mom understand it)? Does it contain the most recent and up-to-date language regarding dispute resolution, limitations on liability, and so on? Second, take a look at some third-party user agreements. Start with those of your competitors. What clauses do they have and how does your agreement compare? Then check out some noncompetitor companies (e.g., sites you visit a lot) and see how their user agreements work. Third, after you get the lay of the land, set up a cross-business team to meet and discuss the user agreement and any changes or updates needed to give your company the best agreement with the most protection. This team will involve the CIO and people from legal, marketing, and business operations. There will likely be others needed and you can figure that out as you move along in the process. Once you get the group together, schedule at least a yearly review of your user agreement to keep it up-to-date going forward.

3. **Is my user agreement enforceable?** This is the million dollar question (literally). The keys to an enforceable user agreement come down to "notice" to and "acceptance" by the user. Did the user have a chance to read and review the user agreement and give some form of consent? If not, you can have the best user agreement in the world but it's useless (and that is not a fun conversation with the C-suite). User agreements are unique because they are contracts processed completely online, they change frequently, and you will not have a physical signature to prove acceptance. Two types of user agreements have emerged: "browserwrap" or "clickwrap." Clickwrap[280] is by far better choice. A clickwrap user agreement requires the users to take some type of affirmative action to acknowledge their consent. Typically, they need to tick a box affirming that they have read and agree to the terms. An even stronger type of clickwrap requires the users to scroll through the user agreement before they have the ability to accept it. The more steps the user must take to "agree,"

---

280 https://termsfeed.com/blog/browsewrap-clickwrap/.

the stronger the odds of enforcing the agreement. Browserwrap[281] agreements, on the other hand, are typically notices or a hyperlink stating something like "by using the site you agree to the terms of use." Courts can be hostile to these types of agreements, especially where the user can complete whatever business they have on the website without having to read or accept the terms. Some businesses favor browserwrap over clickwrap because the former provides less reason for the customer to click away to another site, that is, it's less hassle. If you are going to go with browserwrap be sure to (a) have the agreement link prominently displayed at the top of the page, immediately visible when the user opens your site; (b) make the wording/link a different (bigger) font size and a different color so it stands out; and (c) make sure there is prominent notice/wording that the user is bound by the website legal agreements. Even if you do these things, courts are inconsistent[282] on the enforceability of browserwrap user agreements, which is why clickwrap is a better path.[283]

4. **How do I prove the user agreed to my agreement?** If you are sued by a user can you quickly do the following: (a) know when the user accepted the agreement, (b) prove (technically) that the user accepted, (c) know which version of the user agreement the user accepted (and have copies of all versions of the user agreement), (d) show when modifications to the user agreement were made, and (e) show when the user accepted any modifications? If the answer to these questions is "yes," you are way ahead of the curve. If the answer is "no," then you may not be able to prove that the user agreed to your agreement and all of the elaborate protections you drafted go right out the window. If you are in the latter situation, it's time to sit down with the developers and get the right process in place. In a pinch, you may be able to reconstruct the agreement history by using hard copies you saved of the different versions of the agreement, or locating copies of your website pages from past dates via the Wayback machine at www.Archive.org. That said, don't pin the company's legal strategy on the Wayback machine.

5. **Forum selection/Choice of law.** Take advantage of both of these clauses to best protect your company. A forum selection clause is an agreement as to where any litigation or dispute resolution will be heard. A company typically wants the forum to be in its local courts, for example, the state and federal

---

281 http://blog.ericgoldman.org/archives/2014/08/whats-a-browsewrap-the-ninth-circuit-sure-doesnt-know-nguyen-v-barnes-noble.htm.
282 https://www.venable.com/your-website-terms-of-service-are-unenforceable-11-06-2014/.
283 http://www.sociallyawareblog.com/2016/02/22/clickwrap-browsewrap-and-mixed-media-contracts-a-few-words-can-go-a-long-way/.

courts located in Austin, Texas, or Philadelphia, Pennsylvania. The same is true for arbitration hearings (more on that below). A choice of law provision sets forth which law applies, for example New York law or Utah law. You can have the laws of one state apply in a lawsuit pending in another state. There are many reasons to pick the law of a particular state and you should work through this issue with your outside counsel. That said, for both clauses there should be some reasonable connection between the company and the forum/law, e.g., where your headquarters is located, where you are incorporated, or where you have a large plant or warehouse. If there is no reasonable connection between your business and the forum/law selected, it may appear that you are trying to game the system. If so, a court may not honor the provision. Note that you can also set out a contractual time limit for when claims need to be raised, for example, no more than two-years from the date such claim arose or accrued. For a good example of forum/choice of law provisions in a user agreement read the eBay user agreement.[284]

6. **Arbitration or not?** Confidential arbitration can be an excellent way to resolve disputes. Especially for smaller matters, it tends to be much faster and less expensive/intrusive than litigation in the courts. An arbitration clause plus a class action waiver (see below) can be the difference between quickly resolving a simple customer service issue versus gearing up to spend millions defending a class action in a plaintiff-friendly court. Arbitration clauses are now relatively straight forward; be sure to set out that *all* disputes under, relating to, or pertaining to the use of your website must be submitted to binding arbitration in a forum near your offices. You must be sensitive, however, to the fact that no court will want to see a consumer locked into an arbitration process that seems patently unfair. So, resist the urge to make your arbitration clause aggressively one-sided, especially with respect to smaller size claims. One way to solve this is to provide for a consumer friendly process whereby smaller claims are subject to telephone arbitration (and you potentially offer to pay the filing fees of the user for such claims)—meaning the user will not have to travel to arbitrate and the cost to them to bring a claim is small or zero. Additionally, consider putting in a clause that provides for your costs and nullifies any attempt by the user to bring a claim outside of the provisions of the user agreement. Here is a modified sample from an old Travelocity.com agreement: Mandatory Arbitration—*Any claim where the total amount in controversy is less than US$10,000 shall be resolved via binding arbitration initiated through the American Arbitration Association (AAA). The arbitration will be governed*

---

284 http://pages.ebay.com/help/policies/user-agreement.html?rt=nc.

by the Commercial Arbitration Rules and the Supplementary Procedures for Consumer Related Disputes of AAA (collectively, AAA Rules), as modified by this agreement, and will be administered by the AAA. The AAA Rules are available online at http://www.adr.org or by calling the AAA at 1-800-778-7879. AAA and the parties must comply with the following rules: (a) if either party requests an in-person hearing, the process shall be governed by subsection (c) below, otherwise, the arbitration shall be conducted by telephone, online, and/ or be solely based on written submissions, the specific manner shall be chosen by the party initiating the arbitration; (b) the arbitration shall be conducted by an arbitrator in Tarrant County, Texas, who is approved or otherwise affiliated with the AAA; (c) if either party requests an in-person hearing, (i) the arbitrator shall decide whether a hearing is necessary or whether the arbitration shall proceed as described in subsection (a) above, (ii) if the arbitrator deems that a hearing is necessary, the hearing shall occur at a mutually agreed-upon location, or, if the parties are unable to agree on a location, at a location that is reasonably convenient to you and is selected by the arbitrator, and (iii) either party may elect to participate in an in-person hearing by phone, unless the arbitrator decides otherwise; (d) the arbitrator may award injunctive or declaratory relief only in favor of the individual party seeking relief and only to the extent necessary to provide relief warranted by that party's individual claim; (e) unless otherwise mutually agreed by the parties in writing, the arbitrator may not consolidate more than one person's claims, and may not otherwise preside over any form of a representative or class proceeding; and (f) any judgment on the award rendered by the arbitrator may be entered in any court of competent jurisdiction. If subparagraph (e) above is found to be unenforceable, then the entirety of this Mandatory Arbitration provision shall be null and void. Only a court and not the arbitrator can decide issues relating to the scope and enforceability of this "Resolution of Disputes" section. YOU UNDERSTAND AND AGREE THAT, BY ENTERING INTO THESE TERMS, YOU AND [COMPANY] ARE EACH WAIVING THE RIGHT TO A TRIAL BY JURY OR TO PARTICIPATE IN A CLASS ACTION WITH RESPECT TO THE CLAIMS COVERED BY THIS MANDATORY ARBITRATION PROVISION. *Notwithstanding the foregoing, either party may bring an individual action in small claims court in Tarrant County, Texas.*

Improperly Filed Claims—All claims you bring against us must be resolved in accordance with this "Resolution of Disputes" section. All claims filed or brought contrary to this "Resolution of Disputes" section shall be considered improperly filed and void. Should you file a claim contrary to this "Resolution of Disputes" section, we may recover attorneys' fees and costs up to $1,000, *provided that we have notified you in writing of the improperly filed claim, and you have failed to promptly withdraw the claim.*

Regardless of whether you choose arbitration or not, be sure to include a provision in your user agreement that awards attorneys' fees to the prevailing party in any dispute. Nothing stops bogus lawsuits faster than if a plaintiff has to worry paying your attorneys' fees if they lose.

7. **Class action/jury waiver.** In the pecking order of pain, right after root canal without anesthesia comes a consumer class action lawsuit. A claim that might be worth $1,000 can turn into $10,000,000 if a class is certified. The simplest way around this is to put a class action (and jury) waiver into your user agreement's dispute resolution section (and be sure to carve out class action resolution from the arbitrator's powers in your arbitration provision). Go out of your way to make sure the clause is conspicuous. The clause will read something like this: ANY AND ALL PROCEEDINGS TO RESOLVE CLAIMS WILL BE CONDUCTED ONLY ON AN INDIVIDUAL BASIS AND NOT IN A CLASS, CONSOLIDATED OR REPRESENTATIVE ACTION. IF FOR ANY REASON A CLAIM PROCEEDS IN COURT RATHER THAN IN ARBITRATION WE EACH WAIVE ANY RIGHT TO A JURY TRIAL. Such clauses have been upheld, all the way up to the Supreme Court.[285] One of the companies I worked for (Travelocity) had its user agreement class action waiver/arbitration clause upheld in an antitrust case. Needless to say, the court's ruling[286] was a good day at the office. That said, note that arbitration clauses/class action waivers in consumer contracts are coming under attack as unfair, in particular from the Consumer Financial Protection Bureau here in the United States. It is more important than ever to craft such clauses to be balanced and fair on their face as noted above.[287]

8. **Limit your liability.** You should include limitation of liability provisions in your user agreement. First is a waiver of liability for certain types of actions or problems, for example, the user waives any liability for information provided by third parties or for errors on your website. Similarly, you will want to disclaim any warranties to the extent possible. Second, you should limit the amount and types of damages a party to the agreement can recover. For example, you can preclude punitive damages or consequential damages and you can

---

285 http://media.mofo.com/files/Uploads/Images/130712-Arbitration-Waiver-Covers-Antitrus-Claims.pdf.

286 https://cases.justia.com/federal/district-courts/texas/txndce/3:2012cv03515/222550/93/0.pdf?ts=1376361329.

287 http://www.brannlaw.com/eyes-on-ecom-law/arbitration-clauses-under-attack-again/.

put a cap on the total amount of damages a plaintiff can recover against you. Here is some user agreement language capping the amount of damages: *If, despite the limitation above, the [Company] is found liable for any loss or damage which arises out of or in any way connected with any of the occurrences described above, then the liability of the [Company] will in no event exceed, in the aggregate, the greater of (a) the service fees you paid to [Company] in connection with such transaction(s) on this website, or (b) One-Hundred Dollars (US$100.00) or the equivalent in local currency.*

9. **What is "DMCA" and do I need one in my user agreement?** Yes, you do, especially if you operate a website that allows others to post content (photos, documents, videos, music, etc.) on your site—for example, a travel site with lots of pictures of hotels and attractions. When you allow other parties to post such content, there is a real risk of a potential copyright violation. The Digital Millennium Copyright Act (DMCA)[288] provides a safe harbor to websites that establish and follow specific "notice and take down" procedures. Basically, copyright owners can inform the website of potentially infringing uses. The website then gives notice to the party who posted the content and then blocks further access to the infringing content. There is also a process to unblock the content. The Nexcess blog offers a useful flow chart of how the DMCA process works.[289]

10. **Acceptable use of the website/right to change terms.** Lastly, be sure to spend time on the user agreement provisions that set forth the acceptable uses of your site (i.e., how the site can be used and any limits on what can and cannot be done on your site). The TripAdvisor website offers a good example of such provisions.[290] It's difficult to generalize here because what is written depends on how your business and website operate. So, this is an area worth spending time with the business and outside counsel to figure out the parameters. Finally, include a catch-all provision that provides your company the ability to change the terms of the user agreement at any time upon reasonable notice.

*****

There are a number of user agreement issues I was not able to get to, such as privacy policies, use of "cookies," indemnity, payment terms, end-user license agreement (EULA), linking off to third parties, and intellectual property notices. Fortunately,

---

288 https://www.rocketlawyer.com/article/digital-millennium-copyright-act-%28dmca%29-101.rl.
289 https://blog.nexcess.net/2012/02/22/dmca-process-infographic-flowchart/.
290 https://www.tripadvisor.com/pages/terms.html.

there are resources available to you to get more information regarding drafting and enforcing user agreements.[291] For example, the Association of Corporate Counsel's website (www.acc.com) has some useful materials. Likewise, a simple web search will generate a lot of good information. One website with helpful materials regarding user agreements is the PactSafe website (www.pactsafe.com). Your outside counsel can help as well. The best thing to do, however, is to look at user agreements of other companies (e.g., Netflix, Amazon, Uber, Microsoft). Companies with good businesses and good reputations will have structure and terms that you may wish to work into your user agreement. The most important thing is that you/legal take charge of your company's user agreement process, regularly review the agreement to stay current with the law, understand how the different parts of the agreement work, and ensure the agreement covers the things that are important to how your company operates day-to-day and will pass muster with a court if and when the time comes.

June 9, 2015

---

[291] http://www.lawjournalnewsletters.com/issues/ljn_ecommerce/31_12/news/browse_click_sign_enforce-161020-1.html.

Ten Things:
Partnering with HR (1 + 1 = 3)

One of the most important internal relationships for an in-house legal department is with the HR team. Much of the HR department's day-to-day work directly involves legal issues and analysis. Likewise, some of the nastiest and headline-grabbing litigation[292] involves employees and their claims alleging mistreatment, discrimination, malfeasance, and the like. Regardless of whether there is any merit to such claims, these disputes tend to be very public and can negatively impact your company's brand and reputation (along with economic consequences in the event the company pays a settlement or loses in court). That's why it is very important that legal and HR closely cooperate and align on how to best protect the company from employment-related issues. Working together, one plus one can add up to three.

As general counsel, one of the things I focused on was ensuring that my team (including myself) and HR met regularly to discuss a wide variety of issues and how best to work together to manage them. I was fortunate to work with real professionals both on the legal side and the HR side. Each group brought different viewpoints and skills to table, which was very valuable. Over time we met frequently to discuss different issues, from policy updates and training to cutting-edge legal risks. You and/or your team should consider setting up regularly scheduled meetings with HR throughout the course of the year to stay close on key legal/HR issues. Here are ten important areas that legal and HR should discuss on a regular basis (though focused on the United States, these topics easily apply across borders):

1. **Employee training program.** Most companies have some form of online, live, or combination thereof program to train employees on a wide variety of issues, including things like sexual harassment, compliance, business ethics, and data security. Legal and HR should meet once a year to go through the

---

292 http://www.nytimes.com/2015/03/28/technology/ellen-pao-disrupts-how-silicon-valley-does-business.html?emc=eta1&_r=1.

training program and materials to make sure they are relevant, effective, and updated to capture new issues. There may also be additional training for supervisors[293] (which can substantially reduce liability risks in key areas), and you should review this additional layer as part of any overall process. New hire orientation can be a great place to reach employees and discuss important policies and issues. Work with HR to get legal a "seat at the orientation table" or, if the chairs are full, let you help prepare materials for such sessions. Doing so will pay off down the road through a savvier workforce.

2. **Employee classification.** The process of properly classifying workers as "exempt"/"nonexempt"[294] under the Fair Labor Standards Act is very important. Basically, the classification tells you which employees are hourly and which employees can be salaried. Misclassification of hourly employees as "exempt" can set the company up for severe legal problems and potential big damages with respect to back wages and overtime.[295] You need easy-to-understand guidelines and processes as to when an employee is exempt or not, and you should train all supervisors in this area. Additionally, work with HR to regularly review job descriptions and do periodic auditing of employees earning below a certain threshold (say below $75,000) to ensure they are properly classified—as there is less risk of misclassification at the higher end of the pay scale. This is an especially urgent task, given the proposed new overtime guidelines from the Department of Labor.[296] An additional issue arising from the proposed overtime rules is the need to deal with employee reaction to the changes in their work habits, for example, the need to clock in and out, and lack of "flex time" options.[297]

3. **Interns.** Another area of risk revolves around the use of interns, in particular, "free" interns. The bottom line is that unless you can meet some pretty rigid standards,[298] there is no such thing as a "free" intern. For example, I

---

293 http://www.employerslawyersblog.com/2015/01/five-reasons-to-train-your-supervisors-in-the-new-year.html.

294 http://topics.hrhero.com/exempt-vs-non-exempt-employees/.

295 http://bricker.com/insights-resources/publications/could-this-be-you-preparing-for-and-surviving-a-wage-hour-investigation.

296 http://www.epi.org/publication/what-you-need-to-know-about-the-new-overtime-pay-law/. Note that a Federal District Court stayed the implementation of these new rules and it is not clear whether President Trump will keep them regardless.

297 http://www.employmentandlaborinsider.com/wage-hour/flsa-morale-nightmare-dealing-with-the-new-non-exempt/#page=1.

298 http://www.wcsr.com/resources/pdfs/le071013.pdf.

was approached regularly by colleagues or law school students inquiring as to whether I would be interested in hiring a student intern over the summer months. The intern was not expecting any payment, just the opportunity to get some experience and flesh out a resume. At first I thought it was a great idea and everyone wins—and I was frustrated when HR said "no." But, I quickly came to learn they were right and that despite everyone's willingness to go with such an arrangement, the law was clear that the type of work we had for an intern would not qualify[299] for "free." That said, courts are starting to put more balance into the analysis but the issues around what qualifies for a free intern are still in flux.[300] Given the potential for high penalties and tax exposure, be sure you and HR have a process to vet any and all internships at your company and that you regularly police this area.

4. **Key employee agreements/clauses.** In my experience, legal would draft employee agreements (e.g., confidentiality, noncompete, non-solicitation, IP ownership, arbitration[301] clauses) and HR would administer them. Over time, agreements were modified in a nonuniform manner or older versions of an agreement/clause were used when newer state-of-the-art versions existed. Additionally, when it came time to enforce one of these agreements, we would sometimes find that we could not locate the agreement, or if we did find it, it was not signed by the employee. HR and legal should meet to discuss the preparation and administration of these agreements, including a process to maintain version control and to discuss changes that may be needed given new circumstances or changes in the law (including the recent push in the U.S. to limit the ability to require lower level employees to sign a noncompete).

5. **Employee handbook.** Many companies have an employee handbook containing key policies such as "code of ethics and business conduct," "anti-corruption," "anti-trust," "insider trading," "health and safety," and "trade compliance." Set up a process with HR to go through these policies together and update the handbook and relevant policies as needed (e.g., recent changes in pregnancy

---

299 http://blogs.orrick.com/employment/2015/02/18/class-action-lawsuits-in-vogue-high-fashion-gets-hit-with-wage-and-hour-class-action-lawsuits-over-unpaid-internship-programs/.

300 http://www.outtengolden.com/sites/default/files/unpaid_interns_special_report_oct_2015-1.pdf.

301 http://www.wsj.com/articles/more-companies-block-staff-from-suing-1427824287. This is likely another area where the Supreme Court will need to get involved given the recent decision of the Seventh Circuit around arbitration provisions in employment agreements. See http://arbitrationnation.com/out-on-a-limb-7th-circuit-creates-circuit-split-over-class-arbitration-for-employees/.

accommodation[302]). Note that without proper wording[303] or disclaimers, an at-will employee handbook can become a binding contract.[304] And be aware that the NLRB's general counsel issued a 30-page memorandum[305] on how provisions in an employee handbook can violate Section 7 of the National Labor Relations Act. You should already be thinking about how your handbook matches up to the NLRB's expectations and make revisions[306] as needed.

6. **Employee/contractor classification.** This is another area fraught with risk and traps for the unwary. HR and legal should periodically review all independent contractors each year to ensure they are not being treated like employees[307] (e.g., contractor invited to employee meetings, close supervision and direction of the contractor's work) and therefore entitled to employee benefits. Supervisors and anyone with the ability to engage contractors should understand the proper process around hiring and managing them. I recommend setting up a procedure to flag and review contractors who have been working with the company for a set period of time (e.g., six months), and that there is a review higher up in the organization to look at any decision to keep a contractor beyond the set period of time. If there are not clear guidelines[308] in place around the use and management of independent contractors, your company could be in for some real problems and costly litigation.[309]

7. **Layoffs.** Nobody likes to discuss this topic. Regardless, a proactive legal department will work with HR to be prepared for the possibility of layoffs in

---

302 http://www.laborandemploymentlawcounsel.com/2015/03/test-your-knowledge-employee-handbook-truefalse-quiz/.

303 https://www.laboremploymentperspectives.com/2015/02/16/employee-handbook-mistakes-can-come-back-to-bite-employers/.

304 http://labor-employment-law.lawyers.com/human-resources-law/employee-handbooks-and-at-will-employment.html.

305 http://www.employerlawreport.com/2015/03/articles/labor-relations/nlrb-general-counsel-guidance-memo-on-employee-handbook-policies-is-required-reading-for-all-employers/.

306 http://immixlaw.com/it-may-be-time-revisit-your-employee-handbook/.

307 http://www.twc.state.tx.us/news/efte/independent_contractor_tests.html.

308 http://www.nolo.com/legal-encyclopedia/independent-contractors-avoid-classification-problems-35463.html.

309 https://independentcontractorcompliance.com/2016/03/02/february-2016-independent-contractor-compliance-and-misclassification-news-update/.

any year including a process to reduce the legal risks[310] that can arise when layoffs happen. You should jointly create a simple checklist of all of the steps the company will need to take in the event there is a layoff (e.g., internal/external communications). One key issue is the need for a disparate impact analysis[311] of the potential layoffs to ensure there is no bias against any protected class. You should have in place the tools to run this analysis along with identifying outside counsel to help evaluate the results. Additionally, you should be familiar with the requirements of the Worker Adjustment and Retraining Notification Act (WARN)[312] (or state-specific "mini-WARN" statutes) in the United States and the Transfer of Undertakings (Protection of Employment) statutes (TUPE)[313] throughout Europe (and similar laws in other countries). These statutory worker protections can trip the company up and delay layoffs and/or impose additional costs if not followed. Developing (and keeping current) form severance agreements/releases constitutes good planning and can be helpful when things start to pile up.

8. **Internal investigations policy.** At my last job we (legal/compliance office) worked with HR and internal audit to develop a written investigation policy and protocol. At most companies, internal investigations typically involve the participation of these three groups. We found that, over time, the lines become blurred and that information was not being shared properly between us and there were often duplicative efforts under way to look at the same issue. To fix this, we created a document that clearly set out the roles and responsibility of each group depending on the type of issue presented (e.g., sex discrimination complaint vs. internal fraud vs. business ethics policy violation). In addition, the policy set out how information would be shared, what follow-ups were required, who was copied on what, and the like. We prepared an annual joint communication to all managers sharing and explaining the policy and telling them where they should start in the event they had issues involving employees. Not only did this policy increase cooperation between the three groups; it ended up saving us all a lot of time and effort because we knew who had the wheel for any particular type of investigation and what was expected from our teams.

---

310 http://www.ogletreedeakins.com/shared-content/content/blog/2015/february/tread-carefully-when-implementing-a-reduction-in-force.
311 http://www.acc.com/legalresources/quickcounsel/pacarif.cfm.
312 https://www.doleta.gov/layoff/warn.cfm.
313 http://www.out-law.com/page-448.

9. **Background checks.** Given the potential legal exposure for making a "bad" hire, many companies now do criminal background checks on all potential employees and/or promotion candidates. This is an area to use great care as various cities and states have enacted or are in the process of enacting laws that change the ground rules on when employers can ask job applicants questions about prior arrests (ban the box). Similarly, the Equal Employment Opportunity Commission has set out its expectations with respect to when and how an employer can consider arrest and conviction records.[314] There should also be appropriate due diligence on any third parties your company engages to conduct background checks, in particular around compliance with the Fair Credit Reporting Act, which sets out the general rules[315] of the road for employers in this area. Legal and HR should work together to ensure that the company is in compliance with all of the different laws in the United States (or elsewhere) and fully understands any limitations on use of background checks.

10. **Cutting edge.** Finally, legal should meet with HR several times a year to simply discuss any cutting-edge issues in employment law, for example, work from home[316] policies, BYOD[317] policies, the use of social media[318] by employees, Americans with Disability Act issues, dress codes/religious accommodation guidance, open source/download[319] policies, personal use of company email,[320] service animals, affirmative action plans,[321] unionization efforts, firearms,[322]

---

314 https://www.eeoc.gov/laws/guidance/arrest_conviction.cfm.
315 http://www.icemiller.com/ice-on-fire-insights/publications/if-you-use-applicant-background-checks,-the-fcra-i/.
316 http://www.insidecounsel.com/2015/03/30/9-things-employers-should-consider-when-it-comes-t?eNL=55197043160ba0a81dbf3eb4&utm_source=ic&utm_medium=email&utm_campaign=icscoopenews&_LID=173517506&slreturn=1467335030.
317 https://www.dataprivacymonitor.com/international-privacy-law/bring-your-own-device-everywhere-legal-and-practical-considerations-for-international-byod-programs/.
318 http://blog.hubspot.com/blog/tabid/6307/bid/29441/5-Noteworthy-Examples-of-Corporate-Social-Media-Policies.aspx#sm.00000clsjzbv20dpkr6mlpe4c1krr.
319 https://knowledge.kaltura.com/sites/default/files/7_Myths_IP_Risk_UL.pdf.
320 http://eplirisk.com/takeaways-for-employers-on-the-hillary-e-mail-debacle/.
321 http://www.lexology.com/library/detail.aspx?g=36bf181a-5c9f-4b78-b528-254419faff8f&l=7N-90MHS.
322 http://digital.todaysgeneralcounsel.com/?issueID=29&pageID=32.

wellness programs,[323] inclement weather[324] policies, and ERISA. You do not need to have an answer to all of these types of issues, but you should have a plan to track issues and regularly communicate what legal and HR are seeing regarding the same.

*****

As you can see, there is an endless supply of issues and concerns that legal and HR share. Your company may have the same or vastly different issues than the ones I set out above, but it's a good starting point. The takeaway is the importance of setting up regular meetings between the two staff groups (and this is also an area where outside counsel can be great thought partners and probably give you some free hours to be at the table). If these meetings are not going on today, make it your goal to make the first move and set them up. You'll find that your friends in HR will appreciate the opportunity to work together. Furthermore, talk with other senior company leaders outside of HR and get their views on what employment-type issues or problems they are seeing or think need to be addressed. The company (and you) will benefit from your taking a proactive and strategic role in identifying areas of risk and working to minimize problems down the road.

April 2, 2015

---

323 http://labor-employment-law.lawyers.com/human-resources-law/wellness-programs-may-be-bad-for-employers-health.html.

324 https://www.shrm.org/legalissues/federalresources/pages/inclement-weather-flsa.aspx.

Governance

Ten Things: Basic Corporate Governance for In-House Counsel

I have not spent much time writing about the "corporate" side of the in-house world and would like to discuss some key issues regarding basic corporate law. If this is an area you focus on already, you have it down, but for many in-house lawyers whose practice focuses on litigation, intellectual property, employment, or other areas, it's not something you see every day. If you hope to sit in the general counsel chair one day, it's important to have a solid understanding of several basic areas of corporate law.

Underlying most of everything in corporate law is what I call "basic corporate governance." This includes the formation of the corporation, operation of the board of directors (the board), delegation of authority, annual compliance issues, and so on. This article will discuss ten basic issues regarding corporate governance. While the below is fairly U.S.-centric—as the details of corporate law vary widely by jurisdiction—I will include some reference material for corporate governance issues outside the United States toward the end:

1. **Formation.** There are several different legal entities you can utilize to operate your business, such as a sole proprietorship (i.e., run by an individual), a partnership, or a limited liability company. Professional groups (accountants, law firms) often utilize a special entity designed just for them, for example, a professional limited liability company. The favored business entity in the United States is a for-profit corporation (we'll skip not-for-profit corporations). A corporation is in essence a separate legal "person" (but is not a "natural person") and has the ability to own property, sue and be sued, enter into contracts, and make political donations, and possesses a host of other attributes. A corporation can be privately held (its shares are not generally available to the public) or publicly held (its shares are listed/traded on a public exchange, such as the NYSE[325]

---

325 https://www.nyse.com/index.

or NASDAQ[326]). There are three things that make corporations a preferred entity for business: (a) the shareholders are protected from liability for the debts and actions of the corporation, (b) corporations have perpetual life (i.e., they don't "die"), and (c) corporations operate according to set rules, meaning investors have assurances around key aspects of how the company will operate and how their investment in it will be protected.

In the United States, the rules regarding how a corporation is formed and operates are governed by the state where it is incorporated. State law governs things like the duties of the board, shareholder rights, annual filing requirements, issuance of stock, and mergers. The most popular state for incorporation is Delaware[327] because it has a well-developed body of law regarding corporations (generally favorable to the company/board), business-friendly statutes, sophisticated courts with respected judges, and ease of filing annual or required documents, and investors typically expect these aspects.

2. **Key documents.** There are several core documents every corporation will have in place:
   - *Articles of Incorporation*—This document is sometimes called the "charter" or "certificate." This document is the primary governance document of the corporation and is filed with the state of incorporation. It sets out the name of the corporation, the number and types/classes of stock issued, the registered agent (i.e., the person who accepts notices, lawsuits, and the like on behalf of the corporation), the names and addresses of the incorporators, and other things required by the state law. Incorporators usually try to prepare the least detailed articles[328] with the broadest powers possible, for example, that the corporation may engage in any lawful purpose or endeavor (even if the company starts out making shovels). This allows the business to grow and expand in ways not foreseen at inception. The articles of incorporation can only be amended by vote of the shareholders.
   - *By-laws*—They set out the detailed rules for running the corporation on a day-to-day basis. They are secondary to the articles of incorporation, meaning they prevail in the event of a conflict the articles control. They contain such things as the size of the board, its committees, and the process for holding meetings (including voting by email or allowing telephonic meetings). They contain provisions to resolve conflicts of interest and may contain provisions designed to ward off unwanted solicitations or takeovers

---

326 http://www.nasdaq.com/.
327 http://www.bendlawoffice.com/2011/08/01/reasons-to-incorporate-in-delaware/.
328 http://www.nolo.com/legal-encyclopedia/articles-incorporation.html.

(i.e., "poison pills"). Bylaws[329] do not need to be filed with the state and can be amended by the board, making them superior to the articles in terms of flexibility for the corporation.
- *Shareholder's agreements*—These are very common in privately held corporations and set out the relationship and rights between shareholders, for example, what happens to the stock of shareholder when the shareholder dies. These agreements protect minority shareholder rights and ensure the corporation can function in the event of dysfunction between the shareholders.

3. **Who's who?** There are several important players in operating a corporation:
   - *Shareholders*—They are the "owners" of the corporation and own the shares of stock issued by the company. They vote on key issues, such as mergers and the members of the board. Shareholders can range from owners of a few shares to large institutional shareholders (like billion-dollar pension funds) that own large percentages of the stock of a corporation. The more shares you own, the greater is your influence.
   - *Board of directors*—The directors work for the shareholders and their job is to oversee the running of the corporation by the company's officers and employees. For small companies, the directors may also be owners and officers and heavily involved in the business. For large companies, the directors delegate day-to-day responsibility to management.
   - *Officers*—Most state laws require a corporation to have several officers, including a president, treasurer, and secretary. In Delaware, all that is required is a president and a secretary. Any other officers are simply those created by the company for its own purposes, for example, the general counsel, CFO, CIO. Officers are usually approved by the board and have titles like executive vice president or senior vice president (though you have to be careful of the apparent authority[330] bestowed on any employee based on their title).
   - *Advisory board*—Many corporations have advisory boards[331] made up of experts on certain areas of the company's business or who have other desired expertise. Their role is to give nonbinding advice as requested by the business. An advisory board is not the same thing as the board of directors and is not subject to the same governance standards and other duties.

---

329 http://smallbusiness.chron.com/definition-corporation-bylaws-3964.html.
330 https://www.law.cornell.edu/wex/apparent_authority.
331 http://www.stengelsolutions.com/tips19.htm.

4. **Duties of the board of directors.** The board members have a number of duties they owe to the shareholders of the company. First, they need to regularly attend and actively participate in the meetings of the board and any committees they are assigned to. Typical committees include audit, compensation, and governance. There can be a committee for just about any purpose. Many large corporations have executive committees (that can make decisions when the full board is not available) and technology committees (dealing with cyber risk). Directors are usually paid for their work in a combination of cash per meeting and equity in the company.

    Directors make decisions on material issues facing the company, for example, a merger or a stock offering. In doing so, they owe the company/shareholders a *duty of care* (to act with the care that an ordinarily prudent and careful person would use in similar circumstances) and a *duty of loyalty* (to act in good faith for the benefit of the corporation and its shareholders—not for their own interests). Directors are usually immune to legal liability under the business judgment rule,[332] which states that so long as a majority of the directors have no conflicting interest in the decision, their decision will not later be second-guessed by a court if it is undertaken with due care and in good faith. The business judgment rule applies even if the business decision later turns out to have been a bad decision. Most corporations provide for the indemnification of their directors and officers directly in the bylaws and through the purchase of directors and officers (D&O) insurance.

5. **Delegation of authority.** The owners of the corporation, the shareholders, are the ultimate authority. Unless the corporation is very small, the shareholders cannot effectively make day-to-day decisions. Authority is usually delegated from the shareholders to the board via the articles of incorporation and bylaws (with some decisions reserved for shareholder approval). The board is usually not in a position to be involved in every day-to-day decision either and, in turn, delegates the authority for many actions to the CEO/president of the corporation. The CEO has the ability to delegate authority down to his/her direct reports (i.e., the other officers of the company who handle the various staff groups and lines of business). Additional delegations run all the way down to the lowest levels of the company hierarchy. As in-house counsel, one important task you have is to be familiar with the delegations of authority for your company (which may be a rather complex document) and understand who does—and does not—have authority to take certain actions or make certain

---

332 https://www.law.cornell.edu/wex/business_judgment_rule.

decisions. You do not want a situation where you are about to sign a contract or close a transaction only to find out that you do not have a person present authorized to make the decision or sign the document. Lastly, keep in mind that any powers not specifically delegated by the board are reserved to the board. For example, if the CEO/president can authorize an acquisition worth less than $10M, then only the board can approve an acquisition worth more than $10M.

6. **Resolutions/Minutes.** One important task of a corporation is to ensure proper records are kept of its actions. This is done through either resolutions or the minutes of board or committee meetings. A resolution is a formal written document that sets forth an action of the board and records the vote. Most resolutions are voted on during meetings (in person or via telephone). In some instances the by-laws permit electronic voting via email. The record of what occurred during a board meeting is called the minutes of the meeting. The minutes, resolutions, and other key corporate documents (e.g., the articles of incorporation, bylaws, and stock ledger) are kept in a "minutes book." Keeping an up-to-date and accurate minutes book is very important, especially in the event of a transaction involving the sale of your company or in the event actions of the board are challenged. This also means that the proper drafting of corporate meeting minutes is very important (especially in these litigious times). Minutes are not a verbatim transcript of what was said at each meeting. Instead, they should focus on things like the following:
    - The meeting date, time, and location.
    - The nature of the meeting (regular, committee, special, telephonic, etc.)
    - A list of all attendees (and a list of directors absent from the meeting and whether a quorum of directors is present).
    - The general topics of discussion, the names of all individuals making specific presentations, and the general nature of their presentations.
    - The meeting agenda and materials distributed before or at the meeting.
    - Confirmation of all actions taken by the board, for example, adoption of resolutions and the vote tally

7. **Publicly traded companies.** Corporations decide to go public for many reasons, including the ability to raise large amounts of capital and the cachet of being listed on a public exchange. While there are many benefits to being publicly traded, there are a lot of additional responsibilities and potential pitfalls as well. Here are some of the key ones:
    - *Basic reporting.* A public company must register its shares pursuant to U.S. securities laws. Once properly registered and available for sale, a public company (unlike a private company) faces a litany of disclosure obligations

under the Securities Exchange Act of 1934,[333] all with the aim of giving investors complete and non-misleading information about the company's financial state and any risks investors face if they buy shares. Key reports are as follows:

- **10Q**—quarterly unaudited financials and other information (e.g., risk, legal proceedings, management discussion of the business)[334]
- **10K**—annual audited financials and other information (more detailed than 10Q)[335]
- **8K**—filed whenever there is a material development with the corporation. The purpose is to disseminate important information about the company to all investors at the same time. An 8K covers the time periods between the 10Qs and the 10K. There is a long list of triggering events such as an acquisition of another company, resignation of an officer of the company, entering into a material contract (or loss of such a contract), and release of earnings reports. Public companies typically have processes in place and disclosure committees to evaluate when a company event requires an 8K disclosure, which must be filed, generally within four business days of when the event occurred.[336]
- **Proxy**—A document given to shareholders prior to the annual meeting that informs them of the business to be taken up at the meeting (e.g., election of directors), solicits a proxy for their votes, provides background and compensation information about the board and key members of management, sets out the financial performance of the corporation, and similar information. The proxy is governed by Regulation and Schedule 14 of the Exchange Act.[337]
- **Forms 3 and 4**—A Form 3 is filed when a person in senior management or the board first receives equity from the company. A Form 4 is filed when there is a change in that equity, either a sale of stock or the grant of additional equity.[338]

---

333 https://www.law.cornell.edu/wex/securities_exchange_act_of_1934.
334 http://whatis.techtarget.com/definition/SEC-Form-10-Q.
335 http://whatis.techtarget.com/definition/SEC-Form-10-K.
336 https://www.wilmerhale.com/uploadedFiles/Shared_Content/Editorial/Publications/Documents/WilmerHale-Form-8-K-Guide-October-2014.pdf.
337 https://www.sec.gov/answers/proxy.htm.
338 https://www.mystockoptions.com/faq/index.cfm/catID/66A10EF1-8DD9-49E6-AFD7161DE-771AC94/ObjectID/D943AA01-30A9-11D4-B9080008C79F9E62.

- *Other issues.* There is a long list of other statutory and regulatory requirements and other issues that public companies must deal with. The cost and administrative burden of complying or dealing with all of the disclosure and other issues is a major reason why some companies do not enter (or drop out of) the public markets:
  - **Sarbanes-Oxley**—passed after the Enron, and other scandals, the Sarbanes-Oxley Act imposed a number of new reporting and other requirements on public companies.[339] The key is that the CEO and CFO are now required to certify (subject to criminal liability) that the statements and financials in the public filings are accurate and that adequate controls are in place at the company to ensure accuracy—which drives a lot of work within the company. Sections 302 (certification)[340] and 404 (internal controls report)[341] are probably the most important sections.
  - **Fair disclosure regulation (Reg FD)**—a requirement that companies provide fair disclosure of material company information and that they do not selectively disclose such information to a chosen few such as large institutional investors or analysts.[342] It's designed to give all investors equal and timely information. In today's world, things like Tweets or Facebook posts can trigger fair disclosure regulation issues.
  - **Proxy advisory services**—these are companies that advise shareholders (especially large institutional shareholders) how to vote on proxy issues.[343] In the United States, two firms are the leading advisors: ISS[344] and Glass Lewis.[345] A third, Manifest,[346] focuses on European votes. These services have become controversial regarding their ratings and other methods (e.g., companies need to pay large subscription fees to get access to the services' rating criteria), and the SEC is looking at new regulation.[347]

---

339 http://www.sarbanes-oxley-101.com/.
340 http://www.sarbanes-oxley-101.com/SOX-302.htm.
341 http://www.sarbanes-oxley-101.com/SOX-404.htm.
342 http://media.mofo.com/files/Uploads/Images/FAQs-Regulation-FD.pdf.
343 http://www.camberview.com/wp-content/uploads/2015/02/Engaging-with-Proxy-Advisory-Services_Chapter-37.pdf.
344 https://www.issgovernance.com/.
345 http://www.glasslewis.com/.
346 https://www.manifest.co.uk/.
347 http://www.wsj.com/articles/reforming-the-proxy-advisory-racket-1405986992.

- **Activist shareholders**—these are investors who buy a large amount of stock in a public company for the purpose of replacing the board or forcing management to make changes or pursue objectives favored by the activist (e.g., sale of a subsidiary, a merger).[348] It is not clear whether, over the long-term, such investors are good or bad for companies.
8. **Failure to keep up corporate "niceties."** The corporate secretary has a key role at a corporation. Among his/her many tasks (which include the operational aspects of the board) is to ensure that the company makes all of the required yearly filings (state and federal), holds the annual meeting, properly records all stock transfers, and pays any required fees (in the state of incorporation and any state where the corporation does business). Companies must file annual reports and pay certain fees to retain their status as a corporation. If they fail to do so, they can lose their corporate status and be prohibited from using the state's court system or worse (for smaller companies) be treated as a sole proprietorship or partnership, which means the loss of limited liability protection for the shareholders. There can also be damage done regarding exposure to taxes; the ability to merge or create subsidiaries, get insurance, and get a loan; and other consequences if the company loses its corporation status. While many states provide generous opportunities to come into compliance, you do not want to be in a situation where you are scrambling to reinstitute the corporation—and explaining to the CEO/board why there are problems with your deal.
9. **Subsidiaries, sister companies, holding companies.** Many corporations set up subsidiaries to conduct business in different countries or in different product lines. One big reason is tax structure. Another reason is to make the subsidiary the publicly traded company while the parent remains private. Likewise, a parent company can limit exposure to itself through the use of subsidiaries, sister companies (i.e., companies that share the same corporate parent), or holding companies (companies that do nothing other than own other companies). Regardless the reason or the structure, all of the same requirements around basic corporate governance apply to subsidiary and sister corporations, which can be especially challenging if the subsidiary is partially publicly traded and there are disagreements as to what is best for all the shareholders vs. the parent corporation).
10. **Resources.** Here are a few resources discussing basic corporate governance that I have found particularly useful:

---

348 http://www.wsj.com/articles/activist-investors-helping-or-hindering-1444067712.

- Perkins Coie, *The Public Company Handbook* (5th ed. 2016)[349]
- The Society of Corporate Secretaries & Governance Professionals[350]
- "Importance and Elements of Delegation of Authority"[351]
- Law 360, "Preparing Corporate Minutes: Time Well Spent" (2012)[352]
- Guhan Subramanian, "Corporate Governance 2.0" (*Harvard Business Review*, March 2015)[353]
- www.cooleygo.com
- "Your Duties as a Director — The Basics"[354]
- Getting the Deal Through — Corporate Governance (multiple jurisdictions)[355]
- Corporate governance in the United Kingdom,[356] Canada,[357] India,[358] Singapore[359]
- Practical Law (subscription required)[360]

*****

As you can imagine, you can do little more than hit the highlights of corporate governance in a chapter like this (e.g., I have left out U.S. state securities (Blue Sky) laws[361]). Hopefully, you now have a better understanding of the basics and some places to go for additional information. As you develop your career as an in-house counsel, it's important to always be curious about other areas of the law,

---

349 https://www.smashwords.com/books/view/628176.
350 http://www.governanceprofessionals.org/home.
351 http://www.yourarticlelibrary.com/management/importance-and-elements-of-delegation-of-authority-business-management/8650/.
352 http://www.sutherland.com/portalresource/lookup/poid/Z1tOl9NPluKPtDNIqLMRV56Pab6T-fzcRXncKbDtRr9tObDdEuaJEp0!/fileUpload.name=/Law360(2-14-2012).pdf.
353 https://hbr.org/2015/03/corporate-governance-2-0.
354 https://www.cooleygo.com/director-fiduciary-duties/.
355 https://gettingthedealthrough.com/area/8/corporate-governance/.
356 https://www.frc.org.uk/Our-Work/Codes-Standards/Corporate-governance/UK-Corporate-Governance-Code.aspx.
357 https://www.osler.com/en/resources/governance/2012/the-corporate-governance-review-canada-second-ed.
358 http://www.corpgov.net/2015/05/corporate-governance-in-india/.
359 http://www.wongpartnership.com/index.php/files/download/761.
360 http://us.practicallaw.com/.
361 https://www.sec.gov/answers/bluesky.htm.

especially areas that go to the fundamentals of how your company operates. Look for ways to flesh out your skills. You do not have to become an expert. Being conversant and knowing the basics can go a long way even if it's just knowing when to spot an issue and ask someone for help.

April 18, 2016

Ten Things: Dealing with the Board of Directors

I want to continue to write a bit about basic corporate law issues. In the previous section, I wrote about corporate governance.[362] Now I'd like to discuss dealing with the board of directors (the board). The members of the board are elected by the shareholders of a corporation. Their job is to manage and supervise the company's officers and management and to look out for the interests of the shareholders. Directors owe the shareholders/company a duty of care and a duty of loyalty while serving on the board.

The legal department interacts with the board in several ways. Typically, the corporate secretary (the person who manages the operational aspects of the board along with other duties related to maintaining the corporation) sits in legal. Often the general counsel is also the corporate secretary. The corporate secretary works closely with the chairman of the board and the governance and nominating committee. The chief compliance officer may also sit in legal and works closely with the audit committee. Similarly, any significant litigation, contract, acquisition, or other material legal event will come to the attention of the board and may require its input or approval in some instances. The board will take up these legal matters at regularly scheduled board or committee meetings, or at a special meeting if the circumstances warrant. When these ad hoc legal events come to the attention of the board, various members of the legal department may be invited to the meeting in order to present the issue to the board or be a subject matter expert for any questions the members may have. Any in-house lawyer can be intimidated the first time he or she meets the company's board of directors or prepare materials for them (even if it's just responding to an email). Here are some pointers on how to deal with the board:

1. **Do your homework.** If you are meeting members of the board for the first time (or even the second), be sure to take some time to learn more about them.

---

362 See page 219.

The easiest way to do this is to ask people who deal frequently with your board (i.e., others in legal, finance, corporate secretary function, etc.). Some boards operate very formally, with everyone in suits and ties, and stick to a strict agenda/schedule and very specific protocols. Other boards are informal; the members dress casually and work through an agenda but varying from it often to discuss other things. Know which type of board you will be dealing with. If there is any question, always bet on "formal" because it's hard to go wrong if you pick that path. Take your cues from other company employees in the meeting with you. Don't be a jokester—that rarely is appropriate and can be the kiss of death in the wrong circumstances. Do some background research on the Directors. The websites of most companies, especially publicly traded companies, will contain director bios, and so will the annual report (Form 10K) and the proxy. If you are invited to a board dinner or lunch, knowing a bit about each director's background (e.g., their college or where they work and live) can be a real asset and conversation saver. Learn their names and their roles on the board, that is, committees, lead director, activist director representative, and the like. Finally, try to get a sense of their personalities. Again, this is one information where you'll need to ask people who meet with the directors frequently. Most directors that I have met are great. They are warm and friendly, super smart, and very dedicated to the company. Every once in a while you meet one who is not. Going in to the meeting knowing where the traps are personality-wise is priceless information.

2. **Understand where your duty lies.** As an in-house lawyer, you need to understand who your client is at all times. Under the ethical rules here in the United States, an in-house lawyer's client is the corporation.[363] It is not the CEO or the CFO; it is not any one director. It is the company as a whole, that is, the shareholders' interests as represented by the board of directors. Your job is to be sure your advice and your actions match up with this obligation to your client. Watch out for any one director attempting to influence what you do or how you think based on his or her self-interest. While rare, it is something to be on guard for. If you think you have an issue with any particular director, go talk to the general counsel or corporate secretary (or someone in senior management if necessary).

3. **Transparency.** I remember a valuable piece of advice a board member once gave me. He said, "Do not hide things from the board. Be transparent and even-handed in your advice to us." What he was telling me was don't try to "game" the board or play it cute with your advice and counsel. Give the board

---

363 See page 279.

all the facts. Discuss the pros and cons of any situation in evenhanded manner and do not try to shade things so you can get a certain result from the board. And never try to hide things from the board. Your integrity and reputation are two of the most important things you bring to the table. If the board feels you lack integrity, you will tarnish yourself beyond repair in their eyes. Get all of the potential outcomes on the table. Do not let the board get surprised by something they did not know was a possibility—for example, if the other side in litigation has asked for an injunction that would shut down part of your business. Be sure that is noted to the board when discussing or writing to them about the litigation, even if you think there is virtually no chance the court will grant it. If you're wrong and there is an injunction (which you failed to mention was one of the claims), you will have a lot of explaining to do.

4. **Keep it simple.** As you present to or discuss issues with the board, don't overwhelm them with text and legal-speak. One of the most valuable skills an in-house lawyer can have is the ability to make complex topics simple and straight forward. You need to learn how to do this to be successful. This goes for any presentation materials you prepare for the board, emails discussing legal issues, or other types of memoranda and correspondence. Writing and presenting as an in-house lawyer is different from being with an outside law firm. Do not pack your PowerPoint or memo with paragraphs of text or spend time on case citations and detailed footnotes, or use Latin phrases or other legal buzz words or acronyms. If you have visuals, keep them simple and uncluttered as well. Whenever you have the opportunity to get information to the board, think long and hard up-front about the following:

- What is it that I want/need to say?
- What information needs to be included so the board has the full picture?
- How can I set out and discuss the issues (and my advice) in the simplest manner possible?
- Am I teeing up what needs to be done by the board and setting out their options?

Directors have limited time to consider company business. They already have a ton of material to go through leading up to any board meeting (board books, financials, draft resolutions, etc.), they usually have other jobs or commitments to other boards, and they have personal lives as well. At the meeting, assume they have read your materials in advance and get to the point quickly. You can even say something like "I'm going to hit a few highlights of the background and then move on to the key issues we need to discuss. But, if anyone has questions as we work through the materials, please let me know." Read the room as you present. If they are staring out the window, pick up the pace and/or move to the heart of what you're after—ditch the script if necessary. Everything you can do to be clear and straightforward and not just another lawyer babbling on about things will be noticed and appreciated. Brevity is your friend.

5. **Anticipate questions.** If you are meeting or talking with the board, odds are good that you are there as a subject matter expert on the topic (e.g., the litigation, the contract, the acquisition). If so, spend a significant amount of time anticipating what type of questions you might get from the board and how you will answer them if asked. This is harder than it sounds as questions can seem to come completely out of "left field" as we say here in the United States. Place yourself in the shoes of the directors and think about what questions you would have if faced with the material you are presenting. What are the three or four critical questions that come to mind? Review everything you have set out in the materials and think about whether anything will beg a question or require further elaboration. If it does, is it really a question you want to beg from the board? If not, cut it. Consider having someone else read the materials and see what types of questions they come up with (whether or not you can do this and with whom depends on the sensitivity of the materials).

6. **Honesty.** Closely related to all of the above is the need for honesty when dealing with the board. Obviously, you never want to lie flat out to the board. This issue often comes up in those situations where you do not know the answer to a question asked by a member of the board. The bottom line is don't try to wing it or cobble together something that you do not know for sure to be correct (and you definitely do not want to give them an incorrect answer). Instead, just say you do not have the answer to the question right now but you will find out and report back to them as soon as possible. It's okay for this to happen on occasion. There is just no way to possibly know the answer to every question that might come up (even though you've tried to anticipate as many as possible). That said, if you say "I don't know" a lot, it does not reflect well on you and it will come across as either a lack of preparation or a lack of intellectual horsepower. Neither is a good label.

7. **Be professional.** When dealing with the board, you need to be polished but not overly formal. Some deference is good, but too much makes you look weak. When you talk, watch out for the "ums" and the overuse of the word "like." It is difficult to trust and take seriously someone who sounds like they are in high school. If you know you are going to be speaking with the board in advance, that is, it's not a surprise call/meeting, practice your presentation or the key points you want to make. You may be an awesome speaker when you stand up in front of your team and speak off the cuff but don't try this with the board. It is a vastly different experience. When discussing things with the board, be

prepared to back up your points with evidence and facts. Show that you have been thinking through the angles. Likewise, dress appropriately. You cannot go wrong leaning to the formal side, that is, suit, sport coat, conservative dress and shoes—all of which reflect well on you as a professional.

As an attorney, remember to ensure the proper use and preservation of the attorney-client privilege. Don't forget to include the members of the board when you are educating employees and senior management about how the attorney-client privilege works[364] and how best to ensure that documents and emails containing attorney-client privilege material stay privileged. This means ensuring the board uses the proper labels and specifically asks for legal advice versus business advice (and understands the difference), and that the members of the board do not accidently waive privilege. Don't assume just because they are on the board, they understand how the privilege works.

8. **Always be helpful.** As you engage with the board (and hopefully that engagement grows as you become more senior in the legal department), keep an eye open for things that are helpful to the members. For example, at every regular board meeting we provided a short update (10 minutes) on any material developments in the law dealing with corporate governance and their duties as directors (e.g., regulations, case law, articles). Likewise, if I—or my team—came across something we thought would be useful to our board members, we would share it, along with a short note explaining why the materials were important. Of course, don't overdo it. This is a once-in-a-while type thing and do it only when there is something of real value to share. Additionally, there are always the basics:
   - Promptly return emails and phone calls from board members (even if it's just to say "I have your request and am working on it")
   - Understand that requests from the board usually go straight to the top of your to do list
   - Be on time (i.e., early) to meetings and conference calls with the board
   - Ensure that members of the board receive the meeting materials and have extra copies available in case someone forgets theirs
   - If working on a big project that has the board's involvement, make sure the right people have your contact details just in case someone needs to reach you

9. **Spot risk/have a plan.** One of the most important obligations of the board is to constantly be on the lookout for risk to the company. While this usually

---

[364] See page 263.

conjures up images of "bad" things, risk can also mean opportunity, such as the risks associated with the acquisition of another business. In your dealings with the board, be aware of their need for help in spotting risk (good or bad) and developing a plan to deal with it.[365] The latter is one thing that many in-house counsel often skip over, that is, they are great at pointing out risk or problems but not so great at having a plan or potential solution in hand. Whenever you are dealing with the board and discussing risks, be sure to have in hand your ideas on how to solve the problem or take advantage of the situation. For example, the board is focused on a potential merger but is concerned about opposition from the antitrust regulators. One potential way to help solve the problem is to identify experts (economic, others) who have helped companies get similar deals approved in the past and bring those names and those successes to the attention of the board. While there is no guarantee your deal will get approved, engaging outside experts who have dealt with issues similar to those you anticipate having can help a lot in terms of both getting your deal approved and bringing some peace of mind to the board that the company is doing all it can to get the deal approved.

10. **Keep the CEO up to speed.** There may be times when a member of the board reaches out to you directly with a question or a request. That is generally fine. In fact, you should be flattered they are coming directly to you. Regardless, you need to keep the CEO (and the general counsel) up to speed if this occurs. You do not want them to be blindsided by anything going on at the board level. Be sure they know not only that a board member reached out to you but also be sure they know how you responded, including ensuring they get a copy of anything you send to the board. This gets tricky if the request involves some type of investigation of the CEO or the board member asks that you not tell the CEO about the contact. The former is actually a bit easier to deal with because there should be a process in place at your company with respect to investigations of employees, in particular senior management. If you get a request like this, go to your manager for help with how to proceed. If the request is simply "don't tell the CEO," it gets harder and you are now in a tough spot. How you deal with this will depend on the circumstances and your position in the company's hierarchy. The safest play here is to speak with your manager or the general counsel. If that's not a good option, contact outside counsel you trust for advice.

*****

---

365 See page 239.

There is nothing here that is overly complicated. Rather, most of it comes with experience. And everything mentioned above should be weighed based on how your board *actually* works (either from your own firsthand knowledge or from information you glean from others). It can be a bit scary the first time you're invited to meet a member or members of the board of directors. But, the fact that you are meeting them is a good sign for your career. Look for opportunities to get in front of the board. If you become aware that something you are working on is going to the board, ask your manager if there is a way you can participate or just sit in. It may not be appropriate but they will remember that you are interested and will likely look for opportunities for you down the road.

April 29, 2016

Crisis Readiness and Risk Management

Ten Things: Spotting, Analyzing, and Managing "Risk"

It's difficult to be part of any business and not hear about "risk." It's everywhere. If risk were a woman, it would be the Hollywood "It Girl" of 2016. Put another way, risk is the new black. It's on the lips of every CEO, CFO, and board member, as it should be. And, anything that is important to the board and the C-suite is important to the legal department. In fact, over the past five or so years, one of the key responsibilities businesses are placing on in-house lawyers is spotting and managing risk. The business wants its in-house lawyers to be the ones who sniff through virtually *every* situation looking for risk (legal or otherwise). What this means is that, more and more, in-house counsel need to be masters of the company's business operations and strategy (both short and long term), because you cannot successfully spot and manage risk unless you understand how the company operates and where it wants to go.

Generally, when asked about risk, most in-house lawyers respond *retroactively*, that is, they talk about risk in terms of things the company has already experienced—a recent lawsuit, a data breach, an internal investigation, and so on. While this is helpful, it is only part of the calculus of identifying risk. The harder part (and the more valuable skill) is being able to look forward and see risk. Although it is a more valuable skill, my experience is that there is little to no training around *how* to "look for risk," let alone how to evaluate it or report it out. For many in-house lawyers, it is largely a self-taught skill. My goal here is not to write a treatise about risk or risk management. I have read enough of those types of articles to know that they look really impressive and have complicated charts, graphs, and formulas, but most are hard to apply in the everyday, fast-paced in-house world. I want to set out ten simple ideas and processes you can use to spot and identify forward-looking risk and to evaluate and manage that risk alongside the business. Below I will discuss a few guidelines that will help you be better able to fulfill the demand from the business that you become "risk spotter in chief" or, as I was often called, the "risk guy":

1. **What is risk?** When we think of "risk," we tend to think only of bad things. Yet, not all risk is negative. Avoiding all risk is not the way to run a successful

business, sports team, legal department, research facility, military, or pretty much any organization you can name. Taking risks is important to the success of any endeavor. There is risk in any merger for example, but companies still take that risk every day because there may be a big financial payoff. There is risk in "going for it" on fourth down in American football, but teams still take that chance because it may allow them to win the game.

2. **The risk continuum.** It is important to not always view risk as negative. For simplicity, think of risk as a continuum of "degrees of consequences" ranging from negative outcomes to increasingly positive outcomes:

Risk/Outcome Continuum

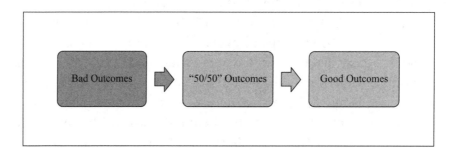

The key is your ability as in-house counsel to understand the different consequences of what you, or the company, want to do, where those consequences fall on the above continuum, and how everything balances out when the good and the bad are added up (i.e., "value creation" vs. "value destruction"). Where the negative consequences clearly outweigh the positive consequences and the downside is material, you probably do not take the risk or vice versa. The really hard part is when the negative and positive consequences are close or nearly equal. Now you have the premise of what I call the "risk conundrum," that is, how do you best manage a situation that has nearly equal negative and positive outcomes? As they say, that's why the C-suite gets paid the big money. And because the C-suite wants to keep making the big money, it wants the in-house lawyers to help spot and manage risk with the goal of helping the business get to positive outcomes.

3. **Types of risk—legal.** As in-house counsel, I made it simple for myself and categorized risk as either "legal" or "strategic." Legal risks are what lawyers are very familiar with, including such broad categories as:
   - Compliance risk
   - Litigation risk
   - Regulatory risk
   - Security risk (e.g., is the physical plant a "safe" work place?)
   - Information risk (e.g., data breach, theft of trade secrets)

4. **Types of risk—strategic.** Strategic risks are risks that the business leaders tend to focus on that are critical to the survival of the business, such as:
   - Financial risk
   - Marketplace risk (e.g., competitors, disruptive technology/business model risk)
   - Succession risk (e.g., sudden death or departure of a CEO)
   - Major political uncertainty risk (e.g., a political coup, currency devaluation)
   - Natural disaster risk (e.g., pandemic, earthquake, flood)
5. **Overlapping risk.** The lists above are not exhaustive and my two categories of risk are not mutually exclusive. In fact, they often overlap.

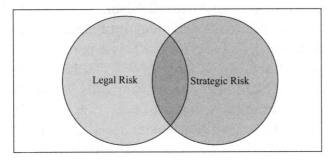

For example, the bank/financial markets meltdown in 2008 in the United States (and elsewhere) included both strategic risks (severe financial problems for most companies, governments teetering on default) and legal risks (regulatory and litigation problems for many companies tied to financial problems). Similarly, in the United States, there is a constant battle in Washington over H1-B visas (i.e., visas given to highly skilled foreign workers so they can fill jobs U.S. employers have difficulty filling from the domestic work force). Companies may have a strategic risk in that if they cannot find enough qualified employees with the right skills to perform critical jobs, the business will be negatively impacted. The company also has a legal risk in that regulations limit the number of H1-B visas and the cap number fluctuates year to year, typically running out in the first or second calendar quarter. Thus, companies must promptly begin the legal process of applying for H1-B visas or risk getting shut out. The most valuable in-house lawyers see the company's strategic and legal risks, analyze how they interconnect, and advise the company on what to do next (e.g., lobby the U.S. government to add to the number of available visas, a process to ensure applicants are qualified for H1-B visas). Lastly, on a global front, the impact of the "Brexit," the United Kingdom leaving the European Union, is fraught with both legal risk and strategic risk for companies. Smart in-house lawyers are already planning on how to deal with the fallout.

6. **Spotting risk.** Risk is everywhere. While the company wants you to spot *every* risk, doing so is impossible. In order to make it manageable, you need to know what types of risk are most important to the company and where to look to get information about those risks. Here are three things to do:
    - *First*, you need to either create or become part of a team that spots risk and/or determines what types of risks are important to measure. Many companies have an enterprise risk management department. If so, this is the group you want to insert yourself into in some manner, that is, as a member, partner, or subject matter expert. If not, you may need to organize a group yourself. This would include internal audit, finance, legal, information security, and members of the primary lines of business. The goal of this risk team, however constituted, is to regularly identify and consider the company's key strategic, operational, and legal risks. This group will need to evaluate the company's opportunities and threats across all businesses and staff group functions. And this team will need to constantly update its work product to account for changes in facts, circumstances, or law.
    - *Second*, keep your eyes and ears open in meetings: board meetings, C-suite meetings, town hall meetings, strategy planning meetings, staff group meetings, and so on. There is an amazing amount of information flowing at these types of meetings. As different topics are introduced, quickly run through these questions:
        - *Is this something a regulator might be interested in?*
        - *Is this something that could make customers or vendors upset or bring on litigation?*
        - *Is this something that if it becomes public or goes "badly" could damage the reputation of the company?*
        - *Is this something covered by specific laws and does it comply?*
        - *Is this something you have seen other companies (competitors, etc.) have problems with?*
        - *Is this something that could severely injure someone (e.g., a safety or environmental mishap)?*

    This is not an exhaustive list, but it is a "good enough" list that if you hit on any of these, it tells you to do some more digging about the risks associated with the project or idea. You can also use this same list (or any list you care to create) as you read documents or emails discussing the company's business or when you read or watch third-party information sources (newspapers, television, magazines). As in-house counsel, you should be constantly on the lookout for risk. A list of questions like these gives you a tool to use as you do so.
    - *Third*, create a simple "alarm" system to tell you if something bad might be coming your way. Set up an alert in each of the main Internet search

engines: Google,[366] Yahoo!,[367] and Bing[368]. Use the name of your company (or any of its subsidiaries) when setting up the alert. You can also add specific topics if helpful. Anytime the search engine finds an article containing the name(s) or terms in the alert, you will get an email with a link to the article. You can also monitor social media regarding your company's brand. There are many articles online that list a number of ways to do this for free.[369] Most of what you get back from these tools can be quickly discarded but every once in a while you'll find something that requires more attention.

7. **Evaluating risk.** In order to evaluate risk and potential outcomes, you need to understand three things:
   - *The company's business goals and strategy.*
   - *The company's level of risk tolerance, that is, how much risk will the company accept?*
   - *The right questions to ask.*

   The company's business goals and strategy (short and long term) should be easily available to you and the risk team mentioned above. Again, as an in-house lawyer you need to fully understand how your company operates in order to understand its goals and strategies. Educate yourself—and help others in the legal department educate themselves as well. Once you know the goals and strategy, you can be on the lookout for developments that could impact either one (negatively or positively).

   The company's level of risk tolerance comes primarily from the board of directors and the C-suite (or in small businesses directly from the owner(s)). Some companies are very conservative; some not so much. Company policies (e.g., business ethics) also set the bar on risk tolerance. Additionally, internal audit and the individual business units/staff groups (including members of the compliance department and the legal department) can and should weigh in on acceptable risks. The most straightforward method of getting this information is to ask the right people through interviews, surveys, workshops, offsite meetings, and so on. When you ask the right people, it is fundamentally important that you also ask the "right" questions. By this I mean finding a way to go beyond discussing historical failures or problems and, instead, attempting to peer into the future and spot new or different types of risks. For this, you and the risk team need

---

366 https://support.google.com/alerts/answer/4815696?hl=en.

367 http://smallbusiness.chron.com/can-yahoo-mail-give-alert-75123.html.

368 http://answers.microsoft.com/en-us/bing/forum/bing_users/how-to-set-up-bing-news-alert/92ac3efb-3e15-4db7-89f5-73b6f7202407?auth=1.

369 See, e.g., http://www.procommunicator.com/free-monitoring-tools/

to be able to explain to those you are interviewing what you are trying to accomplish with respect to gathering information about risks. If you don't, and just ask them to "set out any risks you see for the company next year," you will probably get a recitation tied to *past failures*, but get little about new potential risk arising from future problems. Regardless, think about the things you need to know from your source, including the following:
- *What type of risk is it?*
- *Under what scenarios would the risk arise/happen?*
- *What is the likelihood of the risk occurring?*
- *Can third parties cause the risk to the company?*
- *What type of harm can arise from the risk?*
  - *Monetary?*
  - *Operational?*
  - *Criminal?*
- *What are the best case, worst case, and most likely case for the company in terms of harm?*
- *What are the ways we can deal with the risk to minimize bad outcomes and maximize good outcomes?*
  - *Policies/training?*
  - *Contractual terms?*
  - *Insurance?*
  - *Operational controls?*
  - *Take a "bigger" risk?*
  - *Preparation for the risk?*[370]
- *Are there benchmarks or standards we can use to measure against?*
- *How can we best monitor the risk/what are the trigger points?*

You will likely/should come up with your own tailored list of questions for your company, but the above list covers a wide swath of what you need to know.

8. **Estimating risk.** Once you have spotted and analyzed risk, you will likely want to estimate the "cost" or "value" of the risk, depending on whether the risk is negative or positive in nature. There is a relatively simple and standard formula for this:

Risk value = Probability of event × cost/value of event if it occurs

For example, you are faced with a large breach of contract claim. While the dollar value claimed is high ($1M), you estimate the probability of losing to be

---

[370] See page 239.

low (25%). The risk value is then: *.25 (probability)* × *$1M (cost)* = *$250,000*. On the positive side, if you have a merger worth $25M in incremental operating income every year if consummated and you think the odds that regulators approve the merger is high (80%), the risk value is: *.80 (probability)* × *$25M (value to company)* = *$20M*. An additional tool for estimating risk is a risk impact/probability chart mentioned in the "resources" section below.

9. **Reporting risk.** You need to report risk to the business. This will occur in one of two ways:
   - A formal risk assessment report (usually prepared by the risk team), or
   - An *ad hoc* report (made when necessary).

   The formal report will likely go to the board of directors/audit committee and the C-suite. It will be written and follow a fairly rigid process and established format. An *ad hoc* report may be an email to the general counsel, a memo to the CEO, or an off-the-cuff discussion during a meeting. Regardless of the way the risk is reported, you need to ultimately cover five things: (a) what the risk is, (b) the likelihood of the risk occurring, (c) the range of outcomes the company could face, (d) the options the company has for dealing with the range of outcomes, and (e) a recommendation about which option the company should choose and why.

   If you are reporting the risk in writing, be sure to take the necessary steps to preserve any privilege that might apply.[371] If you fail to do so, understand that any writing (email, report, presentation, etc.) may have to be turned over to the other side in the event of a government investigation or civil litigation. This means you need to spend time with the nonlawyers helping them learn to write smart[372] and to know when to appropriately involve the legal department so as to preserve any privilege. Both are important because poorly drafted or thought-out documents discussing risk could be as harmful to the company as the worst risks they describe. Keep in mind that if you work for a publicly traded company, then you will need to identify material risks to the business in the "risk factors" section of your public filings.

10. **Resources.** Here are several resources you can use to help you spot, analyze, and manage risk:
    - Institute of Risk Management[373]
    - Risk Management Society[374]

---

371 See page 263.
372 See page 45.
373 https://www.theirm.org/.
374 https://www.rims.org/resources/ERM/Pages/default.aspx.

- Risk Factor Disclosures for Publicly Traded Companies[375]
- *Risk and Compliance Magazine* (free e-magazine)[376]
- Risk Impact/Probability Chart[377]
- *Risk Management Magazine* (free online)[378]
- Harvard Business Review—Risk Management[379]
- *Wall Street Journal—Risk and Compliance Journal* (subscription needed)[380]

*****

You will not spot *every* risk your company faces and that's okay. But you need to have a plan in place to catch the most important ones. The above sets out some simple ideas and processes to help in-house counsel spot and evaluate risk. A lot of it you probably already know or intuitively understand based on your legal training (though thinking about risk as potentially "positive" can be new). The challenge is translating your understanding and knowledge of risk into something the business values and can use to maximize the success of the company, and therefore the interests of the shareholders, customers, and employees. Being able to spot and communicate risk (and solutions/options) is a core skill you need to develop on the way to becoming general counsel.[381] The key takeaways here today are as follows: (a) be constantly alert for risks to your company; (b) don't just report risk, but be prepared to discuss the potential outcomes and options for the company; and (c) don't create additional "bad" risk by not putting a lot of thought into writing documents discussing/analyzing risk (or failing to teach your fellow employees how to draft smart documents).

June 28, 2016

---

375 https://www.linkedin.com/pulse/20141118140929-132518611-risk-factor-disclosures-for-reporting-public-companies.
376 http://riskandcompliancemagazine.com/.
377 https://www.mindtools.com/pages/article/newPPM_78.htm.
378 http://www.rmmagazine.com/.
379 https://hbr.org/topic/risk-management.
380 http://blogs.wsj.com/riskandcompliance/.
381 See page 5.

Ten Things: Crisis Preparation 101

As in-house counsel you can sum up your priorities in two categories: "Maximize Value Creation" (e.g., M&A) and "Minimize Value Destruction" (e.g., defending "bet the company" litigation). Pretty much all legal work you or the department do will fall under the above. A "crisis" situation falls under potential value destruction and can come in many forms, including major litigation, data breach, government investigation or criminal indictment, environmental catastrophe, social media "meltdown," product recalls, death of the CEO, campus intrusion, and Foreign Corrupt Practices Act claims, just to name a few. How you and the company respond to a crisis will go a long way to preventing or limiting damage to the company, including its reputation and brand. In-house counsel should play a key role in the strategy and plans to manage these risks should they arise. Ask yourself this question: "If [*pick a crisis*] happened today, do I know the exact steps the company and I would take in the next 24 hours?" If the answer is "no," then it's time to get cracking.[382]

Below I set out ten things for in-house counsel to help manage a crisis situation both before there is one and if one occurs. It is impossible to set out everything you should know or do in a crisis situation, but you will get the building blocks to put plans in place and do further research[383] yourself. This is also an opportunity to show thought leadership, vision, and strategic thinking to your board of directors and your CEO (and other executive team members) by ensuring them that the company is taking the right steps to be ready for a crisis situation.

---

382 http://deloitte.wsj.com/riskandcompliance/2015/03/02/creating-value-from-risk-owen-ryan-ceo-deloitte-risk-advisory-services-2/.

383 http://www.continuitycentral.com/OrganisationResilience.pdf.

Pre-Crisis

1. **It *can* happen to you.** One challenge in the area of crisis planning is to get the business to understand that bad things don't always happen to the "other guys." You should have a discussion with the CEO, CFO, and head of corporate communications (and/or others) about what plans, if any, the company has in place in the event of a crisis and how to go about updating or implementing those plans in a repeatable and systematic manner. It may be an easy sell or it may be a harder sell depending on the audience. If necessary, you can easily find very public examples of crisis situations[384] that went badly and use those situations to stress the importance of having a plan.
2. **Evaluate your company's most likely risks.** You cannot plan for everything but you should be able to think through and prepare for the most likely five to ten situations that would—given your business—present a crisis to your company. The first step is to create a cross-company team to flesh out the risk scenarios (finance, tax, HR, internal audit, legal, CIO, business units, CFO, etc.). You may be the leader of such a team or you may just be part of such a team. It doesn't matter which. Your job is to help ensure the process of crisis planning gets under way. A broad cross-section of the company will give insight into the risks you should be most concerned about. This will enable the team to prioritize the most likely crisis situations and put together the right plans to deal with them.
3. **Have a written plan.** The next step is to prepare a written plan. You can have one overarching plan that contains sections dealing with different types of crisis situations or separate plans for each type of crisis. I would lean toward the former but either option can work. Part of the effort may be gathering crisis plans that already exist in different parts of the organization and bringing them into one document. Regardless, the purpose of a written plan is to give the leadership team basic step-by-step guidance as to what to do in the event of a crisis. Here is a nonexhaustive list of things you will need to cover in your plan:
    - Clear definition of roles and responsibilities.
    - A process to triage the crisis, that is, how serious and widespread the problem is, including impacts on customers and other parties, litigation risk, what facts are known, and what needs to be determined.
    - Where to meet (including an off campus location in the event you are not able to meet at your headquarters).

---

384 https://storify.com/FUTUREPersp/top-crisis-pr-stories-2014.

- How people will be notified of a crisis situation (e-mail, phone call, etc.).
- Crisis bridge-line number and instructions (including how to dial in from foreign countries).
- Who needs to participate (including primary backups in the event someone is not available). Your crisis team will likely consist of the CEO, CFO, the general counsel, COO, chief compliance officer, HR, corporate communications, marketing, investor relations, and internal audit. Likewise, the heads of the various business units should be part of the team.
- Who is in charge of any particular type of crisis; that is, depending on the issue, it may be the general counsel, human resources, CFO, and so on. It is not a good idea to have the CEO in charge of the crisis team. While he or she will be part of the team and may have a key role in communications, the nitty-gritty details of operating the crisis team day-to-day should rest with someone else.
- Contact information for internal people, including alternative phone numbers and alternative email addresses should the company's email server go down.
- Contact information for external people including the board of directors and any outside resources you may need including outside counsel, media relations, security, police/FBI, etc. As in-house counsel, you will want to think about who you would call in the event of a particular crisis. It may be a different lawyer for a data breach versus a litigation crisis. Make sure you have multiple contact numbers for them and have a backup person you can contact. Let your outside counsel know they have been identified by you as someone to help in the event a crisis hits. They will appreciate it and may have useful ideas for you to consider in terms of crisis preparation.
- Communications plan for dealing with external media, social media, employees, investor relations, board of directors, and regulators, as well as who is in charge of developing the messaging and making contact with each group. While you cannot develop the exact messaging language in advance of the crisis, you can develop standard templates (format, language, etc.) that will save time.
- A clear process and timeline to develop and distribute communications, updates to the team, and other documents. With respect to outside communications it will be very important to set out in detail how communications get approved as you can lose valuable time if it's not clear who needs to "sign off" on something before it goes out.
- Where the plan is stored and how it is accessed, and who is the "keeper" of the plan.

- A process to update the plan regularly. Do a health check on the crisis plan at least annually or, ideally, twice a year. Be sure to get a broad set of viewpoints about risks the company faces, in particular if you have new executives joining the company or your business has expanded into new areas.

4. **Practice the plan.** Once you have your plan in place, create "table top" exercises to practice different scenarios over the course of the year. You can eliminate a lot of the uncertainty and confusion that come with a crisis by running through a training exercise so people know what to do and what to expect. This is an area where you may want to invest money in having a third party[385] help you with developing and running the exercises.

5. **Invest in media training for your executive team.** Communication, both internal and external, is a key element of a crisis response plan. You and your executive team may be called upon to speak publicly, for example, via a newspaper, trade magazine, or television. Many companies provide basic media training to their executives. If your company does not, you should raise the issue in terms of at least considering it. Moreover, you should consider more advanced media training for those people who are designated as spokespeople for the company in your crisis plan.

During a Crisis

6. **Stay calm.** When the crisis hits, the most important thing you can do as in-house counsel is stay calm. Many in the business will take their cues from you. Even if your stomach is churning with worry, you will need to be a rock and bring perspective to the situation. If you've done the right type of planning, you will already know what to do, whom to call, and what to say. You need to set the tone and keep people focused on the task at hand.

7. **Follow the plan.** Trust the plan you've put into place and follow it. There may certainly be good reason to deviate from it, but the first meetings and responses regarding a crisis should track what you already have down in writing. This is especially true when it comes to media and other communications. You need to speak with one voice and stay on message. In these days of instant communication, you and your company will be bombarded with questions about your crisis (from both outside and inside the company). The worst thing that could happen is for someone to freelance a response or speculate without knowledge

---

[385] http://www.optimalrisk.com/Risk-Security-Consulting/Business-Continuity-Planning-and-Crisis-Management.

of the facts. And make sure your board of directors is properly updated. If the directors are learning of material issues from other sources first, you will be off to a very bad start. If your company is publicly traded, you will need to be on top of any necessary 8K filings.

8. **Outside help.** In a serious crisis situation, it is highly likely you will need outside help. It can be in the form of experienced outside counsel, public relations team, or other experts. You should have these resources identified in advance and have their phone numbers on speed dial. Moreover, depending on the nature of the crisis, it may involve litigation or regulatory review. If so, it will be important to ensure that parts of your investigation are appropriately protected as privileged communications.[386] This is an area where your outside counsel can be particularly helpful. If appropriate, you will want either the legal department or outside counsel to direct and lead the investigation as doing so will maximize the availability of various privileges.[387]

9. **Communications review.** You need a process in place for legal to review all substantive communications with an eye toward possible litigation down the road. The legal department must work hand in hand with corporate communications in this area. Your instinct as a lawyer will be to say as little as possible. In many circumstances, however, this simply is not possible. You will need to be flexible with respect to communications and look to balance[388] business needs (simple, digestible messaging) versus legal needs (all the complexity and nuances of litigation) as best as you can. You should explain to corporate communications your concerns from a legal viewpoint and listen closely to their concerns from a business communications standpoint. Working together—with some flexibility on both sides—you will be able to balance these needs. One good way to build a better relationship with your communications colleagues is to provide them with training about legal issues generally and the pitfalls of poorly drafted documents, especially in the event of litigation, and vice versa in terms of having communications present to the broader legal team about business messaging.

---

386 http://calfee.com/court-upholds-privilege-and-provides-expanded-protections-for-internal-investigations/.

387 http://www.lexology.com/library/document.ashx?g=3d428f5a-b508-4dfe-b1cd-594bb0c84abe.

388 https://www.lexisnexis.com/communities/corporatecounselnewsletter/b/newsletter/archive/2015/01/08/why-general-counsel-should-manage-complex-corporate-crises-lessons-learned-from-a-crisis-communications-veteran.aspx.

After the Crisis

10. **Postmortem.** When the crisis is over[389] (and it will be), you should invest time in reviewing what worked, what didn't work, and how best to revise your plans, behaviors, and other actions going forward. This is a great place for the legal department to take the lead and add value.

*****

At some point, you and your company will be faced with a crisis situation. The time to prepare for that crisis is now. Planning will not prevent a crisis from happening, but it will make managing the process much easier on everyone (including you) and will help minimize the potential damage to your company. Put crisis planning at the top of your to do list this year.

March 3, 2015

---

389 http://www.businessinsider.com/the-art-of-the-post-mortem-2011-3.

Ten Things: Preparing for When "Bad Things" Happen

Unfortunately, the world we live in can go from good to shockingly awful in a matter of hours. There is no starker reminder of this than the horrific events in Paris on November 13, 2015, followed by the terrorist assault on a hotel in Mali just days later. Besides terrorism, disasters arising from natural events (hurricane, pandemic, earthquake, tsunami) and man-made events (plane crash, fire, cyber attack, workplace violence) lurk in the shadows as well. This is true for both individuals and businesses: tragedy does not discriminate.

One of the most important tasks you have as in-house counsel is to help ensure that your company is prepared for when disaster—man-made or natural—strikes. Protection of your fellow employees and corporate assets/shareholder value should always be at the top of your mind. In some companies, planning for disaster falls within the risk management department[390]; in others, it's a mixture of different departments, including the legal department. Some companies simply have not gotten around to planning for disaster. Regardless of where your company sits on this continuum, legal has a role to play in assisting the company plan for dealing with a crisis. If not already the case, you should ensure legal has a seat at the table for such planning. Here, I want to set out ten things you can do as in-house counsel to help the business plan for when bad things happen:

1. **Business continuity plan.** Every business should have a business continuity plan (BCP).[391] It is the gold standard in disaster planning. However, it is a big endeavor and not something that can be thrown together over the course of a week or two. A properly prepared BCP describes—in great detail—how a company will continue to carry on business in the event of a disaster. Ideally, the BCP will be structured with checklists and step-by-step instructions that

---

390 http://www.marquette.edu/riskunit/riskmanagement/whatis.shtml.
391 https://www.ready.gov/business/implementation/continuity.

allow management to quickly focus on the specific things they need to do to get the business back up and running. Given that the depth and breadth of a properly prepared BCP could easily be a separate book, I will not go into detail here about how to prepare a BCP. There are some resources noted below that can help you get started preparing or updating one. Instead, I will touch on a few BCP basics and then discuss key parts of the plan (or related issues) so as to give you the ability to get some things into place now versus waiting on creating an entire plan. Basically, a BCP requires the company to think through risks and vulnerabilities to the critical parts of its business, and then set out in detail how it will manage any such risk should it come to pass. The key takeaways are as follows: (a) have a plan, (b) disseminate it to management and employees, (c) train on and practice it, and (d) review it annually and update as needed.

2. **Identify the crisis team.** Your planning will start with identifying which executives/employees will make up the crisis team, that is, the people who will gather immediately once a crisis is declared and who will put the BCP into effect. They will also help create and update the plan. The team will largely be made up of senior executives from key lines of business and staff functions, with the goal to cover the entire business. Everyone's role and responsibilities should be clearly set out (e.g., crisis team chair, communications, security, IT, legal). You must establish succession planning with clear instructions about who takes over for whom in the event that someone is not available to act. Contact phone numbers and email addresses should already be listed and made available to everyone on the team. Remember to get alternative phone numbers and alternative email addresses in case the primary numbers/email are not available. It is critical that everyone know how—and be able to—contact other team members. Additionally, identify contacts at key third-party vendors (name, phone, email, description of service/products provided, etc.), as it is likely that some of your company's vendors will need to be involved in dealing with your crisis. The list of third-party vendors should include local utility companies.

3. **Travel.** Your plan will need to cover executive and employee travel, that is, what happens if there is a serious problem and how to avoid problems.[392] First, it is best practice to ensure that not all of your senior management will be on the same flight.[393] That way if there is an incident with the plane, other

---

[392] http://www.oncallinternational.com/blog/travel-risk-management-5-steps-protecting-traveling-employees/.

[393] https://www.shrm.org/hr-today/news/hr-news/pages/limitnumbersameflight.aspx.

executives will be available to deal with the problem. Second, your company should know where its traveling employees are at all times. Your travel agent can help with this and likely has tools to automate the process. All traveling employees should have phone numbers and other ways to contact their travel planner in the event an emergency arises and travel plans need to change. Third, if your employees are traveling to foreign countries, they should take steps to notify their government. In the United States, you notify the State Department via the Smart Traveler Program,[394] which is a free service that allows U.S. citizens/nationals traveling abroad to enroll their trip with the nearest U.S. embassy or consulate. By doing so, travelers will receive important information from the embassy about safety conditions in their destination country; help the embassy contact[395] them in an emergency of any nature; and help the traveler's family and friends get in touch with him or her in an emergency. Fourth, your company should have plans regarding medical emergencies and provide employees with information about what do to if they become ill or are in need of medical attention while on the road. Lastly, you should have detailed plans around what to do if there is a kidnapping[396] involving one of the company's employees.

4. **Temporary headquarters.** In a crisis you should, if possible, have a dedicated room for managing the situation. This room can be on-site or off-site. The key is to plan for the room before it is needed. You will want phones, Wi-Fi, printers, and other key services available (all of which are especially important if the crisis room is off-site). Moreover, it may not be possible to continue to operate your business from its existing location (fire, biohazard, earthquake, bomb, etc.). Your plan should discuss where and how management and employees will work and communicate if this is the case. Many employees may be able to work from home or will simply be idle for some portion of the crisis. Others will need to be present at a temporary work location. Identifying a location (or a process to secure a location) in advance of a problem is an important step.

5. **Identify/know first responders.** For each company location local executives should know whom to call for which type of emergency. In the United States, the most likely first responders will be police and fire (typically, call 911).

---

394 https://step.state.gov/step/.
395 https://travel.state.gov/content/passports/en/emergencies.html.
396 http://www.riskandinsurance.com/detention-risks-grow-for-traveling-employees/.

But don't forget about poison control,[397] public health officials,[398] the Federal Emergency Management Agency,[399] the FBI,[400] Centers for Disease Control,[401] Homeland Security (federal[402] and state[403]), and other public safety officials. Most countries will have similar agencies. Your security manager should reach out to each and touch base. First, just knowing whom to call in an emergency is critical. Second, having a conversation with these officials now, before there is a problem, can provide access to other resources, information, and guidance on how best to prepare for the worst. Once you identify the correct officials, their names, offices, and contact information should go into your BCP (and be sure to refresh the first responder information regularly).

6. **Workplace readiness/security.** In this day and age it is very important to make sure the work environment is as secure and safe as possible. There are no guarantees, but preventing a crisis will be easier if your building is properly readied and secure[404] before there is a problem. The most common ways to do this are registration desks, security guards, entry checkpoints, cameras, properly maintained secured access (e.g., card reader), well-lit facilities and parking areas, clean grounds, unobstructed exits, proper fire suppression system, fire extinguishers, and other safety-related items. The list of what makes a building safe and secure is long.[405] Additionally, there should be well-marked and properly stocked first aid kits throughout the facility. Defibrillators are becoming more and more common as well—in fact, some U.S. states require them.[406] Paramount on your list should be plans for and practice of building evacuations in case of fire, violence, weather, and other emergencies (including having alternative locations for employees to gather in the event one selected location is not safe).

7. **Develop a culture of security.** In addition to securing your building and premises, you need your employees to be on the ball as well. Developing a culture

---

397 http://www.aapcc.org/.
398 http://www.naccho.org.
399 http://www.fema.gov/about-agency.
400 https://www.fbi.gov/contact-us/field-offices.
401 http://www.cdc.gov/contact/.
402 https://www.dhs.gov/direct-contact-information.
403 https://www.dhs.gov/state-homeland-security-and-emergency-services.
404 https://www.wbdg.org/design/provide_security.php.
405 http://hsema.dc.gov/sites/default/files/dc/sites/hsema/publication/attachments/Security%20Guidance%20FINAL_0.PDF.
406 http://www.ncsl.org/research/health/laws-on-cardiac-arrest-and-defibrillators-aeds.aspx.

of security awareness[407] can saves lives and property. For example, all employees should be on the lookout for people who do not belong on your premises. The easiest way to do this is to train employees to, politely, challenge (or report) people not wearing badges. Employees should also be on the lookout for anything out of place, including strange vehicles, packages/backpacks left unattended, or anything else that just does not "feel right." There should be training as to what to do under such circumstances and posters or signage with reminders and phone numbers of whom to call should be utilized. Think about the old World War II poster "Loose Lips Sink Ships." A simple reminder to civilians about an important issue at the time. The Department of Homeland Security has a similar saying: "If you see something, say something."[408] This can easily be incorporated into your own program. Additionally, providing first aid training, CPR training, and defibrillator training can be an excellent way to help develop the right culture—and provide valuable skills in the event of a crisis. Support and participation by senior management cannot be overemphasized. While it can be annoying to stop what you're doing to wander outside for a "fake" fire drill, it is very important that management get behind the importance of such drills and participate when the testing begins (i.e., no one should think they are too important or busy to participate in the drill). If the senior management does not take the drill seriously, then neither will the employees. As with many things, the tone at the top will help determine if security and crisis planning becomes second nature or is just another one of those "programs" that fails to catch hold because it only received lip service from the executive team. Lastly, all employees should be aware of the general parameters of your crisis plan and where to go for information if they suspect a problem or there is a problem (e.g., website, designated persons). The overall goal here is to combat complacency among your employees when it comes to security and safety. You don't want to overdrill and rehearse but you also want to keep the training and messaging current so that people know what to do in an emergency and understand the need to be watchful and on guard.

8. **Insurance.** Get some. Any planning for business continuity needs to contemplate insurance coverage for some part of the risk, especially catastrophic risk. Many companies have "business interruption" insurance[409] to cover interruptions. Likewise, many companies also carry kidnapping insurance and other

---

407 https://emilms.fema.gov/is906/wsa01summary.htm.
408 https://www.dhs.gov/see-something-say-something.
409 https://www.irmi.com/articles/expert-commentary/when-does-business-interruption-insurance-coverage-stop.

types of specialized insurance. See my discussion on insurance law basics.[410] A call to your insurance company may be among the first you make in the event of a crisis. Know whom to call. Additionally, keep in mind that many insurers are generally happy to work with you on spotting issues, training, and planning around the risks they are insuring—kind of free consulting services. And everybody likes freebies. Your insurance broker can be very helpful here as well. You should be regularly reviewing the company's insurance coverage and making sure it matches up against potential risks.

9. **Communications.** One of the most important parts of your crisis planning is the communications process—both internal and external. Several key points here (and also see my earlier discussion about Crisis Preparation 101).[411] First, you want to speak with one voice in the event of a crisis. Determine who that will be in advance and ensure that everyone knows who is authorized to speak for the company with respect to which issues. Typically this will be the head of corporate communications. You can prepare templates (email, press releases, etc.) in advance as well so that your communications have a uniform tone and look. With respect to internal communications you have two audiences. The first is the crisis team itself and ensuring that the communication flows back and forth without problems. Crisis team members should identify an alternate, that is, someone who will sit in for them if they are otherwise unable to perform with the team, and their contact information added to the plan. These people should be notified that they are the alternate and should be part of any training, meetings, and the like involving the crisis team so they are current and up to speed. The second internal audience will be the general employee base.[412] They will be anxious for news about what is going on, what the company is doing in response, where they can go for more information or regular updates, and what they should be doing during this time of trouble.[413] There is certainly a place for "all employee" communication blasts but also think about a cascade method of communication where different levels of the organization receive a message and are then responsible for getting the message down to their teams (along with any group-specific information they need or wish to add). For external messaging,[414] be prepared to deal with questions from the

---

410 See page 93.

411 See page 247.

412 https://www.melcrum.com/research/engage-employees-strategy-and-change/top-tips-10-point-guide-effective-employee.

413 http://www.snapcomms.com/solutions/internal-crisis-communications.

414 http://www.bernsteincrisismanagement.com/the-10-steps-of-crisis-communications/.

press, shareholders, government officials, family members of your employees, and the like. Having a website page dedicated to making the most recent/current information available 24/7 is a good idea and the shell can be prepared in advance of a crisis. Similarly a 24/7 recorded message on a toll-free line is also a good way to mass communicate. If you have a call center and/or central reception area, you will need to keep them in mind as you prepare materials so they have guidance and talking points for any inquiries that come their way. Finally, consider having all of your senior executives go through formal media training.[415]

10. **Sources for more information.** Here are some excellent sources (United States and international) I have found over time to help create a BCP and otherwise understand and plan for business interruptions, terrorist incidents, and other types of crisis situations.
    - Protecting Against Terrorism[416]
    - Company Primer on Preparedness and Response[417]
    - Strategy Guide for Business Continuity Planning[418]
    - Lawyers Guide to Disaster Planning[419]
    - Creating a Business Continuity Plan[420]
    - Expecting the Unexpected[421]
    - SAFETY Act[422]

    Among the sources, I would like to give special mention to the "SAFETY Act."[423] This little known program of the U.S. government provides protections to a wide range of technologies (including products, services, software, etc.) that are designed to identify, detect, deter, or respond to harm arising from

---

415 http://www.instituteforpr.org/crisis-management-communications/.
416 http://www.cpni.gov.uk/documents/publications/2010/2010002-protecting_against_terrorism_3rd_edition.pdf?epslanguage=en-gb.
417 http://www.bens.org/document.doc?id=10.
418 http://www.stamfordct.gov/sites/stamfordct/files/u118/strategy_guide_for_business_continuity_planning.pdf.
419 http://www.americanbar.org/content/dam/aba/events/disaster/surviving_a_disaster_a_lawyers_guide_to_disaster_planning.authcheckdam.pdf.
420 https://www.ready.gov/business/implementation/continuity.
421 https://www.gov.uk/government/uploads/system/uploads/attachment_data/file/61089/expecting-the-unexpected.pdf.
422 https://www.safetyact.gov/pages/homepages/SamsStaticPages.do?path=samspagesBenefitsToYourCompany.html.
423 https://www.safetyact.gov/jsp/faq/samsFAQSearch.do?action=SearchFAQForPublic.

an act of terrorism. If your products or services are "designated" by the government under this program, then, in the event of a terrorist act, the following terms apply: (a) liability is limited to the amount of insurance recommended by Homeland Security, (b) no joint and several liability for noneconomic damages, (c) no punitive damages or prejudgment interest, and (d) any recovery is reduced by amounts from collateral sources. If your products are "certified," then there is complete immunity. This program should be very appealing to a lot of businesses (and may even provide competitive advantages). For example, and one most pertinent given the attacks in Paris, sports venues[424] can obtain SAFETY designation or certification. A number of U.S. sports leagues and venues (and other businesses)[425] are now designated or certified. Other governments may have similar programs (or other programs relevant to this discussion and it's always worth finding out as those resources are usually very well prepared and free).

*****

There is way too much information on preparing a BCP to do anything other than skim the surface and provide some high-level guidance. But, with the list above, you and the legal department can become proactive and go to the business ready to raise and/or discuss the process to update or implement BCPs and get a seat at the table. Simply put, raise your hand and take the initiative. The skills needed to prepare such plans fit nicely into the skills most lawyers bring to the table already. If you are a young in-house lawyer, this can be a real opportunity to work with senior executives across the business and to work with and manage teams and complex issues. If a BCP is well off in the future, pick and choose among the items above where you can go ahead and get started. Getting any of these plans into place or at least started will make your company and its employees safer and protect your shareholders' investment in the company.

November 24, 2015

---

[424] http://catalystdc.com/2015/10/akmal-ali-discusses-safety-act-designation-for-sports-teams-and-venues/.

[425] http://www.sportsbusinessdaily.com/Journal/Issues/2015/10/05/Facilities/Safety-Act-Comerica.aspx.

Representing the Organization

Ten Things: The Attorney-Client Privilege— What You Need to Know

You're having lunch with someone from the business and talking about a project that's not going well and could lead to unhappiness on both sides—your company and the customer. Your buddy is spilling her guts about several of the problems she is encountering on the project and her concern that the company may not be performing up to the contract terms. Your first thoughts are that she's being overly harsh on herself and the team as some of the things she is mentioning may not be a big deal and there is time to correct them. Then she tells you not to worry about it too much because she and her team have been marking all of their emails and other documents discussing the problems as "attorney-client privilege" so that the team can write down whatever they want and it will never be seen by the customer. Oh crud (or words to that effect), you think. This is a real problem.

One of the in-house lawyer's most valuable tools is the attorney-client privilege and the ability of the client to ask pointed and raw questions for the purpose of obtaining legal advice. If not utilized properly, however, this tool can turn into a ballistic missile aimed right at your company. The applicability and proper use of the attorney-client privilege is a very misunderstood area, especially in the in-house world. There are a number of things both counsel and the client need to know in order to avoid common mistakes and provide the best possible case for claiming the privilege. Since some courts are looking at in-house counsel assertions of privilege with a wary eye, it is now more important than ever to get this right. Today I will discuss ten things you need to know to claim and preserve the attorney-client privilege:

1. **What is the attorney-client privilege?** The attorney-client privilege protects from disclosure to third parties: (a) confidential communications, (b) between an attorney and client, (c) made for the purpose of obtaining or providing legal advice. Unless all three of these prongs are met, the communication is not privileged. The purpose of the privilege is to allow clients to discuss issues openly in order to obtain legal advice from both in-house and outside counsel

without fear that those communications will be disclosed to third parties. The parameters of the attorney-client privilege in a particular situation depend on the law of the state where the communication took place. Consequently, it's important that in-house counsel have a good understanding of how the privilege applies in the state (or country) where their headquarters is located and/or the state (or country) where the attorney practices if it is not the same as the headquarters. The discussion here is general to the United States and not specific to any state or other country. Just know that the attorney-client privilege outside the United States can be very limited or may not exist at all.[426]

2. **Why should I care?** If you or the business get the privilege "wrong," there may be numerous long-term consequences for your company. First, if people mistakenly think documents are privileged, they might be careless in how they write things down, thinking the document will never be seen outside the company. I am not implying anyone would be untruthful, just that people are more precise, thoughtful, and professional if they know what they write may be seen by third parties. Second, if you waive the privilege for one document, chances are high that you may have waived the privilege with respect to other documents covering the same subject matter. Third, overly aggressive use of the "privileged" label can cause judges to think that the company is attempting to hide documents and find that such documents—even those legitimately privileged—should be turned over to the other side. Any of these developments can severely jeopardize your chances of winning in litigation and could lead to a damages award to the other side, as well as the release of potentially embarrassing documents the business thought were privileged.

3. **How does it work?** The attorney-client privilege applies in limited circumstances, in particular to the following:
   1. Requests for legal advice from a client to an attorney.
   2. Requests for information from an attorney for information needed to formulate or provide legal advice.
   3. The legal advice actually given by the attorney.

   Many lawyers (in-house and outside counsel) mistakenly believe anything they write for any reason is protected by the attorney-client privilege. They are wrong. Unless the communication meets the test of (a)–(c) it is not privileged. Below, I discuss some ways to help best ensure that truly privileged communications are treated as such. That said, it is up to you to take care to ensure that your communication is privileged or, if at all debatable, that you write the

---

426 http://www.acc.com/chapters/gny/upload/Tab-02-ACC_Seminar_Attorney_Client_Privilege_4-1-14.pdf.

document with the understanding that it may be seen by third parties, including any adversaries of the company. See my earlier section on "writing smart."[427]

4. **Legal advice versus business advice.** In order to invoke the attorney-client privilege, the communication must deal with legal advice. Legal advice is broader than just litigation-related communications, that is, it covers all legal advice including transactional and regulatory. Business advice, however, is never privileged and—for in-house counsel in particular—the line between the two can appear blurry. To add to the fun, different judges see things differently with respect to what constitutes legal advice and what constitutes business advice, that is, what one judge sees as protected legal advice, another judge will see as just business advice and subject to litigation discovery (i.e., turned over to the other side). You need to be constantly vigilant regarding the scope of your communications with the business and understand when you are or are not giving legal advice and, if you are, that you take the extra step to clearly note in the communication that you are providing legal advice.

5. **Who can be in the loop?** A key test of whether the privilege applies depends on who receives the communication. If a document that is otherwise privileged is shared with third parties, then the privilege is lost. A third party is generally anyone other than (a) the company's lawyers, (b) employees of the company with a need to know, (c) certain agents of the company and the attorney, and (d) any parties with whom the company has a joint defense or common interest agreement. The key here is to limit distribution of privileged communications within the company to those with a "need to know" as the bigger the circle of recipients, the greater the chance a court may rule the privilege does not apply. Sometimes it can be difficult to determine which third parties qualify as proper "agents" of the company. If you get it wrong, the privilege may be lost. For example, sharing privileged communications with third-party contractors/consultants,[428] public relations firms,[429] insurance brokers,[430] and other third parties may destroy the privilege. Whether or not this is so depends on the facts and the laws of any particular state.

6. **You must keep legal advice confidential.** It is absolutely critical that you and the company keep legal advice confidential. It cannot be passed along outside that company—a common problem with business colleagues who do not

---

427 See page 45.
428 http://www.mondaq.com/unitedstates/x/422032/trials+appeals+compensation/Procced+with+-Caution+AttorneyClient+Privilege+and+Communications+with+ThirdParty+Consultants.
429 http://www.lexology.com/library/detail.aspx?g=f7bd67f0-8aee-4ead-af6e-ad5b9dc8fb96.
430 http://www.riskandinsurance.com/privileged-communications-2/.

understand the problems doing so can cause. Likewise, everyone needs to be extremely careful when discussing or accessing privileged communications in public areas, for example, restaurants, elevators, airplanes, trains, and sporting events. I have personally overheard or seen numerous privileged communications in such places. As a lawyer, you need to maintain situational awareness at all times, and if you must discuss or access privileged information in a public area, take extra precautions to not be overheard and not expose your laptop screen to prying eyes. If that is not possible, you should simply defer the conversation or work until you can get to private area. Likewise, as much as you love your spouse or significant other, you cannot discuss privileged information with him or her. And, as noted above, the more people in the loop on privileged communications, the greater the chance that someone trips up on the confidentiality prong. *Bottom line*: the fewer people receiving the legal advice, the better. Only those with a need to know should receive privileged communications (and you should spend time thinking this issue through before sending out any privileged communication).

7. **Confidential does not mean privileged.** A common misperception among the business is that all confidential information is privileged, or if they label the communication as privileged, they can keep the documents out of the hands of third parties. As we've seen, this is not correct and the fact that there is a nondisclosure agreement or other type of confidentiality agreement in place will not make a document privileged nor will it preserve the privilege if it is disclosed to a third party. Many businesspeople also believe that if they simply include a lawyer as a recipient of the email, then the contents of the email are privileged. It is very important that you take the time to train your business colleagues and fellow lawyers on this issue. First, labeling something privileged does not make it privileged. It depends on whether the communication is for the purposes of obtaining or receiving legal advice. If that is not the case, there are no magic words that transform an everyday business communication (sensitive or not) into a privileged communication. Second, the business needs to understand that simply copying a lawyer on the communication (or inviting a lawyer to a meeting) does not make it privileged either. The communication still needs to meet the test of asking for or providing legal advice. Another vulnerable spot for privilege issues is attachments to emails.[431] Unless the attachment on its face or by its contents reflects that it is for the purpose of obtaining legal advice, there is a real risk that a court may

---

431 https://presnellonprivileges.com/2015/01/29/developing-issue-attachments-to-privileged-emails-not-necessarily-privileged/.

not view the attachment as privileged, and thereby separating the "privileged" cover note/email from the "nonprivileged" attachment and causing headaches for the company.

8. **Waiving the privilege.** Unfortunately, it is easy to waive the attorney privilege. If you disclose a privileged communication to a third party, it is very likely waived. You can also inadvertently waive the privilege. This typically arises in the context of exchanging documents during the discovery process in litigation, especially when the parties are exchanging a large volume of documents. Federal Rules of Evidence, Rule 502(d),[432] provides a simple and effective mechanism to cure an inadvertent disclosure of privileged documents during discovery. Moreover, if privileged documents are accidently produced, not only is there no waiver in the instant case, but also under FRE 502(d) there is no waiver in any other federal or state proceeding. With respect to the discovery process, while it is expensive and painful, it is very important that in-house counsel be highly involved in any document production for litigation and that there is a robust plan[433] designed to locate and cull out privileged documents. Additionally, companies are seeing regulators such as bank regulators[434] demanding that the attorney privilege be waived regarding certain documents (e.g., internal investigations) as part of any deal to settle or resolve an investigation. Finally, there are issues around whether a party forced to disclose privileged communications in one jurisdiction due to a subpoena[435] has waived the attorney-client privilege in general regarding those documents or if a company can engage in a selective waiver[436] of the privilege. If you find yourself in any of these situations, you should engage experienced outside counsel to advise you.

9. **Other privileges.** The attorney-client privilege is not the only privilege available to you. Though beyond the scope of this discussion, here are some

---

432 http://www.natlawreview.com/article/federal-rule-evidence-502d-underutilized-safety-net-document-intensive-litigation.

433 http://www.insidecounsel.com/2015/05/05/a-stitch-in-time-making-proper-privilege-calls-the?sl-return=1467767906.

434 http://www.americanbanker.com/bankthink/do-financial-institutions-have-any-attorney-client-privilege-left-1076390-1.html.

435 https://presnellonprivileges.com/2015/01/13/judge-lamberth-finds-no-waiver-where-party-produces-privileged-documents-pursuant-to-a-subpoena/.

436 http://www.wilmerhale.com/uploadedFiles/WilmerHale_Shared_Content/Files/Editorial/Publication/Rethinking%20Selective%20Waiver_NYLJ.pdf.

short descriptions of several others that may apply to your situation and are worth investigating:

- *The attorney work product privilege.* The attorney work product[437] privilege protects from disclosure to third parties materials that are prepared by or for a party or its representative motivated by or in anticipation of litigation. Note that it does not protect documents prepared for commercial transactions[438] or other nonlitigation-related legal work (which may still fall under the attorney-client privilege however). A key document used to determine if the attorney work product privilege applies is the litigation hold. Generally, documents prepared after a litigation hold is put in place and which are otherwise motivated by or in anticipation of that litigation are protected. Documents created before a litigation hold is in place may be protected but you can see the problem that arises if you claim litigation was anticipated but you did not put a litigation hold in place. The privilege also applies to documents prepared by nonattorneys, if prepared at the direction or under the supervision of lawyers.

- *The self-critical analysis privilege.* In some jurisdictions, the self-critical analysis privilege[439] is a qualified privilege that encourages companies to honestly evaluate themselves in light of some problem or incident yet protects the company from that report or analysis from being used against it in litigation. Note that whether or not this privilege exists at all is under debate. This is also the time to mention that internal investigations require special attention when it comes to privilege issues. Never begin an internal investigation[440] with potential legal issues without consulting with counsel (in-house or external). You will want to maximize the ability to claim privilege from the beginning, generally by having legal run the investigation.

- *Joint defense/common interest privilege.* These privileges—really just extensions of the attorney-client privilege—allow separate companies with common legal interests to share privileged communications between them so long as the communications otherwise meet the test for attorney-client communications. The agreements do not need to be in writing (though it's obviously better if there is a written agreement). Moreover, common

---

437 https://www.mcguirewoods.com/Client-Resources/Privilege-Ethics/Privilege-Points/2015/6/Courts-Disagree-Basic-Work-Product-Doctrine-Elements-I.aspx.

438 http://www.fr.com/fish-litigation/transactional-attorneys-work-product/.

439 http://apps.americanbar.org/litigation/committees/products/articles/summer2014-0714-self-critical-analysis-privilege.html.

440 https://www.wilmerhale.com/pages/publicationsandnewsdetail.aspx?NewsPubId=17179879305.

interest[441] (or community of interest)[442] privilege can apply to more than just litigation, that is, it can apply to mergers or other situations where legal interests are aligned.

10. **Best practices to preserve the attorney-client privilege.** There are several things you (and your business colleagues) can do to ensure the best possible outcome with respect to protecting the privilege:
    - The most important thing you can do is to be sure to properly label communications that meet the test for attorney-client communications. The document/email should be labeled "Attorney Client Communication—For Purpose of Legal Advice."
    - Be sure that the document/email clearly states that the person is seeking legal advice or that you (as attorney) are responding to a request for legal advice—for example, "I am providing you legal advice regarding [X]," or "I am seeking your legal advice regarding [Y]." Be sure that any attachment you are being asked to review (or have reviewed and are sending back to the client) is also properly labeled, that is, "Privileged and Confidential—Legal Advice/Review Sought." This will give you a better opportunity to claim that the privilege applies to both communications. It may sound a little silly, but using seven or eight words to clearly state in the cover note/email or on the face of the attachment that legal advice/review is the purpose of the communication can go a long way in convincing a judge that the privilege should apply.
    - If legal advice is being sought in any email or a memorandum, be sure that the business puts the lawyer in the "to" line versus the "cc" line. It is difficult to argue that the privilege applies when it appears that the lawyer is not the primary recipient of the communication.
    - Limit circulation of legal advice and privileged communications internally to those that need to know.
    - Keep the communication confidential and do not permit the legal advice to be circulated outside the company.
    - Don't claim the privilege when it's not applicable. Not all of your communications are privileged. If you or your colleagues are incorrectly labeling everything as "attorney-client communication," you can blow your chances of keeping truly privileged documents safe because a judge will, quite

---

441 http://apps.americanbar.org/litigation/committees/trialevidence/articles/fall2014-0914-common-interest-privilege.html.

442 http://www.goulstonstorrs.com/NewsEvents/InteractiveMedia?find=55701.

frankly, not believe you on the ten actual privileged documents when there are dozens or hundreds of incorrectly labeled documents.
- Write smart regardless of your level of confidence that the attorney-client privilege applies. You should always anticipate that anything you write may ultimately end up in the hands of your adversaries.
- Know the applicable laws in your state regarding the attorney-client privilege. Everyone on the legal team should know and understand the basics. Be zealous in your review of documents in production for litigation, and if you think the judge got it wrong, strongly consider appealing the judge's order and moving for a writ of mandamus if necessary.
- Understand that outside the United States privilege issues get tricky, and you should be very careful with respect to what you think might be a privileged communication.
- Train the business on all of the above and find teachable moments when you see something that jeopardizes the privilege or is not a proper use of the privilege.

*****

The attorney-client privilege is a valuable asset of your company. Treat it as such. Identify outside counsel to help answer questions about the privilege and ask them for a free CLE/presentation on the scope of the privilege in your state. Train yourself, your team, and the company on best practices. Be constantly vigilant and in teaching mode on the issue—and fight like hell to preserve and maintain the privilege when challenged. Finally, here are two of my favorite blogs: Presnell on Privileges[443] and McGuire Woods Privilege Points.[444] Subscribe to these blogs and keep them handy for reference; they are well written and full of very helpful information on privileges.

September 30, 2015

---

443 https://presnellonprivileges.com/.
444 https://www.mcguirewoods.com/Client-Resources/Privilege-Ethics/Privilege-Points.aspx.

Ten Things: How to Run a Government Affairs Campaign

If you are in-house counsel and are not paying attention to government officials and regulators (state, local, federal, international), you are making a big mistake. A company acts at its peril (e.g., Google, Microsoft, Airbnb, and Uber) if it underestimates the importance of being aware of what various government regulators are up to or thinking. Your company can be impacted dramatically (good or bad) by what happens through government action (or inaction). Government action can come in many forms, for example, taxation, new rules and regulations (business specific or general), government sanctions, import-export controls, legal reform (tort law, patent law), merger control, data privacy/security, public company regulation, and dozens of other areas. Recently, I have read articles on government action around patent reform, product regulation outside the United States, data privacy, Internet/net neutrality, Fair Labor Standards Act regulations, and regulation of financial advisors. Depending on your company's business, some of these issues could have a direct impact on the bottom line. In short, some part of your company's business is affected daily by government action (or in-action) either in or outside your home country. To be a truly effective in-house lawyer, you need to be on top of this important area. Moreover, being attuned to positive and negative governmental developments is an area where you and the legal function can add great value to the company and show strategic vision.

In my last job, the government affairs team was part of the legal department and all of the company's government relations work and strategy came through legal. We worked domestically and internationally, dealing with government officials and regulators in the United States, Canada, South America, the Middle East, Asia, and Europe. Your company may not have a formal government relations office set up or it may not report into the legal function. Regardless, as in-house counsel, you should look to stay up to speed on what various governmental or regulatory bodies are doing and consider being part of any effort your company may want or need to make to influence the outcome. Here are ten basic points regarding running an effective government affairs campaign. To keep things simple, I will focus on the United States but the points below generally apply anywhere.

1. **Set the table with government officials.** One of the most effective things you can do in the area of government relations is meet with officials *before* there is a problem. Meaning, make time to simply introduce yourself and your business to local, state, and national government officials with no "ask" on the line. For example, if your business is regulated by the Department of Transportation or the Federal Communications Commission, make time to meet the regulators and explain your business to them and give them a point of contact in the event they ever have questions. Or meet with the U.S. Trade Representative. Likewise, establish relationships with the offices of key congressional members (e.g., your state's delegation or the chairs of key committees that can impact your business). If you operate internationally, almost all U.S. (and foreign) embassies have a commercial interests section.[445] They are more than happy to meet with you and get a sense for how your business operates in that country (and can be helpful in the event you run into problems in that country or need to understand the lay of the land). Finally, don't forget your local and state officials. The governor's office, the mayor, the city council, and others will typically all be willing to meet with you to get to know a company operating in their states/towns.

2. **Identify your issue(s).** If you have a formal government affairs department, part of their job is to keep an eye out for regulatory actions, new laws, hearings, and other matters that could impact your company. If you don't have a formal department, or just to supplement your government affairs team, develop your own resources to stay on top of new issues. Newspapers, websites,[446] government-related publications,[447] blogs,[448] television, newsletters, word of mouth, and trade associations[449] can all be valuable sources of information about what's going on in Washington, internationally, or locally. You should regularly and systematically sort through all of your information sources to spot issues (tax laws, trade, patent reform, export restrictions, etc.). You'll want to stay close to your business partners and the CEO/CFO (or the general counsel if that's not you already) to help identify the issues worth spending time

---

445 http://www.referenceforbusiness.com/encyclopedia/Clo-Con/Commercial-Attach.html.
446 http://thehill.com/.
447 https://www.congress.gov/congressional-record.
448 http://www.politico.com/.
449 https://www.uschamber.com/.

on. You will need to prioritize issues as you probably cannot devote time and resource to every issue you spot. You or the department should start out each year with a list of potential government-related issues you'd like to tackle (and be prepared to change your list as circumstances warrant throughout the year).

3. **Build a coalition/Go solo?** Once you have identified your issue(s), you should think about whether it makes sense to go forward alone or as part of a larger group. For simple issues, say your company is opposed to its hometown changing a zoning law near your offices, you're probably fine going forward alone. If the issue is more complicated or more controversial (e.g., the company does not want to be seen by itself as against or for the particular issue), you will want to build or join a coalition of similarly minded businesses/organizations. This can be as simple as working through an existing trade association your company belongs to or as complicated as building a coalition "of the willing" from scratch. If you go the latter route, you will start with companies that operate similar businesses as they are most likely to have the same viewpoint on the issue (and petitioning the government is a proper way competitors can act together). Next, think of companies outside your competitive circle that would have a similar interest in the outcome of the issue (e.g., customers, vendors, general e-commerce companies). Additionally, you may be able to link your coalition or trade association up with other trade associations, coalitions, or public policy organizations that support your position. The key is to spend time thinking about who might be your allies in your campaign (and it may not always be the most obvious businesses) and build your circle outward. The rub of being part of a coalition, however, is that it will require a good deal of compromise as you'll need to accommodate the different needs and risk tolerance of each coalition member. It will not be your way or the highway unless you want your participation in the coalition to be short-lived.

4. **What's the end goal?** Before you launch your campaign, you need to get agreement from the interested parties (internal or your coalition) as to the end goal. How do you measure success? Is it passing a new law or seeing a proposed law fail? Is it to get a few simple changes made to a proposed regulation or a wholesale rewrite? Is it to see a government regulator take action in some manner or keep the regulator on the sidelines? And no matter what your goal is, prepare yourself (and your business team) up-front to be frustrated. It is difficult to get the government take an action you want, be it passing a bill or writing a new regulation. You will find things rarely happen quickly. It will be inch by inch. It may take years to reach your goal (if ever). As my wise government affairs director once told me, "It's way easier to stop something than to pass something." So, go into this with your eyes open and your patience level set at "high" (and be sure your executive team understands this point as well).

5. **How much resource do you need to expend?** Depending on the importance of the issue, you must determine how much money, manpower, and time you and the company are willing to spend. It may be just a letter to your city council representative, or it may be a sophisticated effort that includes mass and social media, economic experts, public relations teams, lawyers, lobbyists, and other professionals. If it's the latter, being part of a coalition can help spread the cost around while dramatically increasing the ability to bring resources to bear on your issue. And not all contributions to a coalition are money. Sometimes coalition members bring subject matter expertise or the willingness to draft materials or take on other tasks where the cost is manpower versus writing a check. Regardless, you will want to stay close to your business leaders so they understand and agree with the costs and effort involved in any particular campaign (or the value/cost/trade-offs of doing nothing).
6. **Communications campaign.** All government affairs campaigns need some type of media or communications strategy. It can range from an "Op-Ed" by your CEO in the local newspaper to a professionally built website dedicated to your issue with materials written by experts, FAQs, press releases, call to action, Twitter feed, Facebook page, blogs, and other sophisticated media tools and techniques. Keep in mind that many effective media materials can be prepared in-house. Your corporate communications or marketing departments can be very helpful here and usually welcome the chance to get involved. Also, you probably have noticed that the more sophisticated government affairs campaigns usually have a clever name, something positive and catchy like "Americans for Faster Internet Access" or "The Coalition for Fair Taxation." If your campaign is worthy of a name, use care in selecting the name so as not to give negative images or unintended meanings (e.g., acronyms can really come back to bite you).
7. **Key activities.** In addition to a communications campaign, there are several other activities you will want to consider undertaking as part of your effort:
    - Plan on wearing out some shoe leather as part of an effective campaign. There is no substitute for meeting with officials, legislators, regulators, staff members, and others to press your point. This will include identifying the best people to meet with and may even include meeting with people who you think might be/are opposed to your position as there is always a chance you can change their mind on the issue or keep them neutral in the process, that is, they are not actively working against you. You will need to determine who from your company or coalition will be present at any meetings. The importance of the issue may require your CEO to attend for example. Who attends a meeting sends an important message to the folks in government you are meeting with, so be thoughtful here.

- You will typically want materials to hand out at your meetings. There are two main types of written materials. The first is a short "leave-behind" piece that highlights the issues and "the ask" (i.e., what you want the official to do). We called this a "one-pager" because the ideal length is one page (or as close to that as you can get). The second is a "white paper." A white paper is a lengthy and detailed discussion of the issues and "the ask." It will often contain detailed legal analysis or economic analysis usually prepared by an attorney or outside expert (e.g., an economist). The length, level of detail, and content of a white paper will depend on the issue. It will generally be costly to put together but there are times, especially when dealing with complicated regulations or regulatory action, that you will need a white paper to encourage or discourage action on the part of the government. Remember that anything you give to public officials will most likely become public or can become public.
- You may want to or be asked to draft sample legislation (i.e., the text of the law or amendment or regulation you want to see implemented or changed). This is a real opportunity to shape the law and you should always accept an offer like this.
- There may be hearings held on the issue. If so, you should consider having someone testify either in person (most effective) or by drafting testimony that will be entered into the official record. If you have someone testify in person, ensure they are well spoken, are well versed in the issues, and are comfortable speaking and presenting in public. Having the wrong person testify can undo all of the good you may have otherwise accomplished.
- Figure out who outside the government is opposed to your positions and why. You may be able to convince them otherwise, you may be able to reach common ground on acceptable compromises that enable you to join forces, or you may just have to agree to disagree. At a minimum, you will want to understand the arguments in opposition to your views and figure out how to best respond to them as they will come up as you go forward.

8. **Grassroots.** Politicians and regulators listen to citizens. Voices count, and the more voices supporting your position the better. Consequently, getting citizens involved through meetings, testimony, phone calls, emails, letters, petitions, and so on can be tremendously helpful. This is called a "grassroots"[450] campaign. Consider asking your employees to engage and make it easy for them to (a) understand why the issue was important to the success of the company and (b) sign a petition or send an email/write their congressional delegation. Think

---

450 http://www.capitolimpact.com/2011/11/08/3-keys-to-running-a-successful-grassroots-campaign/.

about asking customers, vendors, and others to get involved. For example, you can put a link on your consumer-facing websites with information about the issue and easy ways for people to get involved. You can also work to create general public interest about your issue via many mechanisms, including social media like Twitter and Facebook, short web videos, press releases, or other media events. Above all, keep your message simple and be sure you include a call to action so that people who want to get involved know how to make their voice heard. A good example of grass roots is the Ebay Main Street[451] website and the emails they send out several times a year asking people to get involved on key issues.

9. **Use of consultants.** There are times when you will need professional help with a campaign and you will need to seriously consider hiring a lobbyist,[452] that is, a professional with relationships and/or expertise needed for your particular issue. Lobbyists can be extremely valuable additions to your campaign, and part of your planning should be dedicated to thinking about whether or not you need such help. Lobbyists will be able to help you put together the strategy (including all of the items mentioned above), will know which officials and staff members are the most important to speak with about your issue, and can help you understand the arcane twists of the governmental process, including how legislation makes it out of committee and to a vote (it's a lot more complicated than Schoolhouse Rock's "Bill on Capitol Hill"[453] led you to believe). A close second is a professional public relations firm to help develop and execute your communications strategy. Using consultants will be costly. A coalition can help reduce these costs by sharing them across members.

10. **Know the rules.** As you develop your campaign, be sure you (and/or your coalition) understand the legal boundaries. Companies with active government affairs efforts usually have some type of political action committee (PAC) to make contributions. You need to be sure that any and all donations—and the operation of the PAC—are done well within the rules of the road.[454] There will be limits on things as simple as lunches, even token gifts. You will need to be well versed in anti-bribery laws around the globe (especially if you have employees on the ground in foreign jurisdictions who may be involved in your campaign). Finally, if you are working with competitors you will need to be

---

451 http://www.ebaymainstreet.com/.
452 https://www.americanexpress.com/us/small-business/openforum/articles/should-you-hire-a-lobbyist/.
453 https://www.youtube.com/watch?v=tyeJ55o3El0.
454 http://www.fec.gov/pages/brochures/contriblimits.shtml.

cognizant of competition law issues. If you're serious about government affairs, you will want to take some professional advice from a law firm or other entity that specializes in the nuances of campaign financing and anti-bribery issues. Take this part seriously as the damage to reputation and other harm that can come from not following the rules is huge.

*****

A well-run government affairs group or campaign can help your company succeed in the business world. It takes hard work, patience, strategic vision, and good deal of creativity to be successful—all skills in-house lawyers have or should have. Stay in touch with and on top of governmental issues that could affect your company and take steps to ensure that your company makes informed decisions about whether to get involved and, if so, what steps are needed to have the best chance of success.

February 17, 2015

Ten Things: Common Ethics Issues for In-House Counsel

I was in-house counsel for over 20 years and served as chief compliance officer for a good part of that time. One of the challenges I recall for me and my legal team was finding practical advice for in-house counsel around ethics issues. We held a number of CLE presentations on ethics every year—helpful in terms of yearly mandatory ethics-related CLE hours. While welcomed, the presentations generally left me less than satisfied because most of them were heavily focused on parsing out the text of the relevant rules of professional responsibility (in our case, Texas), with a lot of focus on words like "shall" and "may." I am not saying this is not important, but what I came to realize is that many of the ethics issues I dealt with as in-house counsel were broader than what a specific section of the rules did or did not mandate me to do. Instead, what I really needed was a general awareness of my different ethical obligations (including those under the rules) and whether I knew or could easily find the answer to my problem, or if I needed to ask someone for help to figure out the next move.

Below I will take on that challenge and discuss ten of the most common ethics issues faced by in-house counsel and how to deal with them or what to keep in mind as you analyze the situation. There are definitely some traps out there for the unwary. Hopefully, after reading this, you'll have a better understanding of some of the key things around ethics you need to keep in mind as in-house counsel and when you may need to ask for help. Apologies to my international readers as this is a pretty U.S.-centric discussion though I think the themes apply globally.

1. **In-house is different.** If you read through the ABA Model Rules of Professional Conduct[455] or your applicable state rules,[456] you will see that most of the

---

455 http://www.americanbar.org/groups/professional_responsibility/publications/model_rules_of_professional_conduct/model_rules_of_professional_conduct_table_of_contents.html.

456 http://www.americanbar.org/groups/professional_responsibility/resources/links_of_interest.html.

rules seem to be written for lawyers in private practice. The rules specifically addressing in-house counsel appear as a small fraction of the rules (but in-house counsel must comply with all of the rules nonetheless). There are several reasons for this disparity: there are no fee disputes for in-house lawyers, no client trust account issues, no advertising issues, and the in-house lawyer is an employee of the client. Moreover, the in-house lawyer's deep involvement in the day-to-day business can lead to a higher level of accountability in ways not affecting lawyers in private practice. For example, in-house lawyers are now more frequently in the crosshairs of regulators and are expected to be "gatekeepers" whose job is, in part, to keep the company honest in ways that do not fall clearly within the rules of professional responsibility. This requires a very delicate balancing act that outside counsel is often immune from. Understanding that things are different in-house will give you a lens to consider the different ethics issues that pass your way.

2. **Resources.** There are a number of resources available to you regarding ethics issues. Start with the rules of professional responsibility for wherever you practice law. A complete set should be available for free online via your state bar association. Next are the *ABA Model Rules of Professional Conduct*. Since most state rules are based in large part on the ABA Rules, I will refer to various sections of the ABA Rules below (but understand that not all of the ABA Rules are adopted by every state). Likewise, you can find court and disciplinary panel decisions online. The ABA Center for Professional Responsibility website[457] is very helpful, and blogs are an excellent way to gain insight into key issues — the Legal Ethics Forum,[458] the Law for Lawyers Today,[459] and the Compliance and Ethics blog.[460] Regardless, when faced with an ethics question (under the ABA Rules or otherwise), think about the following when deciding what to do: (a) the rules of professional responsibility, (b) common sense, (c) your conscious, (d) how will your actions (or inaction) appear to your peers and colleagues (or your mom), and (e) how will your actions (or inaction) affect the company's reputation and shareholder value. Running through this list can help get you to the right decision.

3. **Who is the client?** For in-house counsel, the client is the organization and not any individual member of management or employee (ABA Rules §1.13).[461]

---

457 http://www.americanbar.org/groups/professional_responsibility/resources.html.
458 http://www.legalethicsforum.com/.
459 http://www.thelawforlawyerstoday.com/.
460 http://complianceandethics.org/.
461 http://www.americanbar.org/groups/professional_responsibility/publications/model_rules_of_professional_conduct/rule_1_13_organization_as_client.html.

This can be difficult to remember at times because your business colleagues often think of you as their lawyer. That is okay at times, that is, to the extent the employee is an extension of the company, but it must always be clear between you and the business client that you represent the interests of the company and not them individually. This means you have to watch out for things like the senior management "squeeze"—"what I'm about to tell you is only between you and me as my lawyer." You must be able to recognize situations where separate counsel may be needed and to advise your business colleague to get their own lawyer if needed. This occurs most often in the context of internal investigations. Under such circumstances, it's important that you give your business colleague what is known as an "Upjohn" warning.[462] You must make it clear to the employee you are interviewing (including senior management) that you represent the company and not them and they have the right to obtain their own counsel (ABA Rules §1.13(f)).[463] The best practice here is to have a standard written warning that the employee signs. There are plenty of sample warnings available online.[464] Failure to give this warning can waive the attorney-client privilege and lead to other problems.

4. **Confidentiality.** As a lawyer you are required to keep confidential information confidential—this is broader than the attorney-client privilege (ABA Rules §1.6).[465] Moreover, you must always take steps to preserve the attorney-client privilege (whether the privilege applies outside the United States depends on the country involved and you should familiarize yourself with the rules of that jurisdiction as the level and types of privileges vary by country).[466] You also have a duty to preserve client files and documents, and not just for purposes of a litigation hold (ABA Rules §1.6(c)).[467] You should regularly back up[468] your email and hard drive (talk with your IT department about the best way to do

---

462 http://www.gibsondunn.com/publications/Documents/Dunst-Chirlin-RenewedEmphasisOnUpjohnWarnings.pdf.

463 http://www.americanbar.org/groups/professional_responsibility/publications/model_rules_of_professional_conduct/rule_1_13_organization_as_client.html.

464 http://www.pepperlaw.com/publications/internal-investigations-upjohn-warnings-are-required-2011-01-07/.

465 http://www.americanbar.org/groups/professional_responsibility/publications/model_rules_of_professional_conduct/rule_1_6_confidentiality_of_information.html.

466 http://www.acc.com/chapters/gny/upload/Tab-02-ACC_Seminar_Attorney_Client_Privilege_4-1-14.pdf.

467 http://www.americanbar.org/groups/professional_responsibility/publications/model_rules_of_professional_conduct/rule_1_6_confidentiality_of_information.html.

468 http://www.pcworld.com/article/2065126/the-absurdly-simple-guide-to-backing-up-your-pc.html.

this). The old saying "Loose lips sink ships" is 100 percent relevant in the in-house world. Be careful of your discussions in restaurants, elevators, and especially when you are on the phone in a public place—since most people seem to feel they must speak louder when talking on a phone. Similarly, create strong passwords,[469] that is, a combination of numbers, letters, and symbols, to use for your company accounts. Secure your laptop and smartphone, and if you use your own personal devices to conduct company business or store company documents, you need to secure those as well and use strong passwords at home (see Comment 18 to ABA Rules §1.6).[470]

Confidentiality also applies to your use of social media: (a) don't embarrass yourself or the company, for example, complaining about your bad personal experience with the services of a customer of the company—that can come back to bite you, (b) don't comment on legal matters involving the company, (c) don't "torch" the judiciary, no matter frustrated you may be, (d) don't give out confidential information or destroy privilege, and (e) be constantly alert for social engineering "phishing" scams[471]—and not just the ones where the "King of Nigeria" needs your help with a money transfer.

5. **Up-the-ladder reporting.** When companies run afoul of securities laws or criminal laws, you will often see someone ask "where were the lawyers?" Unfortunately, this means that, more and more, in-house counsel are under the microscope,[472] and regulators are expecting you to act as gatekeepers to prevent fraud and bad acts by the company. The bottom line is that you cannot assist in a crime or fraud and you must act to take steps to prevent bodily harm (ABA Rules §1.2,[473] §1.6,[474] and §1.13[475]). Furthermore, if you work for a publicly traded company, you may have obligations under Sarbanes-Oxley

---

469 http://www.howtogeek.com/195430/how-to-create-a-strong-password-and-remember-it/.
470 http://www.americanbar.org/groups/professional_responsibility/publications/model_rules_of_professional_conduct/rule_1_6_confidentiality_of_information/comment_on_rule_1_6.html.
471 http://www.eweek.com/security/advanced-phishing-scam-targets-ceos-cfos-for-phony-cash-transfers.html.
472 http://blogs.wsj.com/law/2012/10/01/former-glaxo-vp-the-criminalization-of-the-practice-of-law-is-here/.
473 http://www.americanbar.org/groups/professional_responsibility/publications/model_rules_of_professional_conduct/rule_1_2_scope_of_representation_allocation_of_authority_between_client_lawyer.html.
474 http://www.americanbar.org/groups/professional_responsibility/publications/model_rules_of_professional_conduct/rule_1_6_confidentiality_of_information.html.
475 http://www.americanbar.org/groups/professional_responsibility/publications/model_rules_of_professional_conduct/rule_1_13_organization_as_client.html.

§307[476] to report material violations of the law "up the ladder." Know whom to go to if this happens (and consider having trusted outside counsel lined up with whom you can discuss concerns and the proper path forward). Likewise, under the Dodd-Frank and SEC whistleblower rules,[477] keep in mind that the company may not engage in any retaliation against a whistleblower. All in-house legal departments should have guidelines in place (and training) on what to do if an in-house lawyer suspects that a crime has been or will be committed by the company. Depending on the circumstances, consider documenting any actions taken by you or the department to comply with your obligations (or expectations) as this may be useful in the event there is some reason outsiders are asking "where were the lawyers?" at your company.

6. **Lawyer versus business partner.** There is a Jekyll and Hyde component to being in-house counsel that revolves around the fact that the business often wants you to act as both a lawyer and a business partner.[478] Acting as a business partner however runs the risk of hurting claims to attorney-client privilege, which applies only when you act as a lawyer providing legal advice. Since being part of business decisions is a reason many of us went in-house legal in the first place, you must ensure that you participate properly in either role. This is made more complicated when the business wants you to act as a business partner on occasion, but communicates with you as though everything is legally privileged. Courts generally are becoming more hostile[479] to claims of attorney-client privilege involving only in-house lawyers and their business clients, often presuming (unfairly) that your communications are more business than legal and therefore not deserving of protection. It is critical to always take steps to (a) properly mark privileged communications, (b) set out the legal purpose of your communication at the beginning of the email or in the body of the document/attachment, (c) separate business advice from legal advice, ideally through separate documents but if it is not possible at least by separate and clearly marked sections of the document, and (d) train the business on the difference between legal and business advice and when the privilege properly applies and how to request legal services versus business advice (and be sure all of the lawyers in your department understand the process as well).

---

476 http://www.cailaw.org/media/files/SWIICL/ConferenceMaterial/2015/bootcamp/sarbanes-ppt.pdf.

477 https://www.tnwinc.com/11404/5-insights-from-the-sec-whistleblower-hotline-that-will-impact-your-2015/.

478 https://www.reedsmith.com/files/uploads/Documents/Placing_the_Attorney_Client_Privilege_at_Risk_How_to_Avoid_a_Waiver.pdf.

479 http://www.yettercoleman.com/wp-content/uploads/2014/07/Texas-Lawyer-July-14-2014.pdf.

7. **Competence.** As a lawyer you have an obligation to maintain competence regarding developments in the law that are important to your client (ABA Rules §1.1).[480] For in-house generalists, this is a broad mandate. You should focus on learning skills that the company needs both in the near term and as you look out five years into the future (which is a good exercise for legal departments to undertake every year). Build around the following: (a) Take continuing education requirements seriously. CLE doesn't not have to be pure drudgery and a "let's get this over with" moment. Instead, it can truly help you develop or refine skills that are important to you and your company; (b) Your obligation of competence may include understanding the basics of e-discovery and litigation holds given how quickly things can go wrong for the company if there is a failure here; (c) Spend time on business ethics and compliance training; (d) Improve your legal research skills generally (and cast a wider net in terms of the tools you use); and (e) Become savvy with technology,[481] including social media and digital security (see Comment 8 to ABA Rules 1.1).[482]

8. **Conflicts.** Conflicts matter to in-house counsel. For instance, in-house attorneys frequently deal with client conflicts (joint ventures, subsidiaries, outside counsel) and with conflicts of interest (usually internal to the company). Regarding the latter, always be mindful of your own conflicts, including prior advice and actions and how your current actions—or ability to be impartial—may be impacted by what you said or did previously. Be sure that the advice you give and the work you are doing now reflect your best efforts and thinking, even if it means you may have to backtrack from what you said or did in the past. Keep your eyes open for conflicts of interest among the executives, board of directors, and employees (and understand the company's policies on such conflicts). If you spot a conflict, follow your process and find a way to help resolve it in the best interests of the company. Client conflicts can take the form of who you wish to hire as outside counsel (and your process to deal with their conflicts) or who you bring on as a new attorney to the department. For example, in *Dynamic 3D Geosolutions vs. Schlumberger* (1:14-cv-00112-LY (W.D. Tex., March 31, 2015)),[483] an entire in-house legal department was disqualified from working on a company matter because the new lawyer had

---

480 http://www.americanbar.org/groups/professional_responsibility/publications/model_rules_of_professional_conduct/rule_1_1_competence.html.

481 See page 129.

482 http://www.americanbar.org/groups/professional_responsibility/publications/model_rules_of_professional_conduct/rule_1_1_competence/comment_on_rule_1_1.html.

483 https://www.hklaw.com/Publications/Entire-In-House-Legal-Department-Disqualified-Following-Lateral-Hire-04-21-2015/.

previously worked for the defendant in litigation and the company (plaintiff) failed to properly screen them from meetings and actions related to the litigation (ABA Rules §1.9).[484] Plaintiff's outside counsel was also disqualified as the conflict was imputed to them as well. This became a huge, expensive mess and the general counsel had the unpleasant duty of explaining to senior management and the board how all of this happened. The simple message: conflicts matter, even to in-house attorneys and in ways you might not expect, so keep alert.

9. **Communications outside the company.** A common request to in-house counsel by a client is for you to sit in on a call "with the other side"[485] during a contract or other type of discussion. Be careful here because if you know the other side is represented by counsel (and most companies of any size have dedicated in-house lawyers) you need permission from the lawyer (not the client) to be part of that call—if counsel for the other side is not otherwise present (ABA Rules §4.2).[486] The same is true if for some reason a business person on the other side of a deal or dispute calls you directly in hopes of potentially speeding things up. While it's a positive sign, you still need to explain that you cannot talk with him or her unless their lawyer grants you permission to do so. If you are speaking with someone unrepresented by counsel, you have an obligation under the rules not to mislead them about your role as a lawyer and do not provide them with legal advice (other than advice to secure counsel of their own) (ABA Rules §4.3).[487] One of the most difficult areas to deal with is your obligation of candor when dealing with the other side or with the court (ABA Rules §3.3,[488] §4.1,[489] and §4.2[490]). As to the former, there are exceptions made for negotiating (and the puffery that naturally comes with that process)

---

[484] http://www.americanbar.org/groups/professional_responsibility/publications/model_rules_of_professional_conduct/rule_1_9_duties_of_former_clients.html.

[485] https://www.milbank.com/images/content/5/9/5998/032009-BLN-Ex-Parte-Communications-in-a-Transactional-Practice.p.pdf.

[486] http://www.americanbar.org/groups/professional_responsibility/publications/model_rules_of_professional_conduct/rule_4_2_communication_with_person_represented_by_counsel.html

[487] http://www.americanbar.org/groups/professional_responsibility/publications/model_rules_of_professional_conduct/rule_4_3_dealing_with_unrepresented_person.html.

[488] http://www.americanbar.org/groups/professional_responsibility/publications/model_rules_of_professional_conduct/rule_3_3_candor_toward_the_tribunal.html.

[489] http://www.americanbar.org/groups/professional_responsibility/publications/model_rules_of_professional_conduct/rule_4_1_truthfulness_in_statements_to_others.html.

[490] http://www.americanbar.org/groups/professional_responsibility/publications/model_rules_of_professional_conduct/rule_4_2_communication_with_person_represented_by_counsel.html.

but there is no bright line as to when puffery crosses over into deceit or dishonesty[491] (ABA Rules §8.4(c)).[492] For that you need to rely to some extent on paragraph 2(a)–(e) above.

10. **Supervisors/Outsourcing.** As in-house counsel you are responsible for those you supervise and for taking reasonable steps to ensure they comply with their ethical obligations (ABA Rules §5.1).[493] Likewise, you are ultimately responsible for third-party vendors acting on your behalf (ABA Rules §5.1 and §5.3[494]). This is particularly true given the rise of outsourcing of certain legal services (document processing, simple contract preparation, cloud storage,[495] etc.). In addition to ethical behavior, you need to ensure that neither you, nor your employees or vendors engage in the unauthorized practice of law (ABA Rules §5.5).[496] For you and your team, it's about keeping your license current (including obtaining the appropriate amount of continuing legal education). In some places in-house counsel must be licensed in the state where they perform legal work for the company. In other places, they do not. The ABA has a helpful chart of the licensing requirements for in-house counsel in all 50 states.[497] In a similar vein, you need to ensure that your vendors are either properly licensed or are properly supervised by licensed lawyers (you, your team, or outside counsel). This is an area where due-diligence about your vendor is a smart idea. Bad things can happen if you engage (or allow) the unauthorized practice of law, with the mostly likely problem being no attorney-client privilege where you thought one existed.

*****

---

491 http://www.americanbar.org/content/dam/aba/administrative/labor_law/meetings/2009/2009_ethics_a.authcheckdam.pdf.

492 http://www.americanbar.org/groups/professional_responsibility/publications/model_rules_of_professional_conduct/rule_8_4_misconduct.html.

493 http://www.americanbar.org/groups/professional_responsibility/publications/model_rules_of_professional_conduct/rule_5_1_responsibilities_of_a_partner_or_supervisory_lawyer.html.

494 http://www.americanbar.org/groups/professional_responsibility/publications/model_rules_of_professional_conduct/rule_5_3_responsibilities_regarding_nonlawyer_assistant.html.

495 http://www.americanbar.org/publications/gpsolo_ereport/2012/september_2012/ethics_cloud_computing_lawyers.html.

496 http://www.americanbar.org/groups/professional_responsibility/publications/model_rules_of_professional_conduct/rule_5_5_unauthorized_practice_of_law_multijurisdictional_practice_of_law.html.

497 http://www.americanbar.org/content/dam/aba/administrative/professional_responsibility/in_house_rules.authcheckdam.pdf.

It is certainly important to be familiar with the specifics of the applicable code of professional responsibility. You should have a copy of the rules (or a "link" to an online version) handy. That said, the following points will probably solve 90 percent of the day-to-day ethics issues faced by in-house counsel:
- Remember who your client is
- Protect the attorney-client privilege
- Know when to go "Up the Ladder"
- Use strong passwords and keep company records safe
- Keep you license current and stay up-to-date on legal developments and technology
- Be smart with social media and on guard for "phishing" scams
- Identify "go-to" counsel for ethics questions—don't fly solo

There is a target on the backs of in-house counsel these days. A bit of diligence and common sense is your best defense.

August 18, 2015

Additional Resources

Ten Things: Best Legal Blogs for In-House Counsel (2015)

Back when I was general counsel I once told my team that if you send me something I will read it, pretty much no matter what. I am not sure if that is a positive or a negative, but it certainly kept me informed about what was going on in legal and around the company. I'm not saying that everyone needs to have the same approach I have to reading things. In fact, sometimes it's nice if someone can point out things worth reading (vs. having to dig them out yourself). That's my plan here.

Over the course of the last several years, legal blogs have exploded. There are probably several blogs for just about any topic of law you are interested in. Blogs can be very helpful tools for in-house counsel (or any lawyer for that matter), in particular for finding answers to legal questions quickly or for staying on top of new issues. Over time, I have identified a number of blogs that I like to read regularly and that I think are particularly well written and useful to in-house counsel. There are many very talented legal writers out there, covering really interesting topics, and below I will list some of my favorite legal blogs (and the topics they cover). I highly encourage you to check these out over the next several weeks, and if any interest you, follow them regularly. Or just keep the list handy in case you need it later down the road:

1. **Presnell on Privileges** (www.presnellonprivileges.com/). It discusses issues and case law around various privileges such as attorney-client and work product, as well as those not as well known such as accountant client, common interest, self-critical analysis, and insurer-insured. There is a very handy index as well.
2. **Adams on Contract Drafting** (www.adamsdrafting.com/blog/). It provides excellent posts on common and not so common issues regarding drafting contracts. Sometimes the author writes about specific contract clauses; sometimes it may be just a common phrase or sentence used frequently in contracts. It is always interesting and always helpful. Also good is **The Contracts Guy** (http://www.thecontractsguy.net/).

3. ***Corruption, Crime & Compliance*** (www.blog.volkovlaw.com/). It has well-written discussions about compliance and ethics topics including white-collar crime and anti-bribery. Second place is ***FCPA Professor*** (http://www.fcpaprofessor.com/).
4. ***Employment and Labor Insider*** (www.employmentandlaborinsider.com/). It is a one-stop shop for issues involving employment litigation, including age discrimination, the Americans with Disabilities Act, noncompetes, sexual harassment, telecommuting, and wage and hour issues.
5. ***Chronicle of Data Protection*** (www.hldataprotection.com/). This is my "go to" blog for all things data security or data privacy related. It is always on top of breaking issues and always putting forth practical solutions to data privacy issues. Also check out: ***Privacy Law Blog*** (http://privacylaw.proskauer.com/).
6. ***Electronic Discovery Law*** (http://www.ediscoverylaw.com/). If your company has lawsuits involving e-discovery (and who doesn't) this is almost indispensable. Access to case law, statutes/rules, and timely articles on cutting edge issues involving electronically stored information.
7. ***Global Regulatory Enforcement Law*** (www.globalregulatoryenforcementlawblog.com). A smorgasbord of information about all things involving global regulatory enforcement including antitrust, government contracts, and government investigations. (Plus I finally got to use "smorgasbord" in a sentence…).
8. ***Trademark and Copyright Law*** (www.trademarkandcopyrightlawblog.com). Everything you could want to know about trademarks, copyrights, unfair competition, domain disputes, defamation, and more.
9. ***The In-House Advisor*** (www.in-houseadvisor.com). There is always something interesting discussed in this blog. It's aimed squarely at in-house lawyers and covers a wide variety of issues especially on litigation and risk avoidance.
10. ***Arbitration Nation*** (www.arbitrationnation.com). Hmmm, I wonder what this blog is about. Kidding aside, an excellent resource for all things arbitration. Honorable Mention: ***JAMS ADR Blog*** (http://jamsadrblog.com/)—mediation/arbitration issues around the globe.

A few other very helpful "nonblog"/"blog-ish" resources for you to consider: *Above the Law*,[498] *Risk and Compliance Magazine*,[499] *Lexology.com*,[500] *Corporate Disputes Magazine*,[501] and *Corporate Counsel Connect*[502] (*disclaimer*: I write articles

---

498 http://abovethelaw.com/.
499 http://riskandcompliancemagazine.com/.
500 http://www.lexology.com/.
501 http://www.corporatedisputesmagazine.com/.
502 http://legalsolutions.thomsonreuters.com/law-products/ns/news-views/corporate-counsel/2015-december.

for *Corporate Counsel Connect* but there are many other excellent writers contributing as well).

*****

As you can imagine, there are dozens of great legal blogs out there. An easy way to find a good blog is to use a search engine with the general topic (e.g., "e-discovery") and the word "blog" in the search box. Also, the blogs I listed above tend to focus on U.S. law. If you look, you will find a number of blogs dealing with the law in non-U.S. jurisdictions.

December 29, 2015

Ten Things: A To Do List for In-House Counsel

One of the hardest tasks I recall as in-house counsel was the yearly process of setting of goals for the legal department,[503] both as a member of the department and as general counsel for two companies. To me, it feels like there is something inherently difficult about setting legal department goals when probably 75 percent of what the team will work on in the upcoming year is still unknown and won't really be knowable until it appears on their plate.

Despite these particular limitations, it is possible to create a useful and measureable set of goals for legal. Below I will set out a to do list that you can adopt in full or in part as part of your yearly goal planning. These are all tasks that need to be done, pretty much regardless of the size of your company or the number of attorneys in your legal department. Moreover, they are designed with the CEO and other C-suite executives in mind so that they can see how the legal department is proactively scoping risk to the company and its various lines of business and (more importantly) taking steps to deal with those risks.

Yearly Legal Department To Do List

- Work with Human Resources to review and update the following company policies/employee agreements:[504]
  - Employee handbook (ensure compliance with NLRB guidance memo)[505]
  - Non-solicitation/noncompete agreements (ensure language meets standards for key states or countries where company operates)
  - Employee confidentiality agreement

---

503 See page 103.
504 See page 209.
505 http://static.ow.ly/docs/GC%2015_04%20Report%20of%20the%20General%20Counsel%20Concerning%20Employer%20Rules.pdf_36Fc.pdf.

- Intellectual property ownership agreements
- Exempt/nonexempt and employee/contractor classification health check
- Email/document drafting policy[506]
• Create processes and a set of operations metrics to effectively manage legal department budget and spend:[507]
  - Implement or plan to implement an e-billing system
  - Create monthly report based on key operations metrics about legal spend
    - Average hourly rate (year over year)
    - Average hourly rate by firm versus "market" rate for similar work
    - Partner/associate ratio (by project)
    - Spend versus budget/forecasted spend (by project and overall)
    - Get outside counsel to help/buy-in with process[508]
  - Update "outside counsel guidelines" and send to all current outside counsel and at outset of every new matter
  Meet with outside counsel before the start of any material legal project to set cost and team expectations of both parties, and, at the completion of the project, do an honest post-project analysis of what worked and what didn't work (for both the company and the law firm) and determine how can we improve project management going forward
• Compliance health check.[509] Review and update key compliance-related policies and update/implement means to test compliance:
  - Employee training process (how we teach employees about compliance)
  - Anti-bribery policy (FCPA, etc.)
  - Antitrust compliance policy (including trade associations)[510]
  - Record retention policy/including legal hold process
  - Revise/update company business ethics policy
  - Ensure all employees know how to report an ethics/compliance concern (emails, posters, town hall meetings, etc.) and put into place/test hotline, compliance office email, and other mechanisms in place to allow employees to communicate concerns
  - Work with internal audit to test key parts of compliance program
    - Educate the legal department and the company management and employees about the proper use of the "attorney-client privilege"[511]

---

506 See page 45.
507 See page 115.
508 http://www.law.com/sites/articles/2015/12/07/what-will-it-take-to-run-legal-departments-of-the-future/.
509 See page 145.
510 See page 149.
511 See page 263.

- Review company website:
  - Update user agreement[512]
  - Update privacy policy update[513]
  - Ensure proper legal and/or contractual grounds exist for transferring personal data (customer, employee, etc.) out of European Union to United States or other country[514]
  - Review/update employee training around IT security (password policy, "phishing," malware, etc.)
- Review processes and procedures around litigation or otherwise highly disruptive events:
  - Ensure that company contracts have well vetted dispute resolution clauses/procedures, including choice of law, arbitration, choice of venue, mediation, limitations of liability, indemnity, etc.
  - Review procedures for the intake of new litigation[515]
  - Review procedures to keep the CEO and board of directors up to speed on material litigation[516]
  - Ensure appropriate crisis preparation procedures and plans are in place[517]
  - Ensure appropriate business interruption (i.e., "bad things happen") plans are in place[518]
  - If you work for a publicly traded company, work with the CFO and Investor Relations to develop a plan to deal with activist investors[519]
- Create and distribute a client satisfaction survey to company management and employees (i.e., gather feedback about how your internal clients feel about the legal department) and engage more closely with business:[520]
  - Distribute survey mid-year so as to get results in time for year-end review and next year planning
  - Post results (or selected results) on legal department intranet web page so they are available for company employees to see
  - Create an action plan based on the results to improve the delivery of legal services

---

512 See page 201.
513 See page 155.
514 See page 171.
515 See page 49.
516 See page 53.
517 See page 247.
518 See page 253.
519 http://deloitte.wsj.com/riskandcompliance/2015/04/23/shareholder-activism-how-will-you-respond/.
520 See page 135.

- Place members of the legal department at weekly/monthly staff meetings of the businesses or business groups so as to help ensure that legal is knowledgeable about issues that concern the business and is able to provide guidance in real time
- On quarterly basis ask CEO and other C-suite members to tell you what keeps them up at night and determine if the legal department can assist in mitigating issue or concern

- Identify key government-related actions (domestic or international) that present either risk or strategic advantage to the company and create a government affairs plan around the same:[521]
  - Identify a proposed law or regulation (domestic or international) that is helpful to your company and design a government affairs campaign to support it
  - Identify a proposed law or regulation (domestic or international) that presents risk to your company and design a government affairs campaign to oppose it
  - Identify key government/agency officials who can significantly impact your business and set "get to know you" meetings with them over the course of the year
- Review insurance policies to ensure the insurance the company has is what it wants and needs:[522]
  - Check specific policies:
    - D&O
    - Cyber risk
    - E&O
    - CGL
  - Other policies important to your company's specific lines of business
  - For each policy, ensure the legal department and appropriate people in the business and staff groups understand the process of determining whether insurance might apply to a claim along with when and how to provide notice of a claim to the insurer
- Take/Update an inventory of the company's intellectual property (patents, trademarks, copyrights), trade secrets, and other confidential information and ensure proper policies and procedures are in place to protect the information:[523]
  - Employee training
  - Agreements and procedures
  - Exit interview process

---

521 See page 271.

522 See page 93.

523 See page 183.

- On-boarding process
- Securing the office (e.g., "clean desks")/proper sign-in and escort procedures for guests
• Create a five-year technology-plan for the legal department to increase efficiency and lowers costs. The goal is to implement what you can this year but set out long term plan to account for/budget for needed or improved technology over the course of the next five years, including:[524]
  - E-billing system
  - Matter management system
  - Document management system
  - Legal research tools
  - E-discovery software (with state-of-the-art legal hold management tools)
• Improve quality of life within the legal department itself:
  - Satisfaction survey of legal department members and 360 reviews of the department leaders
  - Improve the content and quality of staff or department meetings[525]
  - Plan for an off-site for the entire department
  - Find simple but effective ways to reward and retain your team members[526]
  - Help each lawyer create a development plan that provides opportunities for growth and responsibility so that they can become successful in-house lawyers at your company[527]
  - Ask each team member to prepare a detailed check-list about one key facet of their job to be compiled into a booklet that will provide the tools and instructions needed if that employee leaves the company or is otherwise unable to do that particular task when needed
• Create a "calendar of action" setting out the specific day or week during the year so that repeatable tasks set out in your to do list become institutionalized and part of the normal yearly-flow of activity of the legal department.

*****

My goal here was to give you a solid playbook for recognizing and planning important high level tasks for the upcoming year. As always, there are dozens and dozens of other tasks and sub-tasks (and detailed descriptions) that could be added to or layered on the above list. The important thing for you as in-house counsel is to

---

524 See page 129.
525 See page 121.
526 See page 109.
527 See page 3.

use the list above (all, part, or none), your own list, and other input (e.g., the business leaders and/or C-suite) to create a framework of key things that "need to get done" this year (and ideally every year). Equally important is assigning the work and tracking progress. Many legal departments now use "key performance indicators"[528] to track how they are doing.[529] In addition to tracking progress, keeping the goals in front of your team at meetings or with updates, and using examples of how different work or achievements of the legal department fit into the goals are helpful to ensuring that these important tasks do not become just another piece of paper gathering dust in the drawer.

January 12, 2016

---

[528] http://www.insidecounsel.com/2015/07/06/key-performance-indicators-part-1-four-kpis-that?slreturn=1468771191.

[529] http://www.insidecounsel.com/2015/07/22/key-performance-indicators-part-2-putting-advanced?&slreturn=1468771222.

Ten Things: "Cool Tech" for In-House Lawyers (2016)

I was one of the lunch-time speakers at the 2016 State Bar of Texas 15th Annual Advanced In-House Counsel Course in San Antonio, Texas. My panel's task was to discuss ways to "Work Smarter, Not Harder." A lot of what we discussed involved the use of technology (along with some good old-fashion "nontechnical" ideas). If you know me, you know I love gadgets and technology. Give me some neat technology to play with and I am off to the races, trying to think of all the ways I can use it in my work and personal life. And there is always something new to try. I have written about using technology to increase efficiency in the legal department.[530] There I focused a lot on some of the bigger technology efforts most in-house legal departments now require, for example, matter management, e-discovery, along with some of my favorites like Practical Law and Getting the Deal Through, etc. Everything I wrote about then is still relevant and it's worth re-reading that one. But, since time does not stand still and there are plenty of new programs, apps, and other tech bits for me to write about, below I will discuss ten "cool tech" items for in-house lawyers. I should point out that I do not receive anything to endorse the technology below; it's just my opinion on what I think in-house lawyers, located just about anywhere in the world, might find useful:

1. **Pocket.**[531] This has become one of my favorite "everyday" bits of technology. Whenever I come across interesting articles or videos or whatever on the Internet, I would either email them to myself or print them out. Pocket has changed all of that. You download Pocket to your favorite web browser and whenever you find an article, blog, video, website, etc. you would like to read or visit later, you just click on the little Pocket icon on your tool bar and it's saved for later—whether you are connected to the Internet or not. Great for storing up stuff to read on the plane or while you're waiting for that next meeting to start.

---

530 See page 129.

531 https://getpocket.com/.

It's integrated with over 1,500 apps (e.g., Twitter, Flipboard), works on your lap top, smart phone, and tablet. Best of all, it's free. The only downside is now you actually have to read all those articles you saved!

2. **Free Conference Call.**[532] Wow, talk about truth in advertising. This is, well, a *free* conference call service. And it works great! Not only do you get your own bridge-line (and password) to host free conference calls, you also get toll free dial-in numbers for just about any country. You can also set up and present free webcasts and video streaming, just like GoToMeeting, only this is 100 percent free. And you can host up to 1,000 callers or webcast viewers. You can even record and share your calls/webcasts. The good folks at FCC host training webcasts several times a week along with easy to understand online tutorials. It takes about 30 seconds to sign up for this service. I use FCC almost every day. Highly recommended.

3. **Stanford Law School—Foreign Corrupt Practices Act Clearinghouse.**[533] This is a brand spanking new website from Stanford Law School in collaboration with Sullivan & Cromwell. If your legal department deals at all with anti-bribery issues, the FCPAC is a tremendous free resource containing a massive amount of information and data, including a repository of original source documents, detailed information all relating to enforcement of the FCPA (i.e., cases, fines, etc.). There are also data analytics available—which is always helpful when the C-suite or board asks you, "Well, what happened with other companies?" Additionally, the site contains data, maps, "heat" maps, alerts, articles, etc., all dealing with the FCPA. Following is a passage from the website:

   The goal of the FCPAC is to provide investors, policymakers, scholars, judges, lawyers, the media, and the public at large with a comprehensive website for all things FCPA-related. Users can review relevant laws, read articles about FCPA compliance and enforcement, and view, search, and sort data about FCPA enforcement actions according to their individual needs and interests.

4. **ContractSafe.**[534] When I was general counsel, one of the projects we started and stopped numerous times was purchasing a contract management tool. Like many companies, our contracts were stored in many different places, in different types of repositories, with different capabilities to get data. While we did have guidelines for storing contracts, we lacked a central system. And there were numerous times, litigation, due diligence, etc., where we could have

---

532 https://www.freeconferencecall.com/.
533 http://fcpa.stanford.edu/.
534 https://www.contractsafe.com/.

saved an immense amount of time and expense if we could have quickly located contracts, let alone the missed opportunities by not having key contract dates and terms automated. The problem was most of the systems we looked at were way too complicated and way too expensive. The folks at ContractSafe appear to have solved that problem. Cofounder (and lawyer) Ken Button gave me a demo of the product a few months ago and I was very impressed. It was simple, did all the core things you would want (i.e., searchable, deadlines, access from anywhere, etc.), and was fairly inexpensive. If this were available several years ago we would have definitely given it a hard look. There is a short four-minute video (narrated by Ken himself) you can watch on YouTube.[535] Check it out.

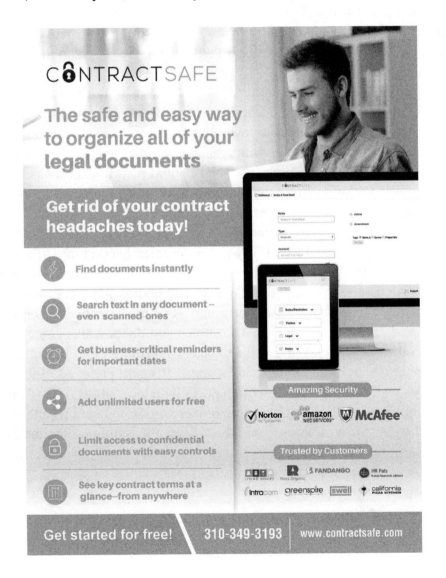

---

535 https://www.youtube.com/watch?v=t3iGxKAp0YU&feature=youtu.be.

5. **SnapDat.**[536] For some of the newer generation, business cards seem like a fossil or something grand-dad used to carry around with him. Yet, there are dozens of times during the week or the weekend where you wish you had a business card (or even a "social card") to share with colleagues, opposing counsel, potential clients or customers, new friends, etc. If you didn't happen to pack a few in your wallet or purse, or you left them back at the hotel room, you're out of luck. Unless you have downloaded the free SnapDat app. SnapDat allows you to create an electronic business card and share it as a v-card with just about anyone electronically, including anyone in your contacts list. You can use your company logo or create one using a template. You can even include a photo and links to your social media accounts like Twitter or LinkedIn. There are a bunch of other features[537] as well. Never get caught without a professional looking business card again. Be sure to watch this two minute video on YouTube.[538]

6. **Notability.**[539] Believe it or not, "Mr. Tech" here is fairly new to the tablet world, finally buying an iPad (though I still love my laptop). I am also a heavy note-taker, that is, writing out notes by hand in my paper notebook (which is a much better way of learning/remembering than typing notes into a laptop or tablet). I recall that sometimes I wished I could record what I was listening to so that, in addition to my notes, I could hear exactly what was said (e.g., an interview with a witness). Eventually I figured out that I can record audio on my iPad and that, with the proper apps, I can either type or write notes by hand on it. Then I discovered Notability which seamlessly combines all three in one ass-kicking app. With Notability you can sync audio recordings up to your hand written notes. You can draw with it, add photos and other images, import and embed documents—all directly into your documents. It even has "left-hand" and "right-hand" modes. Your notes and documents can be saved as a pdf or other file formats and you can back everything up to iCloud, Dropbox, Google Drive, or other cloud based storage. It's a bit pricey ($7.99 on iTunes) but if you want to meld hand written notes with technology, it's worth it. Here is a helpful video[540] describing some of its features. Oh, and go ahead and buy a good stylus for writing on your tablet. I like the Bamboo Fineline 2.[541]

---

536 http://www.snapdat.com/.
537 http://www.snapdat.com/features.html.
538 https://www.youtube.com/watch?v=sbFg8WAbM9Q.
539 http://www.gingerlabs.com/.
540 https://www.youtube.com/watch?v=6563A5_bUiM.
541 http://www.wacom.com/en-us/products/stylus/bamboo-fineline-2.

7. **Slack.**[542]—Slack is the hot collaboration tool of 2016. It allows you to build a team site and put all of your team communications in one place (called "channels"). You can utilize real time messaging and file sharing, and one-to-one messaging for private conversations, and you can search all of the information in your Slack project channel, including documents and conversation threads. You can download the mobile app or a desk top version (or both). You can create channels for teams or for specific projects. Slack allows you to drag and drop all of your files, images, pdfs, documents, and spreadsheets into Slack and then share them with anyone you want. If you use Dropbox, Google Drive, or similar services, you can paste the document link into Slack for everyone to access (and it becomes searchable as well). Slack can reduce the wear and tear on your email inbox dramatically. There is a free version so you can try it out and see if it's something that works for your team and then, if necessary, upgrade to one of the paid versions with more features and storage. Here is a short video[543] with some of the basics of Slack. This is a great tool for legal projects both within the legal department and within the company—you can even invite people from outside the company to join a project. Just remember that you need to be *very careful* about attorney-client privilege issues[544] and work product issues when using a platform like this. Be sure to label privileged communications and documents properly and ensure everyone using the tool understands how the privilege works and is "writing smart,"[545] that is, not using the tool in a way that can come back to embarrass the company or worse. Those jokes just aren't as funny when you see them thrown up on a giant screen at trial.

8. **Typeform.**[546] Earlier I discussed how to prepare a client satisfaction survey for the legal department.[547] There I talk about using Survey Monkey or Zoom as the technology engine. Those are still great tools, but I found one that is better. Typeform allows you to easily create great surveys, and provides templates containing numerous ways to ask survey questions, from "yes/no" to multiple-choice, to scales of 1–10, open text, or whatever. There is even "skip-logic" that allows you to take the user to different questions depending on the

---

542 https://slack.com/.

543 https://www.youtube.com/watch?v=3OGM0QMjYbA.

544 http://www.corpcounsel.com/id=1202762836347/Should-InHouse-Lawyers-Use-Slack?kw=Should%20In-House%20Lawyers%20Use%20Slack?cn=20160719&pt=Daily%20Alert&src=EMC-Email&et=editorial&bu=Corporate%20Counsel&slreturn=20160708162606.

545 See page 263.

546 www.typeform.com.

547 See page 135.

answer he or she selects in an earlier question. You can create online payment forms, job applications, event registration forms, polls, integrate with common apps, and a dozen other uses. There is a free version with unlimited surveys and other basic templates, and you can download the results of your survey into a spreadsheet or use the online analytical tools. The paid versions give you even more features and options. Besides client satisfaction, you can use Typeform for your next legal department offsite, to get feedback on things going on in the legal department (e.g., the department meeting), or many other things. Any time you think feedback might be useful, Typeform can help you automate the process of gathering the data and make it easy for people to give you the feedback you want.

9. **Safe PST Back Up.**[548] I save a lot of my emails to folders I have created in Outlook on my laptop hard drive. I have also experienced the joy of the "tech guy" updating my laptop and losing all of my folders. Twice. So, let's just say I have learned my lesson here: backing up your laptop is like voting in Chicago—do it early and often. I use Safe PST Back Up which is a free download that allows you to easily capture and back up your personal email folders (and other things). To simplify, when you save emails off of the email server they become what are called PST files[549] (vs. OST files). Once they are saved as PST files, if you have deleted them from the exchange server, there is no way to get them back if your laptop crashes and the emails stored there are lost. Safe PST Back Up solves that problem. You can back up email, contacts, calendars, tasks, and other folders and you can access them with any version of Outlook. Once you get started, the software only backs up changes/new items to your PST files, saving time and storage space. I use a 1TB Seagate external hard drive to back up my PST files (and my other files, that is, documents, spreadsheets, PDF, etc.). You can back up continuously or at different intervals (hourly, daily, weekly, etc.). Of course, there is a paid version and an enterprise version with more features. But, if all you want to do is make sure you have your save email folders in case something goes horribly wrong, the free version is all you need. There are several excellent short "how to use" videos for Safe PST Back Up on YouTube.[550]

10. **If This Then That.**[551] This is an app you will be hearing a lot about over the next few months. The *Wall Street Journal* calls it the best Internet productivity

---

548 http://www.safepstbackup.com/.

549 https://support.office.com/en-us/article/Introduction-to-Outlook-Data-Files-pst-and-ost-6d4197ec-1304-4b81-a17d-66d4eef30b78.

550 https://www.youtube.com/watch?v=rlvArj7VSM4.

551 https://ifttt.com/.

tool of 2016.[552] "If This Then That" (IFTTT) connects apps and devices through a series of "recipes," that is, if this happens, then do this. It's that simple. It connects two different services (no more and no less). The only limit is your imagination. For example, if you wanted an alert sent to your son to take his allergy medicine every time the ragweed count hits a certain level, you can link together the ragweed alert to your text message system. Or anytime you are tagged in a photo on Facebook, have that photo sent to your Dropbox account. You do all of this through what is called a "recipe" where a "trigger event" causes an action, that is, if this, then this. It's a bit like being a computer programmer. Okay, a very, very simplistic computer programmer! And if you don't feel like reinventing the wheel or want to see what recipes other users have cooked up, the IFTTT community has posted over 400,000 recipes online.[553] There is a good tutorial about IFTTT available online.[554] Well worth the 20 minutes to watch it.

*****

You do not have to be a technophile to use any of the technology above. Trust me, I'm just an "Average Joe" when it comes to technology. But I do love to try stuff out and see if it can improve my work product or make me a better lawyer or leader. The key is to not be afraid to try it. As you can see, there are lots (and I mean lots) of videos on YouTube to help you get started with just about anything noted above. You won't break anything, so give it a shot. One thing I am watching but didn't list above is how in-house legal departments utilize "virtual reality." It's still in its infancy but I think there will be some really neat uses of virtual reality (besides playing video games). For example, you can host a department meeting virtually, or even an annual shareholder meeting if you're really ambitious. You can also attend that deposition you don't want to travel to or sit in the court room while your attorney argues that key motion—all without having to leave your desk. Well, that's what I predict any way.

July 29, 2016

---

552 http://www.wsj.com/articles/meet-the-internets-best-productivity-tool-if-this-then-that-1464793511.

553 https://ifttt.com/recipes.

554 https://www.youtube.com/watch?v=CEAVFU3ELcI.

Index

A

ABA Center for Professional Responsibility website, 280
ABA Model Rules of Professional Conduct, 279–280
Absolute/dogmatic statements, 46
"Accidental" settlement agreements, 66
Activist shareholders, 226
Adams on Contract Drafting, 291
Advisory board, 221
Agenda/writing, 87
Analyzing survey results, 140–141
Answer up-front, summarizing, 28
Answer/options/recommendation, 31
Anticipate questions, 232
Antitrust and Associations Handbook, 154
Arbitration, 204–206
Arbitration Nation, 292–293
Articles of incorporation, 220
Attorney-client privilege, 263–264
    communications, 265
    confidential, 265–267
    joint defense/common interest, 268–269
    legal advice *vs.* business advice, 265
    protection, 269–270
    self-critical analysis, 268
    waiving, 267
    work product, 74, 268
Audit/assessment, 148

B

Background checks, 214
Battles, picking, 15
BCP. *See* Business continuity plan
Being practical, 35–36
Being yourself, 18–19
Birthdays and anniversaries, people goal, 109–110
Blended rates, 116
"Bluebook," 31
Board of directors, 221, 222
    anticipate questions, 232
    CEO, 234
    homework, 229–230
    honesty, 232
    keeping simple, 231–232
    professional, being, 232–233
    risk/plan, 233–234
    transparency, 230–231
    understanding, 230
Bonuses, 112
Budget, 59
    cost, 55
    predict costs, 38
"Budget tool," 115–116
Business and deal terms, 80
Business approvals/buy in, 80
Business communications, 45–46

Business continuity plan (BCP), 253–254
By-laws, 220–221

C

Calendar of action, 299
Calm, during crisis, 250
Cap on rates, 117
Carefulness, 5–6
CEO, board of directors, 234
CFO, litigation, 72
Champerty, 73–74
Chronicle of Data Protection, 292
Class action/jury waiver, 206
Clear/simple communication, 28–29
Clickwrap user agreement, 202
Client, 51, 86, 104, 280–281
Client satisfaction survey, 137–138, 297–298
   action plan, 141–142
   analyzing the results, 140–141
   confidentiality of responses, 137
   purpose, 135–136
   questions, 136–137
   sharing the results, 141
   tools, 136
   weighing the responses, 138–139
   "word cloud," 139–140
Coalitions/Go solo, 273
Commercial General Liability (CGL), 94
Common ethical issues
   client, 280–281
   communications, 285–286
   competence, 284
   confidential, 281–282
   conflicts, 284–285
   in-house, 279–280
   lawyer *vs.* business partner, 283
   resources, 280
   supervisors/outsourcing, 286
   up-the-ladder reporting, 282–283

Communications, 3–4, 37, 251, 258–259, 274, 285–286
Company (sued)
   confidentiality issues, 51–52
   insurance, 50–51
   key documents and witnesses, 49–50
   litigation hold, 50
   outside counsel, 51
   reading the complaint, 49
   settled/resolved, 51
   short summary of lawsuit, 49
Company website, 297
Competence, 284
Compliance-related policies, 296
Confidential, 51–52, 56–57, 64, 187, 265–267, 281–282
   arbitration, 204–206
Conflicts, 284–285
Consultants, 276
Contingencies, 63–64
Contract negotiation, 88–89
Contract provisions, 147
Contracting process
   business and deal terms, 80
   business approvals/buy in, 80
   deal, 81–82
   drafting, 82
   endgame, 82
   form agreement, 79–80
   legal involved, 81
   legal services, 80–81
   nondisclosure agreement (NDA), 81
ContractSafe, 302–303
Control of the defense, ROR, 98–99
Conversations, inappropriate, 151–152
Cookie Directive, 161
Cool tech for in-house lawyers
   ContractSafe, 302–303
   FCPAC, 302
   Free Conference Call, 302
   IFTTT, 306–307

Notability, 304
Pocket, 301–302
Safe PST Back Up, 306
Slack, 305
SnapDat, 304
Typeform, 305–306
Cooperate, ROR, 98
Copernic search program, 133
Corporate governance
  advisory board, 221
  board of directors, 221, 222
  core documents, 220–221
  delegation of authority, 222–223
  formation, 219–220
  officers, 221
  publicly traded companies, 223–226
  resolutions/minutes, 223
  resources, 226–227
  secretary, 226
  shareholders, 221
  subsidiaries, sister companies, holding companies, 226
Corporate secretary, 226
Corruption, Crime & Compliance, 292
Cost of litigation, 72
Cost sharing, 117
Cost *vs.* rate, 37–38
Counsel present, 151
Crisis preparation
  calm, 250
  communications, 251
  following the plan, 250–251
  media training, 250
  outside help, 251
  planning, 248
  postmortem, 252
  practice the plan, 250
  risk, 248
  written plan, 248–250
Crisis team, 254
Culture of security, 256–257

Cutting edge, 214–215
Cyber and privacy liability (cyber risk), 94
Cyber risk insurance, 158–159

D

Damages update, 59
Data breach response plan, 159–160
Data incident *vs.* data breach, 160
Data inventory, 155–156
Data privacy
  cyber risk insurance, 158–159
  data breach response plan, 159–160
  data inventory, 155–156
  data transfer, 159
  documents, 160–161
  impact assessments, 176
  laws/rules, 156–157
  privacy policies and notices, 157–158
  public disclosures, 161–162
  special protection, 156
  vendor contracts, 158
Data privacy officer (DPO), 173
Data processors, 174
Data Protection Authority (DPA), 173
Data transfer, 159
Deal worth, 81–82
Decision trees, 55–56, 59
Declarations, insurance policy, 96
Deductible *vs.* retention, 97
Defend Trade Secrets Act (DTSA), 185
"Definition of Success," 59
Delegation of authority, 222–223
Department award, 112
Department of Justice, 154
Depositions, 59
Digital Millennium Copyright Act (DMCA), 207
Directors and officers (D&O), 94
Director's background, 229–230
Discounted rate cards, 116
Document creation, 153–154

Documents and emails, drafting
  absolute/dogmatic statements, 46
  anger, 46
  business communications, 45–46
  destroy/delete, 47
  "draft-subject to revision," 46
  "gung ho" statements, 46
  knowledge, 46
  legal issues, 46
  profanity/off-color humor, 46
  project names, 47
Drafting, 82
"Draft-subject to revision," 46
Duties of the parties, 97
Duty to defend *vs.* duty to indemnify, 97–98

E

Easy on the eyes, writing skills, 29
E-billing system, 130
E-discovery tool, 130–131
Effective staff meeting
  agenda, 122
  logistics, 122
  making important, 125
  over time, 125
  presenting/talking, 124
  purpose, 121
  solicit feedback, 124–125
  solicit ideas/topics/questions, 122–123
  technology, 123–124
  testing, 124
8K reports, 224
Electronic discovery law, 292
Email
  destroy or delete, 47
  record retention, 168
  reminder, 146
Employee
  agreements/clauses, 211
  classification, 210
  contractor classification, 212
  handbook, 211–212
  training program, 209–210
Employment/labor insider, 292
End goal, 273
Endgame, 82
Enforceable user agreement, 202–203
Enforce/review, 168–169
Enforcing the settlement, 65
Environmental, 94
Equal Employment Opportunity Commission, 214
Errors and omissions (E&O), 94
Estimating risk, 244–245
Ethical issues, 74
Ethical, negotiations, 91–92
"Ethics Every Day," 147
EU Data Privacy Directive, 161
EU data privacy law, 171–172
  collection of personal data, 176–177
  consent, 174–175
  data privacy impact assessments, 176
  data privacy officer (DPO), 173
  data processors, 174
  enforcement, 173
  notification of breach, 174
  regulation, 172–173
  resources, 178–179
  "right to be forgotten"/access, 174
  transfers of data, 175–176
EU Privacy Directive, 159
Evaluating risk, 243–244
Excess/umbrella, insurance policy, 95
Executive
  buy-in, 147–148
  presence, 8–9
Exit interviews, 188–189
Expectations up-front, 119

F

Fair Credit Reporting Act, 214
Fair disclosure regulation (Reg FD), 225

Federal Trade Commission, 151, 154
Fee arrangements, 116–117
First party *vs.* third party, 95
First responders, 255–256
Five-year technology-plan, 299
Fixed fees for specific projects, 116
Flexibility, 112–113
Following the plan, 250–251
Foreign Corrupt Practices Act Clearinghouse (FCPA), 302
Foreign Corrupt Practices Act (FCPA)/ anti-bribery health check
   audit/assessment, 148
   contract provisions, 147
   email reminder, 146
   executive buy-in, 147–148
   outside counsel, 148
   policy, 145, 146
   possibility of bribery issues, 146
   process, 147
   training, 146
Form 3, 224
Form 4, 224
Form agreement, 79–80
Forms and checklists, 24–25
Forum selection/choice of law, 203–204
Free Conference Call, 302
Free hours, fee arrangements, 117
Funding an entire claim, 71

G

General counsel
   carefulness, 5–6
   complicated projects to senior management, 11
   "Dr. Yes," 7
   executive presence, 8–9
   learn the business, 7
   legal skills and credentials, 9
   nonlegal skills and credentials, 10–11
   power dynamics, 11–12
   strategical, thinking, 7–8
Getting paid, 73
Getting the Deal Through.com, 131
Getting things done, 16–17
Getting up an hour earlier, 21–22
Global regulatory enforcement law, 292
Goals
   legal department, 105–106
      budget targets, 107
      build and retain extraordinary team, 106–107
      high-revenue/cost-saving and strategic commercial agreements, 108
      interests of the company, 108
      strategic transactions and initiatives, 108
Governance *See* Corporate governance
Government affairs campaign
   activities, 274–275
   coalition/Go solo, 273
   communications campaign, 274
   consultants, 276
   end goal, 273
   government officials, table with, 272
   grassroots, 275–276
   issues, 272–273
   resource, 274
   rules, 276–277
Government-related actions, 298
Grammar matters, 29–30
Grassroots campaign, 275–276
"Gung ho" statements, 46

H

Honest and truthful, 40–41
Honesty, 232
"Hot docs," 59
HR department
   background checks, 214
   cutting edge issues, 214–215
   employee
      agreements/clauses, 211

classification, 210
   handbook, 211–212
   training program, 209–210
employee/contractor classification, 212
internal investigations policy, 213
interns, 210–211
layoffs, 212–213

I

If This Then That (IFTTT), 306–307
Improvement, outside counsel, 38–39
Informed, keeping, 36–37
In-house advisor, 292
In-house counsel
   agenda/writing, 87
   calendar of action, 299
   client satisfaction survey, 297–298
   company website, 297
   compliance health check, 296
   contract negotiation, 88–89
   ethical, 91–92
   five-year technology-plan, 299
   government-related actions, 298
   insurance contract basics (*see* Insurance contract basics)
   insurance policies, 298
   legal department budget and spend, 296
   listening, 89
   litigation/disruptive events, 297
   policies/ employee agreements, 295–296
   preparation, 85–86
   protection, 298–299
   quality of life, 299
   reasoned positions, 90
   relationship, 89–90
   understanding the leverage, 86–87
   written playbook, 87–88
In-house lawyers
   battles, picking, 15
   being practical, 35–36
   being yourself, 18–19
   budget/predict costs, 38
   communication, 37
   cool tech (*see* Cool tech)
   cost *vs.* rate, 37–38
   getting things done, 16–17
   good people skills, 16
   help/opinions of others, 14–15
   honest and truthful, 40–41
   improvement, 38–39
   informed, keeping, 36–37
   input, valuing, 40
   learning business, 39
   marketing materials/plans, 39–40
   notebook and writing things, 13–14
   outside counsel, over-rely, 17–18
   reading, 18
   risk taking, 15–16
   routine to start day, 14
Instant message (IM) program, 132
Insurance, 50–51, 257–258
   binder, 96
Insurance company/indemnitor, 64–65
Insurance contract basics
   deductible *vs.* retention, 97
   duties of the parties, 97
   duty to defend *vs.* duty to indemnify, 97–98
   first party *vs.* third party, 95
   insurance policy, 96
   litigation, 99
   notice, 96–97
   occurrence *vs.* claims made, 95
   policy limits, 95
   reservation of rights, 98–99
   types, 94–95
Insurance Information Institute, 95
Insurance policy, 96. 298
Insured, 97
Insurer, 97
Internal investigations policy, 213
Internet/social media, 194
Interns, 210–211

J

Jargon, eliminating, 30–31
Jessup, C. *(A Few Good Men)*, 28–29
Joint defense/common interest privilege, 268–269
Judge, 58
Judge/jury research, 59

K

Key documents and witnesses, 49–50
Key motions, 59
Key trade association activities, 152
Knowledge
    email and documents, 46
    litigation process, 50

L

Last year's goals, 104
Lawsuits, defending, 71–72
Lawyer *vs.* business partner, 283
Lawyers of choice, 72–73
Layoffs, 212–213
Learning business, 3, 7, 39
Legal
    involvement, 81
    issues, 46
    risks, 240
    services, 80–81
    skills and credentials, 9
Legal advice *vs.* business advice, 265
Legal blogs
    Adams on Contract Drafting, 291
    Arbitration Nation, 292–293
    Chronicle of Data Protection, 292
    Corruption, Crime & Compliance, 292
    Electronic Discovery Law, 292
    Employment and Labor Insider, 292
    Global Regulatory Enforcement Law, 292
    In-House Advisor, 292
    Presnell on Privileges, 291
    Trademark and Copyright Law, 292
Legal department
    goals, 105–106
        budget targets, 107
        build and retain extraordinary team, 106–107
        high-revenue/cost-saving and strategic commercial agreements, 108
        interests of the company, 108
        strategic transactions and initiatives, 108
    measure success, 105
    potential IPO, 105
    proactive/forward thinking, 105
    skills and talent, 105
    success/failure, 106
Legal department budget and spend, 296
Legal department, efficiency of
    Copernic, 133
    e-billing system, 130
    e-discovery tool, 130–131
    Getting The Deal Through, 131
    IM program, 132
    Lexology, 131
    Practical Law, 129–130
    SigFonts, 131–132
    TRACE, 133
    TripCase, 132
Less expensive firms, 117–118
Lexology.com, 131
Liability
    limitation of, 206–207
Limit use of first-year lawyers, 117
Listening, 3, 28, 89, 111
Litigation
    duration of, 57–58
    hold process, 50, 167–168
    insurance company, 99
Litigation, board and CEO
    budget/cost, 55
    confidentiality, 56–57
    decision trees, 55–56
    judge, 58

outside counsel, 54
process/timing, 53–54
regular meetings/reports, 58–59
success, 54–55
time diversion of management, 56
Litigation financing
cons, 73–74
deal for, 70–71
defending lawsuits, 71–72
definition, 69–70
ethics issues, 74
"pros," 72–73
resources, 75–76
steps, 75
uses, 70
Litigation financing companies (LFCs), 70–75
Litigation process, knowledge, 50
Litigation/disruptive events, 297
Lobbyists, 276
Logistics right, 62–63

M

Management skills, legal budget, 116
Marketing materials/plans, 39–40
Media training, 250
Mediation, 118–119
Meeting. *See* Staff meeting
Membership criteria objective and standardized, 153
Microsoft privacy notice, 161
Mirroring, 90
Money, time/people, 4
Monthly/quarterly report

N

National Advertising Division (NAD), 196
National Institute of Standards and Technology, 161
National Labor Relations Act, 212

New York Times, 19, 46
Nondisclosure agreement (NDA), 81
Nonlegal skills and credentials, 10–11
Notability, 304
Notebook and writing things down, 13–14
Notice, 96–97
Notice process, 160

O

Occurrence *vs.* claims made, 95
Officers, 221
Open-ended questions, 90
Opinions of others, 14–15
Outside counsel, 51, 54, 148
over-rely, 17–18
Outside counsel fees
agree with senior management, 116
alternative fee arrangements, 116–117
"budget tool," 115–116
expectations up-front, 119
guidelines, 118
less expensive firms, 117–118
mediation, 118–119
monthly/quarterly report, 119–120
RFP process, 118
significant costs, 117
Outside help, 251
Overlapping risk, 241

P

Paraphrase, 90
People skills, 16
Percentage contingency fee, 116
Planning for next week/declutter, 25
Playing hooky, 111
Pocket technology, 301–302
Policies/ employee agreements, 295–296
Policy form, 96
Policy limits, 95

Political action committee
  (PAC), 276
Portfolio funding, 71–72
Possibility of bribery issues, 146
Postmortem, 252
Power dynamics, 11–12
Practice the plan, 250
Preparation, 85–86
  BCP, 253–254
  communications, 258–259
  crisis team, 254
  culture of security, 256–257
  first responders, 255–256
  insurance, 257–258
  sources, 259–260
  temporary headquarters, 255
  travel, 254–255
  workplace readiness/security, 256
Presnell on Privileges, 291
Privacy policies and notices, 157–158
Privacy Shield agreement, 175–176
Privilege issues/stay professional, 32
Privileged communications, 265
Proactive/forward thinking, 105
Problems escalated/solved, 197
Process/timing, 53–54
Productive, being
  dedicating set times, 23
  forms and checklists, 24–25
  getting up an hour earlier, 21–22
  the to do list, 24
  planning for next week/declutter, 25
  "small chunks," 23–24
  stop multitasking, 22
  "top three," 22
  truly delegate work, 22–23
Profanity/off-color humor, 46
Professional, being, 232–233
Project names, 47
Protection, 298–299

Proxy advisory services, 225
Proxy reports, 224
PST files, 306
Publicly traded companies, 223–226

Q
Quality of life, 299
Quick awards, 110

R
Reading, 18
Reading the complaint, 49
Reasoned positions, 90
Record retention program
  benefits, 163–164
  categories, 165
  customize, 164
  email, 168
  enforce/review, 168–169
  litigation hold process, 167–168
  location, 165
  resources, 169
  roll-out, 166–167
  types, 164–165
  vendors, 165
  written policy/schedules, 165–166
Regular meetings/reports, 58–59
Reporting risk, 245
Reports, 224
Reputation and brand
  building, 197–198
  Internet and social media, 194
  right tone at top, 191–192
  social media accounts, 198
  social media policy, 193–194
  speak out/quiet, 198–199
  trademarks, copyrights, and domain
    names, 192–193
Request for proposal (RFP)
    process, 118

Reservation of rights letter (ROR), 98–99
Resolutions/minutes, 223
Respond, ROR, 98
Responses, confidentiality of, 137
Retainers, 116
Reverse contingency fees, 72
Reward and retain
   birthdays and anniversaries, 109–110
   charity to support, 110
   department award, 112
   flexibility, 112–113
   listening, 111
   "pick a book," 111–112
   playing hooky, 111
   quick awards, 110
   spot bonuses, 112
   tout your team, 111
"Right to be forgotten"/access, 174
Risk, 239–240
   continuum, 240
   estimating, 244–245
   evaluating, 243–244
   legal, 240
   overlapping, 241
   reporting, 245
   resources, 245–246
   spotting, 242–243
   strategic, 241
Risk taking, 15–16
Risk/plan, 233–234
Roll-out, 166–167
Routine to start day, 14

S

Safe PST Back Up, 306
SAFETY Act, 259
Sample Data Privacy Notice, 161
Sarbanes-Oxley Act, 225
Scope of the release, 61–62
Secretary, corporate, 226
Self-critical analysis privilege, 268

Senior management
   complicated projects, 11
   litigation process, 99
   process/timing, 52–53
   responses, 138–139
   survey results, 141–142
Sense of humor, 3
Set times, projects, 23
Settled/resolved, 51
Settlement agreements
   "accidental," 66
   confidentiality, 64
   contingencies, 63–64
   enforcing the settlement, 65
   insurance company/indemnitor, 64–65
   logistics right, 62–63
   scope of the release, 61–62
   settlement team, 65–66
   tax/accounting implications, 65
Settlement team, 65–66
Settlement/alternative dispute resolution, 59
Shareholder's agreements, 221
Short summary of lawsuit, 49
SigFonts program, 131–132
Skills and talent, 105
Slack, 305
"Small chunks," 23–24
Smart Traveler Program, 255
SnapDat, 304
Social media accounts, 198
Social media policy, 193–194
Spot bonuses, 112
Spotting risk, 242–243
Staff meeting, 125–126
   agenda, 122
   logistics, 122
   making important, 125
   over time, 125
   presenting/talking, 124
   purpose, 121
   sample legal department, 126–127

solicit feedback, 124–125
solicit ideas/topics/questions, 122–123
technology, 123–124
testing technology, 124
Staff/attendees, 153
Stop multitasking, 22
Strategic risks, 241
Strategical, thinking, 7–8
Strategy issues, 59
Subsidiaries, 226
Success, 54–55, 105
Success/failure, 106
Successful in-house counsel
   communicate frequently, 3–4
   fair and honesty, 3
   know your numbers, 4
   learn the business, 3
   listen, 3
   money, time/people, 4
   opportunity, 4
   sense of humor, 3
   simply as possible, 3
   surprised boss, 3
Supervisors/outsourcing, 286
Surprised boss, 3

T

Taking minutes, 151
Tax/accounting implications, 65
Temporary headquarters, 255
10K reports, 224
10Q reports, 224
Time diversion of management, 56
Timelines, 59
To do list, 24
"Top three," 22
Tout your team, 111
TRACE, 133
Trade associations and antitrust risk
   counsel present, 151
   document creation, 153–154
   inappropriate conversations, 151–152
   key trade association activities, 152
   membership criteria objective and standardized, 153
   staff/attendees, 153
   taking minutes, 151
   written agenda, 151
   written antitrust policy, 150
Trade secrets, 183–184
   agreements, 184–185
   catalogue, 184
   confidential, 187
   exit interviews, 188–189
   factors to determine, 184
   plan, 189–190
   right policies, 185–186
   training, 186–187
   warning signs, 187–188
Trademark and copyright law, 292
Trademarks, copyrights, and domain names, 192–193
Transfer of Undertakings (Protection of Employment) statutes (TUPE), 213
Transfers of data, 175–176
Transparency, 230–231
Traveling, 254–255
TripAdvisor website, 207
TripCase.com, 132
Truly delegate work, 22–23
2016 Verizon Data Breach Investigations Report, 161
Typeform, 305–306

U

Understanding leverage, 86–87
Up-the-ladder reporting, 282–283
User agreements. *See* Website user agreements

V

Vendor contracts, 158
Volume discounts, 117

W

"War," 90–91
Warning signs, 187–188
Website user agreements, 201–202
   acceptable uses, 207
   arbitration, 204–206
   class action/jury waiver, 206
   DMCA, 207
   enforceability, 202–203
   forum selection/choice of law, 203–204
   limitation of liability, 206–207
   proof issues, 203
Weighing the responses, 138–139
"Word cloud," 139–140
Worker Adjustment and Retraining Notification Act (WARN), 213
Workplace readiness/security, 256
Writing skills
   action/next steps, 32
   answer up-front, summarizing, 28
   answer/options/recommendation, 31
   "bluebook," 31
   clear and simple, 28–29
   easy on the eyes, 29
   grammar matters, 29–30
   jargon, eliminating, 30–31
   listening, 28
   privilege issues/stay professional, 32
Written antitrust policy, 150
Written plan, 248–250
Written playbook, 87–88

About the Author

Sterling Miller served as executive vice president, general counsel, corporate secretary, and chief compliance officer for Sabre Corporation from June 2008 until retiring in November 2014. Prior to this position, he was the senior vice president and general counsel for Sabre's wholly owned subsidiary Travelocity.com from 2004 to 2008. He currently serves as senior counsel to the Dallas office of the litigation boutique Hilgers Graben PLLC and consults with in-house legal departments.

As general counsel, he advised the board of directors and C-suite on numerous issues, including legal and corporate governance issues. He managed the company's global legal department, government affairs group, corporate secretary office, compliance function, and data privacy team.

Sterling was in-house counsel at American Airlines and Sabre Corporation from 1994 to 2004. He was in charge of litigation and regulatory matters for Sabre Corporation. Prior to that, he was a litigation attorney with the firm of Gallop, Johnson & Neuman in St. Louis, Missouri.

Sterling earned his J.D. degree from Washington University in St. Louis (Order of the Coif and Law Review) and his bachelor's degree from Nebraska Wesleyan University. He is an active speaker on legal and industry panels, including presenting at the 2016 South by Southwest conference. In 2007, *Inside Counsel* magazine named the Travelocity legal department as one of the "Ten Most Innovative" legal departments in the United States. The following year (his first as Sabre general counsel), the Sabre legal department won "Honorable Mention" honors for the innovations implemented under his watch. Sterling was a finalist in the *Dallas Business Journal*'s "Best Corporate Counsel" award in 2007 and 2008.

Sterling serves on the board of directors of Terrasoul Superfoods and the advisory board of Travefy.com. He is a member of the American Bar Association's Task Force for Legal Project Management and a contributor to the book *Using Legal Project Management in M&A Transactions—A Guidebook for Managing*

Deals Efficiently and Effectively. In addition to "Ten Things You Need to Know as In-House Counsel," he writes a column called "The Insider" for Thomson Reuters' *Corporate Counsel Connect* e-zine, focusing on issues critical to in-house lawyers.

Sterling published his first book in December 2015 through Mill City Press entitled *The Evolution of Professional Football: 1920–2015*.

Sterling resides in the Dallas–Fort Worth area with his wife and two daughters.